All Hands and the Cook

THE CUSTOMS AND LANGUAGE OF THE
BRITISH MERCHANT SEAMAN 1875-1975

Captain Barry Thompson has spent almost all his life at sea, or closely associated with ships. This book shares his long-time interest in the language and customs of his shipmates, and the ships in which they served.

I am completely and utterly impressed by the range and depth of knowledge that the book contains. I am sure it will be an invaluable source of information.
Captain J.M.R.Sail MNI National Chairman of The Merchant Navy Association.

The British Merchant Navy had a great and proud history and this book ensures that its everyday language, phrases, and expressions have been admirably recorded before they are lost forever. It will bring back memories of a way of life that has long gone.
Rory Smith. Retired Commodore P & O Cruises.

Cover painting by Charles Wood,
from a British propaganda poster issued during World War 2,
as a tribute to the Merchant Navy. The poster bears the words:
'The life-line is firm thanks to the Merchant Navy'.
REPRODUCED WITH PERMISSION OF THE NATIONAL ARCHIVES.

Other books by the author:
Surveying Marine Damage (A text book)
Deeds not Words – The Story of the New Zealand Coastguard
Spirit of Adventure – The Story of New Zealand's Sail Training Ship
(with Tessa Duder & Cliff Hawkins)

An early steamship of 1879

All Hands and the Cook

THE CUSTOMS AND LANGUAGE OF THE
BRITISH MERCHANT SEAMAN 1875-1975

Captain Barry Thompson

PUBLISHED BY
The Bush Press
ON BEHALF OF THE AUTHOR

First published in 2008
byThe Bush Press
on behalf of the author,
Capt Barry Thompson

Copies of this book are available from:

United Kingdom – Captain M.D.Rushan,
17, The Croft, Bishopstone.
Salisbury. Wilts. SP5 4DF
E-mail: rushan@shoreside.demon.co.uk
Telephone: 0044-(0)1722-780460

New Zealand – Captain C.B.Thompson,
2/126 Selwyn Avenue,
Mission Bay, Auckland, 1071
E-mail: shipmaster@ihug.co.nz
Telephone: 0064-(0)9-521-1204

Prepared for publication by
Bush Press Communications Ltd,
PO Box 33-029, Takapuna, 0740
North Shore City, New Zealand

Printed in China through
Bookprint International Ltd,
6/9 Wilkinson Street, Oriental Bay,
Wellington 6011, New Zealand

ISBN 0-908608-72-1
EAN 9780908608720

DEDICATION

For Charlie Bamford (1924-2003) who was the catalyst for this book and exemplified so many of the finest qualities of the British merchant seaman.

This book is also dedicated to the thousands of British merchant seamen who gave their lives in two World Wars. By preserving some of their language I hope it will pay them a well deserved tribute.

THE AUTHOR
Captain C.B. Thompson R.D. F.N.I. Hon.M.I.I.M.S.

A Londoner by birth, Barry Thompson served at sea with Port Line and P & O before settling in New Zealand after he married a Kiwi.

Becoming a marine surveyor, and later a consultant to the shipping and insurance industries, he was appointed the Auckland Lloyd's Agent and also served on the New Zealand Committee of Lloyd's Register of Shipping.

A Liveryman of the Honourable Company of Master Mariners and, for many years a naval reserve officer, his nautical interests also included time on the Executive Committee of the New Zealand Volunteer Coast Guard, latterly as President, and as both a trustee and volunteer master of New Zealand's two sail training ships, *Spirit of Adventure* and *Spirit of New Zealand*.

As a specialist writer on nautical matters, Barry Thompson has contributed to the diploma courses of the International Institute of Marine Surveying and his book *Surveying Marine Damage* is a standard text, now in its second edition. He has written extensively for maritime magazines both in New Zealand and in Britain.

ACKNOWLEDGMENTS

Over the five years or more that I have been deliberately recalling or being reminded of the many seafaring terms and expressioins recorded in this book, I have enjoyed the enthusdiastic support and encouragement of numerous seafarers, past and present. Many have had the pleasure of recapturing the language which was so familiar to them during their careers while proudly serving under the Red Ensign in many of the finest ships ever built, manned by some of the world's ablest seamen.

There are too many to acknowledge here so I hope the majority will accept this collective 'Thank you'. I am grateful to them all. However, there are a few individuals and organisations without whose help I should probably have been unable, and certainly reluctant, to complete the book. I hope they, and all who read it, will enjoy reliving some of their days at sea or remembering other associations with British shipping and those who manned its ships.

Special thanks to:

In the United Kingdom:

Nautilus (UK), previously NUMAST, the Merchant Navy Officers' Union and Andrew Linnington, editor of its magazine *The Telegraph*.

The Merseyside Maritime Museum.

Captain Hamish Roberts and members of The Southampton Master Mariners' Club.

Captain Reg Kelso (ex Union Castle Line).

Captain Malcolm Rushan (ex Port Line, Orient Line and P & O) – but for his assistance this book may never have been published.

The late John Russell, ex-Secretary of the Radio Officers' Association.

David Thomas (ex- B I and British Rail Ferries).

The late Eric Talbot-Booth, a good friend during my seafaring years with whom I corresponded and discussed ships seen during my voyages. He provided most of the silhouettes and drawings of the ships. (I have been unable to trace a few of those responsible for others and would be pleased to hear from anyone who may be concerned.)

In New Zealand:

The late Captain Brian Scott (ex-Clan Line, Lamport & Holt and Booth Line).

Captain Jim Ellis (ex-Radcliffe S.S. Co).

Mr Bruce Birnie (Shaw Savill and Crusader Lines).

Mr Gordon Ell of Bush Press for his friendship and guidance during the editing and preparation of this book.

Both my wife Tessa Duder, a respected New Zealand writer, and my daughter Kate, a very competent editor, have my special thanks for their valuable advice in making the text more readable.   C.B.T., Auckland.

Contents

The Author page 5, Acknowledgments page 6
Frequently used abbreviations page 8
Author's Notes page 9, Preface page 10
Introduction page 13, Indices page 353

FREQUENTLY USED ABBREVIATIONS

BOT	Board of Trade
EOW	Enginer of the Watch
Fo'c's'le	Forecastle
MN	Merchant Navy
MSA	Merchant Shipping Act
NZ	New Zealand
OOW	Officer of the Watch
RN	Royal Navy
RNR	Royal Naval Reserve
WW1	The First World War (1914 – 1918)
WW2	The Second World War (1939 – 1945)

AUTHOR'S NOTES

(1) Gender

Women at sea were almost entirely confined to the purser's department and little involved with navigation and seamanship, or with the engine room, during most of the period covered by this book. Consequently, and for this reason only, I have almost invariably used the male gender throughout and have retained the terms 'seaman' and 'seamen', rarely using the more modern 'seafarer' and 'seafarers'.

(2) Tonnage and dimensions

The tonnage of a merchant ship is usually given in two ways:
(i) Gross register tonnage. The ship's internal capacity based on 100 cubic feet to the ton and indicated by 'grt'. (Note that it is still 'ton' as it is not a unit of weight.)
(ii) Deadweight tonnes. The weight of cargo the ship can carry before submerging her loadline and becoming overloaded. Indicated by 'dwt'. (Because the term refers to weight it is now metricated as 'tonnes'.)

   The dimensions of ships have been given in imperial measure as these units were in use during most of the period to which this book refers.

(3) References

(i) The symbol * shown to the left of a word or phrase, has an entry of its own elsewhere in the text which may help the reader if referred to at this point
(ii) Words in bold, other than in headings, generally do not have an entry of their own but appear within other entries.They are included in the index as they warrant a reference

PREFACE

The idea for this book came a few years ago when, on a number of occasions over a pint of beer in a services club, I found myself yarning with Charlie, a retired Able Seaman/ Bosun who served for many years in British merchant ships.

We talked of ships and ports we both knew so well and Charlie's yarns were full of language which had almost slipped from my memory after many years ashore. It was peppered with colourful words and expressions once so familiar to me. I gained enormous pleasure just listening to a real seaman recalling experiences, some good, some bad, but all typical of our years at sea in the heyday of the British Merchant Service.

Charlie was the archetypal British merchant seaman of his era – a fine seaman, ever-ready to complain when he felt he was getting a rough deal but, regardless of his personal feelings towards an officer, always respectful of his 'ticket'. Typically, by his own admission, Charlie would have been among the first to pilfer cargo if he fancied winning some attractive item for himself but, like his fellow seafarers, would have regarded the personal gear of his shipmates as sacrosanct.

When I first met Charlie a personal loss had left me at a low ebb but after about an hour of listening to his colourful seaman's language as he spun his yarns, I soon regained my usual *joie de vivre*. I revelled in the memories of ships and shipmates, of times ashore in foreign parts and of the joys of arriving back home at the end of a long voyage.

A Mancunian, Charlie went to sea before WW2 as a fifteen-year-old deck boy and served throughout the period of hostilities in ships of all sorts. One ship was sunk by the German pocket-battleship *Graf Spee* and he bacame a prisoner of war before being rescued later from the prison-ship *Altmark* by HMS *Cossack* near Narvik Fjord. A little later he was serving in another ship which was blown-up at Suez.

After the war Charlie jumped ship in New Zealand only to be

sent back to the United Kingdom by the police, but he later returned to settle legally. He continued to serve in foreign-going ships under the New Zealand flag until the late 1980s when he 'swallowed the anchor' and came ashore. By this time the Red Ensigns of both countries were fast vanishing from the world's seas.

Charlie's language was not drawing-room talk. It was full of nautical expressions and the colloquial language of the merchant seaman. I realised just how much I had forgotten and how readily this language could be lost. With the exception of the professional nautical terms little has been documented. I resolved to record as many of the terms, expressions, and seagoing customs as I could remember, for others to enjoy. Since then fellow seafarers have contributed many more.

Except for ferries and cruise ships, British ships have largely disappeared from the world's oceans and, with them, the British merchant seaman. The Cardiff tramp steamer, the smart twelve-passenger refrigerated cargo ship, the 8,000 ton oil tanker and the true passenger liner have almost entirely vanished. Today's monster ships, the cruise liners, the container and Roll-On, Roll-Off ships, the bulk carriers and super-tankers, often have less than half the crew of their smaller predecessors. The very mention of earlier manning scales, often more than double those today, would be almost enough to cause the 21st century shipowner a paroxysm. The crew of many of today's ships come from non-traditional seafaring nations and many speak little or no English. The little they do speak is almost entirely devoid of the traditional seafaring language.

Charlie epitomised for me, in so many ways, the typical British merchant seaman of a now past age. I hope this book, which makes no pretence at being a scholarly treatise, will go some way towards preserving the memory of such seamen, together with their special language and customs.

AUCKLAND.

April 2008

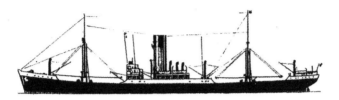

*A cargo ship on the Far East run
between the two world wars.*

Introduction

Many colourful expressions have entered into everyday English from the language of the sea and the landlubber is often unaware of the origin of phrases such as, 'Learning the ropes' and 'Between the devil and the deep blue sea'.

Many excellent dictionaries, and now web-sites, contain nautical language. Common usage aside, there are a number of nautical dictionaries which are concerned only with professional seamanship terms and expressions, most of which originated in the days of sail or during the early steamship era towards the end of the 19th century.

Several good dictionaries have been compiled of the slang and everyday language and expressions of the Royal Navy, much of it originating on the lower deck and often quite colourful. To the best of my knowledge there has not been much attempt to record the slang and colloquial language of the British merchant seaman.

Much of the professional language is still in use at sea today for the day-to-day operation of British ships, and it was never intended that this book should merely repeat it. However, I have included a number of professional words or terms where they relate to parts of a ship or to seagoing practices which have now largely disappeared but were in general use during the period under review. These terms help to convey some idea of the working and social life of the merchant seaman and an understanding of the colloquial terms which arose from it. They too were, of course, also part of the seaman's language.

This book covers roughly the period from 1875-1975, when the British Merchant Service, as we had known it, was a source of such national pride. However, it is not intended that the period under review should be too precise; some of the terms and expressions recorded here would have originated earlier, in some cases in the heyday of the sailing ship. But, as sailing ships gave way to steam ships and then to motor ships, and as new types of vessels were built to serve ever-changing trades, new expressions developed to accompany them.

Language develops to fill a need. As technology changes, and as the way in which a task is carried out alters, so new words are created and become part of the language. Many sailing ship terms were carried into steam ships by those who had crewed the sailing ship and were familiar with them. Some continued to meet the need, but as the steamship developed some sailing ships terms became obsolete, while new ones arose to meet the new technology's needs.

The colloquial language to which this book principally refers is largely that of the era after sail gave way to steam. It became the colloquial language of the steamship and later of the motor ship.

The advent of the steamship in the 19th century, although removing the uncertainty of propulsion and the need for skilled sail handling, really changed very little in the way many things were done at sea. Similarly, the later development of the motor ship, although further improving propulsion, did little to bring about any other changes in ship operation and almost none in cargo handling.

Seamen are traditionally conservative. It was not until the mid to late 20th century that these things began to change, slowly at first but, in the past two or three decades, very quickly indeed.

Flags of convenience, freight containers and mechanical and electronic aids have all reduced manning levels. For these, and other reasons, this trend has been especially marked in the British Merchant Service, contributing to the decline in the number of British seamen.

Technology has brought about enormous changes to the way essential tasks are now carried out. Add to this the changes introduced by the 1995 Merchant Shipping Act which replaced the 1894 Act, bringing about changes to employment in British ships.

Where once fifty or more men sailed together in a typical cargo ship, the numbers now are around fifteen and might include women. Their day to day contact and social life at sea have been drastically curtailed by reduced manning. Except in ferries around the coast of the United Kingdom, British seamen now have very limited occasions when they serve together and even then the nature of their employment gives little social opportunity to develop a colloquial language.

Political correctness has also played its dubious part and even the renowned shipping newspaper, *Lloyd's List,* no longer refers to ships in the female gender as 'she'.

Consequently, many words and expressions have now become, or are fast becoming, obsolete and their inclusion here will recall for many the words and expressions which were once in common use. Of course, the language has not entirely disappeared with the changed circumstances, but much of it is dying as the number of British seamen has diminished. A study commissioned recently by the Department for Transport shows that this trend can be expected to continue for the next 15 years – in June 2005 the number of active UK seafarers, many serving in foreign-flagged ships, had dropped to just a little over 26,000; fewer than the number lost during WW2.

As I know of no previous record of this language, it was inevitable that most of the terms and expressions included here are primarily remembered by those who served at sea during the latter part of the twentieth century. Memories are fallible and it is possible that there are errors as a result, although I have sought second and third opinions wherever possible.

Such was the diversity of British shipping and its trades, it was to be expected that my correspondents would not all have exactly the same recollection of the use of some of the terms. Just as the expression 'different ships: different long splices' conveys the notion that the way some things are done may differ between ships, so it must be accepted that the use of a particular expression varied, albeit usually only slightly, among ships and shipping companies. Spelling has sometimes presented a problem and a few words could have been spelt in more than one way. Where this arises I have opted for the one appearing to have the most support.

In some cases there was more than one word or expression to convey a single thought. I have used the more common as the principal one but have included the alternatives.

It has been very difficult to decide which terms and expressions warrant a mention and which should be left out. A few of those included are also used in the Royal Navy; it is not surprising that some should be common to both sea services. They formed part of the language of the British seaman of the period. However, there is overall a rather surprising difference between the colloquial language of the two services.

Inevitably, the cloistered life at sea with its absence of female restraints, resulted in seafarers developing a number of vulgar expressions. For the sake of the accuracy of the record I have included them and am sure readers will recognise the need for my doing so. They amount to only a very small proportion of the entries.

It may appear that a disproportionately large number of the entries relate to deck officers and deck ratings but upon reflection the reason will be apparent. Until the advent of the steam ship, the crew of the relatively small sailing ships were mostly concerned with sailing and maintaining the ship. Only the cook, sometimes a steward, and later a donkeyman to look after the auxiliary (donkey) engine, its boiler and steam winches, possessed other skills.

By the turn of the 20th century Britain's vast imperial Merchant Service employed over 200,000 mariners from around the world with the majority still deck officers and ratings. By then, steamships were well established but it was still relatively early days in the growth in numbers of engineers and catering staff, and the pattern of ship operations had been established many years earlier. The language of the merchant seaman had been born in the sailing ship era and only slowly did engineers and catering staff influence it, although their numbers grew rapidly as the Trans-Atlantic passenger liners developed in size.

Many of the words and expressions belong principally to the working life of British merchant seamen in the heyday of the tramp ship and 'tween deck cargo liner. Others came with the development of the oil tanker, specialised cargo carriers and the passenger ship. The majority can loosely be said to comprise, forecastle language, (usually abbreviated fo'c's'le) which is the equivalent of the Navy's lower deck language, although it was not entirely confined to the ratings. Much of it found its way amidships into the officers' accommodation too.

A few of the terms and expressions will be unfamiliar to some merchant seamen; some being peculiar to a particular trade or type of ship, e.g. tankers. (Those peculiar to fishing vessels have been excluded.) The Merchant Service, unlike the Royal Navy, did not have its *modus operandum* directed by a single source. It comprised two or three hundred separate companies, each directing the operation of its ships in its own manner. The differences were sometimes very marked. Passenger ships tended to be operated differently from cargo ships and in several large passenger ship companies, naval influence was introduced by officers who served intermittently as naval reservists. But it is probably in tramp ships that the language of the review period became most nurtured and developed.

The crews of British ships came from a number of ports around the United Kingdom but towards the middle of the period when the passenger liner reigned supreme, a large proportion of them came from London, Liverpool, Southampton and Glasgow. Inevitably, particularly in the case of the first two, terms and expressions came from the surrounding areas, significant influencing the language in many ships. Consequently many Cockney and Scouse expressions appear throughout.

As far as possible I have grouped the terms and expressions together under appropriate chapter headings. Each chapter consists of two parts. The first contains a reference to the place aboard ship to which its entries belong, together with a discussion on the practices and customs associated with the subject of the chapter. In many cases these require the use of appropriate professional terms. The second part includes the colloquial terms used by seamen in connection with the subject.

DEFINITIONS

An understanding of the contents of this book requires some knowledge of the administrative structure of merchant ships and a few definitions will assist. But definitions can go only some of the way toward an overall understanding, as there can be subtle difference of meaning, depending on context. Those familiar with a profession, such as that of sea-going, can usually detect quite readily which meaning is applicable but others may experience some difficulty in picking up the sometimes subtle difference.

The Merchant Navy. It was a fitting tribute to their courage and indomitable spirit that, in 1922, after the first of the two world wars, King George V saw fit to honour all British merchant seamen by introducing the collective title, The Merchant Navy for all the many and diverse British shipping companies in which they served. The new name gained a good deal of favour during WW2 when merchant seamen, being civilians and not wearing a uniform ashore, were often little recognised for the essential war work they were performing. Reference to their belonging to the Merchant Navy helped to give them an enhanced status in the public eye alongside their counterparts in the Royal Navy.

The Merchant Service. Although in 1922 Merchant Navy became the official name, Merchant Service has remained a term still widely used by seafarers and others. It was in general use before this date and was still commonly used right to the end of the period under review. (In the USA the equivalent term is 'US Merchant Marine'.)

The Mercantile Marine. This term is almost synonymous with Merchant Service. It had some official recognition in that it was also used when referring to the Government office – the **Mercantile Marine Office** (sometimes also referred to as **The Shipping Office**) – once found in all major United Kingdom and Commonwealth ports. Its Superintendent was responsible for administering the official regulations governing the affairs of merchant seamen in their port district and was known as the **Superintendent of Mercantile Marine.** It was also the term used in The Mercantile Marine (Uniform) Order 1918 and 1921, which introduced the standard uniform.

The Master of the Merchant Navy and Fishing Fleets. The title to which King George V appointed the Prince of Wales in 1928. It added formality and furthrer status to the term introduced in 1922.

The Red Duster. The colloquial name by which the national flag of British merchant ships, the familiar Red Ensign, was commonly known from the latter part of the 19th century. Those who proudly served under this flag, far from showing any disrespect, used the term with affection. Sadly today, except for a few cruise ships and UK-based ferries, it is a rare sight in foreign ports.

The Merchant Shipping Act (MSA). Unless specifically stated otherwise, the Merchant Shipping Act is the Act of 1894 which, for many years, was the largest single item of legislation on the United Kingdom statute book. Amended from time to time, it was the principal Act governing most aspects of the seaman's life until 1995. Then a new Act consolidated all Merchant Shipping Acts and amendments of the previous 100 years, and introduced sweeping changes.

Master. According to the MSA, the master was a person, other than a pilot, in command of, or in charge of, a ship. This accords with the generally understood meaning.

Officer. This term is not defined in the Act but the dictionary refers to an officer as a person holding a position of authority or trust. This is not very helpful as many people on board have a position of trust even though they may lack much authority. Nevertheless, it is a term which is fairly well understood.

The term used by the Act when referring to deck officers is, **mates,** and to engineer officers, **engineers.** The term, 'officers', albeit not included in the Act, is however in general use when referring to all mates, radio operators, engineers, doctors, pursers and sometimes chief stewards. (The only people who actually signed the ship's articles as officers were the radio officers – usually only one in most ships).

Rating. Also not defined in the Act, this is the commonly used term for all other than the master, officers and apprentices or cadets. They made up the bulk of the crew and are usually described as deck, engine room or catering ratings. (The term, 'other ranks', is confined to the Armed Services and is generally not used in merchant ships.)

A level of responsibility and skill separates a small number of ratings from the others. They are often referred to as **senior ratings** and are generally considered as **petty officers** although the Act makes no such provision. They usually possess superior skills to those of the ratings over whom they have authority, some holding a trade qualification. In an average cargo ship they included the carpenter, the bosun, the lamp trimmer, the donkeyman and usually the cook. In passenger ships they are joined by other senior ratings including plumbers, masters-at-arms, the chef, the second steward, the printer and occasionally others.

In the *deck and *engine departments the difference between these senior ratings and other ratings was usually not very evident from their casual working dress but when wearing uniform a badge on the sleeve indicated rank. However, many did not possess a uniform. It was more apparent in the *Catering Department, particularly in passenger ships where they regularly wore a working uniform. A chief steward was usually regarded as an officer, while a second steward, or in a cargo ship the storekeeper, was seen as a senior rating, although in the catering department the distinction was inclined to be a little blurred. The braid on the cuff was a common but not universal distinction; gold for an officer and silver for a senior rating.

Seaman. The MSA stated that this term includes '... every person (except masters, pilots and apprentices duly indentured and registered) employed or engaged in any capacity aboard ship'. In common usage at sea the term frequently referred more to those who worked on deck and employed the skills of seamanship and navigation than to engineers or others in supporting roles on board.

Seamen. As used in the MSA, the plural of seaman. Unless specifically stated otherwise, it is often used in a generic and wider sense referring to all who belong on board a ship, including the master and apprentices.

Deck hand. This is a term often used in lieu of seaman when referring to a rating working on deck as distinct from those employed in the engine room (engine room hands) or those specifically described by any special employment within their department.

Sailor. Although popular talk and literature may describe all those who go to sea as sailors, the term is not used in this way in the Merchant Service. It usually refers to a deck hand, i.e. it is a term specific to ratings in the deck department with seamanship skills.

Seafarer. A general term for all who serve at sea.

Mariner. Another term for those who serve at sea, rarely used for those who have not served in the deck department, and more particularly used when referring to an officer where a greater depth of professional knowledge is anticipated, as in **master mariner.** (The term, master mariner, is correctly applied only to a person holding a Foreign-Going Master's Certificate of Competency.)

Sailorman. A term still occasionally used, often in a slightly romantic sense, harking back to the days of sail. While not specifically excluding any seafarer when used today, because of its past use it is most appropriately applied to a deckhand rather than to others on board.

Crew. The term is not defined in the Act but is commonly used to refer to the entire personnel employed aboard the ship and is used except where the context indicates otherwise.The term, **'ship's company'**, is rarely used in the Merchant Service. It is almost exclusively confined to use in the Royal Navy where the term *crew* is only used when referring to those in a ship's boat.

As generally used, 'crew' included the master, the seamen and apprentices but excluded a pilot whose employment was by separate contract – another way of saying, as in the Act, '… not belonging to the ship'. Adding to misunderstandings, it is unfortunate that 'crew', was sometimes used to refer only to the ratings thereby introducing a small but important variation in meaning. When used in this more limited sense the appropriate departmental adjective was placed before it, as in, 'deck crew' or 'engine room crew'.

Departmental organization. As will be explained in more detail later, most merchant ships had the crew organised into three main departments with the master in overall authority. All ships had a Deck Department with the chief officer (the mate) in charge. (Although the master's promotion path would have been through the **Deck Department** he was usually considered to be above any departmental role).

The Engine Room Department was under the chief engineer. The third department differed in both name and structure between passenger and cargo ships. Usually known in passenger ships as the **Purser's Department**, it came under the Purser. It was often subdivided, one part for passenger services and accommodation, the other for the galley and stores. Cargo ships more frequently referred to it as the **Catering Department,** for which the chief steward was responsible.

PROLOGUE

The British Merchant Seaman

It is not surprising that, growing up in an island community, a large number of Britons turned to the sea for a living. This, in turn, could be expected to make them competent seafarers and over centuries the professional British seaman, whether in the Royal Navy or Merchant Service, or as a fisherman, has enjoyed an impressive reputation. This remains so today but unfortunately their number has dwindled to such an extent that they now represent only a small proportion of the world's seafarers.

During the period covered by this book, approximately 1875 -1975, British merchant shipping was at the height of its supremacy and the change came about very rapidly.

A few years ago NUMAST (now Nautilus UK) the British officers' trade union, fronted a campaign to alert the public and their short-sighted politicians to the perilous state of the country's merchant fleet. They produced a brochure containing a photograph of a Red Ensign (Britain's maritime flag) superimposed over which was the slogan, 'Take a good look. Soon you might not get a chance'.

British merchant seaman, in one form or another, have a history dating almost as far back as the beginning of occupation of the British Isles. Throughout history they have played a vital role in war and in peace, maintaining and developing trade within, to and from, Britain. In 1938 over 130,000 seafarers (and 50,000 Indians and Chinese) were employed in British ships but today their role is quite small in terms of world trade which has been steadily growing. after hundreds of years of

Britain's supremacy at sea the massive change almost all occurred during the past thirty-five years or so in spite of the growth in seaborne trade. For about the past ten years this has grown by around 50% while the share enjoyed by British ships has certainly not been commensurate.

(Comparative figures showing the decline are difficult to come by because not all records use the same criteria – some use gross register tonnage (grt) and other use deadweight tonnage (dwt), some include sailing ships, other do not. In the early part of the period British tonnages often included those of the Colonies and Dominions. Today they are shown separately. Further confusion arises due to the inclusion or omission of coasters with ocean-going ships. The figures for British seamen employed can be misleading too. Some include British seamen only while some include foreign seamen employed in British ships.)

According to figures provided by the Minister of Shipping, between 1975 and 1997 the UK registered trading fleet's tonnage declined by almost 95%, leaving the country with a mere 2% of the world's merchant fleet. Although the introduction of the tonnage tax by Her Majesty's Government has improved the situation slightly, it remains very serious. It is difficult to appreciate the extent and speed of the decline in Britsh shipping although it is pleasing to record that recently the trend has at least been reversed.

In 1875 steam had by no means surpassed sail on all the word's trade routes and there were still many sailing ships under the British flag. (The *Cutty Sark* was launched only six years earlier.) By 1890 steam had clearly overtaken sail, with Britain owning about 12 million grt of shipping. At the start of the twentieth century Britain owned more than 50% of the world's tonnage but only a few years later, during the WW1, the country suffered huge losses of ships and seamen to enemy action. (WW1 losses exceeded 3,300 ships and around 17,000 seamen. WW2 losses exceeded 4,700 ships and about 32,000 seamen, almost 24,000 of whom have no grave but the sea. Their names are inscribed on the Merchant Navy Memorial on Tower Hill in the City of London.)

After WW1 Britain's merchant fleet climbed back to a position of world supremacy and was again the largest merchant fleet in the world with nearly 7,000 merchant ships estimated at 17.5 million grt – about 40% of world tonnage. By 1930 it had grown by another 850 ships to over 20 million grt. Then, in the early part of the following decade it was hard hit by the Depression which affected the shipping industry seriously, about a third of its fleet being laid-up and 60,000 seamen out of a job. Even more were on reduced pay or served in some lower capacity. One well respected company, Port Line (then the Commonwealth & Dominion Line) even operated one of its ships, *M.V. Port Gisborne,* manned on deck by ex-apprentices who held certificates of competency as second mates; 18 of these young men served in the fo'c's'le as able seamen and quartermasters.

Shipping began to recover in the mid-1930s as world trade picked-up again but before the decade was out WW2 had begun, at which time nearly 27% of world tonnage was British owned – 6,843 ships of 1.7 million grt employing about 132,000 seamen.

Sadly the war saw terrible losses again, principally from the German U-Boats whose devastating attacks in wolf-packs took a heavy toll. (In May 1943, 239 U-Boats were operating in the North Atlantic.) This time the losses attributed to submarines alone were put at over 2000 ships and many more were lost to surface raiders and bombing by the Luftwaffe. This number of ships lost was almost catastrophic but even more important was the loss of the skilled seamen who went down with them.

But after WW2 shipping settled down yet again and by 1946 a combination of British, Canadian and American wartime shipbuilding had restored its post-war fleet to somewhere near the tonnage with which it had entered the war. but the seamen were harder to replace. It took time to train them and it took even longer for them to gain the necessary experience.

As Britain went into the 1950s and 1960s it again had an impressive merchant fleet with some of the finest ships and seamen afloat. Many see these as the golden years of British shipping when the Red Ensign was again seen in almost every part of the world. In 1960 the tonnage had increased to 21.1million grt – 16.3% cent of world tonnage. Most of the thirty years that followed the war were prosperous with many British shipowners having some fine ships built in British shipyards.

By 1975 the tonnage on the British register was 33.2 million grt, but by this time the fleets of the flags of convenience had grown and Britain's share was just under 10% of world tonnage. although the number of British ships was lower than previously, their size had increased enormously and the actual tonnage was the highest ever. 73,400 seafarers, including 34,800 officers, were then employed in British-registered ships.

From 1975 both numbers and tonnage of British shipping started to drop. The decline was slow at first but as the century moved into its final quarter it gained momentum. Ships flagged out to the flags of convenience, principally Liberia which finally overtook the tonnage on the British register in 1967, but also Panama and other unlikely 'maritime' countries, compounded the problems of competition now coming from another source – the jet airliner.

There was another factor too. although many ships were bigger than ever the number of seamen required to man them dropped as automation took over. In any event shipowners now began seriously to employ labour from third-world countries at lower wages.

By 1995 the UK owned and registered ships over 500 tons gross, actively trading, had fallen as low as 251. By the end of the 20th century there were only about 10,000 British seafarers all told, about two-thirds of whom were officers, many serving in foreign-flagged ships. The British merchant fleet was at it lowest ebb. Britain had almost ceased to be a maritime nation and this is reflected in the public's lack of interest in ships and awareness of shipping's importance to the nation.

The extent of the decline after the end of the review period is dramatically illustrated by the almost complete disappearance from British ship-owning of P & O, once one of the largest and most successful British shipping companies. In 1974 the company owned 224 ships and had a further 33 on order. Today a mere handful of ferries remain to remind us of one of the greatest names in British shipping. P & O is now owned by a Middle East oil-rich country.

Readers will ask how it came about that Britain's once huge and very successful merchant fleet became so decimated that by the end of the twentieth century it had long ceased to be a significant contributor to world trade when some countries had increased their fleets exponentially. The answer probably lies in several events which occurred about the same time.

One influence was the post-war growth of ship registries set up by small nations whose charges, combined with less demanding standards of safety, were intended to attract the shipowners of the established maritime nations. The arrival of these 'Flags of Convenience' was seized on by some owners who saw an immediate opportunity to save costs regardless of the national consequences. A lesser standard of professional competence and safety became acceptable in many cases and was fuelled by the apathy of members of Parliament. Most did not wish or conveniently failed to foresee the problems. Consequently those British shipowners who embraced some of the less responsible 'Flags of Convenience' soon employed cheaper foreign labour.

For many years British ships had been actively engaged in cross-trades (the carriage of cargo between two countries outside the United Kingdom) and about this time the United Nations began to discourage the practice. It encouraged third-world countries in particular to make a bid for carriage to and from their shores in their own ships. The result was the formation of indigenous national shipping companies in some of these countries and an inevitable reduction of carriage in UK-registered ships.

In spite of sometimes dreadful working conditions, British shipping had been relatively free of labour disputes over the years. However, the seamen's strike in 1960, which persisted in some regions against the recommendations of the National Union of Seamen, followed by a further strike in 1966, simply added fuel to the fire. Whatever the rights and wrongs of these disruptions, they accelerated the flight of shipowners from the UK registry and reduced the employment of British seamen.

Finally, perhaps one of the most significant influences, was the introduction of the jet airliner. In the early 1960s passenger jets quite quickly replaced a large proportion of the passenger shipping on the North Atlantic routes and, before the next decade was out, the jumbo jet had made serious inroads into the ship-borne passenger services to Australia and the Far East. Britain possessed a large number of passenger liners which, until the spectacular growth in cruising towards the close of the 20th century, were particularly hard-hit by the growth of air travel.

With the loss of British ships inevitably came the loss of employment opportunities for its seamen who came from all over the country but, except perhaps in the case of Scotland, principally from areas close to the ports – on the East Coast, Dundee, Leith, Newcastle, South Shields, Hartlepool, Hull and London; Southampton in the south; and on the West Coast, Glasgow, Belfast, Liverpool, Cardiff and Avonmouth.

There were smaller ports too, particularly in Scotland; some of the finest seamen came from the Hebrides, Orkneys and Shetlands where, in many cases, they had been nurtured in the fishing industry.

London, Southampton and Liverpool were the great liner ports from which sailed the pride of Britain's passenger ships, but some of the other ports, principally, Hartlepool, Glasgow,

Cardiff and Newcastle were the home of the country's major tramp ship companies.

In many British ships a large part of the crew came from the Indian sub-continent, Hong Kong, Singapore, West Africa and the West Indies, and local crews were sometimes employed in ships on a local trade, e.g. Booth Line had some ships running up the Amazon with Brazilian ratings. Many of these foreign seamen were very loyal to the British shipowners who employed them and to their officers, but few now remain except in foreign owned ships.

The period 1875-1975 included two world wars when Britain's sea lifelines were stretched almost to breaking point by an enemy intent on destroying its merchant fleet. It is difficult to credit today that in the early part of WW2 a seaman's wages ceased from the time his ship was sunk by enemy action. Fortunately, this shameful situation was put right a little later and appropriately, a few years ago, the British Government declared 3 September (the day on which WW2 broke out) as **Merchant Navy Day.** In some respects the Merchant Navy has at last been formally elevated to equal status with the three armed services and this is reflected in the title of John Slader's book, *The Fourth Service*, about merchantmen at war, which was published in 1994.

The one bright spot on the horizon is that at the time of writing a small number of ships have returned to the British register. Efforts are being made to rebuild the British merchant service and the tonnage tax, introduced about the turn of the last century, is having some favourable effect. In the new millenium the tonnage of shipping on the UK register has more than quadrupled although a significant proportion is foreign owned. (The *Queen Mary II* is under the red ensign although American owned.) Even Norway, a traditional maritime nation has lost some of its ships to the UK register and it is to be hoped that more British-owned ships will be attracted back.

By 2005 the number of British seafarers then serving in British-owned ships was estimated at around 16,000, with many British officers, principally captains and chief engineers, serving in foreign ships. Although in 2007 more ships returned to the Red Ensign, it is unlikely there will be a major increase in British merchant seamen employed, as many of the crew will come from the countries with a lower cost of living. When the *Queen Mary II* went into service in 2004, although under the British flag and boosting the tonnage on the British register, she carried only 200 seafarers from the UK out of a crew of about 1,300.

The introduction of the tonnage tax has seen owners increase their training commitment to British seafarers and the UK Chamber of Shipping is actively campaigning to see a substantial increase in the number of cadets and, in good time, junior officers under training.

It is to be hoped that the trend will continue and although the recovery is quite modest it is encouraging as, at last, the British Government appears to have started to appreciate the important role a merchant fleet can play in the national interest. Although a return to Britain's former glory and pride in its Merchant Service may be a long way over the horizon, at least a start has been made. But many are sceptical of the motives. It is financially rewarding to attract tonnage, and the drive for growth in numbers on the British register has amost certainly been pursued with this clearly in mind.

There was a time when the British merchant seaman was not held in high regard by his fellow countryman. For years seamen tended to be seen as a race apart and it might be true to suggest that, in the past, they have been quite happy with this. In 1776 Sir John Fielding commented that Rotherhithe and Wapping, *'… are chiefly inhabited by sailors, where a man would be apt to suspect himself in another country. Their manner of living, speaking, acting, dressing and behaving are so very peculiar to themselves.'* **

**(From an article in the *Honourable Company of Master Mariners Journal*, Winter 2002/3, which gave a credit as follows – Sir John Fielding, 1776, quoted in Peter Earle, *Sailors:English merchant seamen 1650–1775*, 1998.

Samuel Johnson too was less than complimentary when he said, *'No man will be a sailor who has contrivance enough to get himself into a jail:for being in a ship is being in a jail, with the chance of being drowned.... a man in a jail has more room, better food and commonly better company.'*

Fortunately others have since seen them in a different light. Nicholas Monsarrat, author of *The Cruel Sea (*Cassells, *1951)* after more than three years in corvettes during WW2, some of them in command escorting convoys across the North Atlantic and around the East Coast of Britain, became very familiar with merchant ships. In his earlier book *Corvette Command* (Cassells, 1945) he paid a well-earned tribute to British merchant seamen and those of her allies when he wrote:

'Incidentally, it is the merchant seamen especially who have risen above the peace-time grudge they might well bear, and have glorified their calling by an unmerited generosity.Their valour and spirit have heaped coals of fire:no class in Britain was treated worse, or more brutally disregarded, than the merchant seamen in the early nineteen-thirties, and no class forgot it more quickly and completely when the call to action came'.

Such was the respect of the Poet-Laureate, John Masefield, for the British merchant seamen after their valiant efforts in WW2, that he wrote a poem for the HMSO publication, *Merchantmen at War – Official Story of the Merchant Navy 1939-1944*. The poem concluded with a final verse summing up the nation's gratitude:

'Unrecognised; you put us in your debt:
Unthanked, you enter, or escape, the grave;
Whether your land remember or forget
You saved the land, or died to try to save.'

Of the ships in which they sailed, Masefield wrote the oft-quoted lines:

'They mark our passage as a race of men,
Earth will not see such ships as these again.'

An early post-WW2 cross-channel ferry

CHAPTER ONE

Engagement &
Employment

Towards the end of the nineteenth century and into the twentieth, a number of important changes brought about an improvement in both the competence of British seamen and the manner in which they were employed. Among them were the regulations for the examinations for officers' certificates of competency and the Merchant Shipping Act of 1894. The Act also provided many regulatory measures which improved the lot of seamen and the early part of the twentieth century saw more legislation which went further in improving conditions at sea.

ENGAGEMENT, EMPLOYMENT, DOCUMENTATION
The Board of Trade was the government department whose Marine Department was concerned with the regulation of merchant shipping. An Act of Parliament in 1850 conferred, for the first time on a single department, 'the general superintendence of matters relating to the British Mercantile Marine'. It retained this responsibility until the outbreak of WW2 when a separate Ministry of Shipping was formed. In 1941 the Ministry amalgamated with the Ministry of Transport to become the Ministry of War Transport and, with the return of peace, it was renamed the Ministry of Transport. Later it became the Ministry of Transport and Civil Aviation, then the Department of Trade and Industry (DOTI) – nicknamed Dotty – Department of Transport and finally today, Department for Transport (DfT). (For many the 'Dotty' nickname has remained.)

However, these name changes have had little direct effect on merchant seamen and in this book little heed has been paid to the name of this government department at any one time as seamen continued to refer to it, many years after its first name change, as the Board of Trade – usually abbreviated to BOT.

Engagement:

The Shipping Office. Although the name of this office was officially changed to **Mercantile Marine Office** as long ago as 1862, seafarers continued right through the period of this study to refer to it as 'the Shipping Office'. As the Government office in port areas throughout the United Kingdom responsible for administring and overseeing the provisions of the Merchant Shipping Act, it was involved to a large degree with the engagement of seamen and admnistering the regulation and conditions of their employment.

Shipping Master. The Government employee responsible for running a Mercantile Marine Office. Although his title was also officially changed to **Superintendent** in 1862, the original name remained in constant use through the review period. He, or his deputy, signed on and discharged crews and had extensive powers under the Merchant Shipping Act.

Registrar General of Shipping and Seamen. This office, situated at Cardiff, was responsible for keeping the records of ships and seamen but had little day-to-day contact with them. All the ***Official Log Books, Articles of Agreement** and other papers were kept here. It also had important duties in connection with the Royal Naval Reserve.

Ship's Articles. Or simply 'the articles'. An abbreviated form of **Agreement with the Crew**; the legal contract which included a reference to the terms and conditions relating to the crew's employment, signed in front of a *Shipping Master.

Most Articles, signed by the master and the crew, bound the latter to serve the former for a specified voyage or period, usually a maximum of two years. They contained, the seaman's name, age, date and place of birth, home address, last ship and whether the seaman wished to take up an advance of pay or an *allotment note. Signed by each individual, the ship's articles were 'opened' at the beginning of a voyage and 'closed' at the end of it. A copy of the clauses appearing in the articles had to be posted in a conspicuous part of the ship accessible to the crew.

Foreign-going articles. The crew of the majority of British ships signed these articles as their ships were generally away from UK ports for extended periods but if they returned to an area covered by *Home Trade articles within two years, they had to *Pay off. There were exceptions where crews were on *running agreements to avoid frequent changes of articles. Only foreign-going certificates of competency were acceptable for officers signing foreign-going articles.

Home Trade articles. Vessels operating within **Home Trade limits** (the coasts of the United Kingdom and Europe's coastline between Brest and the River Elbe) signed Home Trade articles which had different provisions from Foreign-going articles.

Running Agreements. The terms of the articles were varied in some special cases. The crew on many of the North Atlantic passenger liners, for example, had six-month running agreements as they were returning to the United Kingdom at short intervals, often no more than a week or two apart, and the paper work involved in opening and closing articles was not warranted.

Bombay or Calcutta articles. Many Indian crews employed in British ships were engaged from these two major Indian ports. Separate articles from those previously opened in a UK port for other members of the crew were opened for them at these ports when they *signed on. A similar arrangement applied to ships recruiting their crews in Singapore and Hong Kong.

Signing on. When the *articles were opened, all on board (except the *apprentices, signed them – the act of 'signing on'. At one time this invariably took place in the shipping office but for convenience, in the latter part of the period under review, the shipping master often attended on board the vessel and the articles were signed there.

Signing off. On completion of a voyage, the Articles of

Agreement would be closed. The seamen would then sign the articles again before the *shipping master (on board or in the office) to conclude the agreement with the master. They then received any pay still due after deducting any drawings during the voyage for shore-going or personal expense, (e.g. *slop chest and *subs) and left the ship. They were then said to have been *signed off or *paid off. If their conduct and ability had satisfied the master, they might be invited to sign on again for the subsequent voyage when the articles were opened either immediately or usually later and closer to sailing day. Seamen might also be paid off at any time during the voyage while in port by mutual agreement, usually for reasons of illness.

Pay-off (or paying-off) table. Often used more metaphorically than literally as the place where seamen would say farewell to one another upon *signing off. In its literal use, it referred to the actual table where the shipping master presided when he signed off the crew. In a cargo ship it was usually the Saloon table.

On articles. The period between *signing on and *signing off.

Sea time. Time on articles was rated as 'sea time' for the purpose of time required to qualify for certificates of competency and other seagoing qualifications. Time spent in port qualified so long as the seaman was on articles but, in a home port, officers in particular would often serve temporarily in a ship off articles and, somewhat illogically, not earn sea time. This delayed the date at which they could present themselves for examination for certificates of competency which required a specified period of sea time.

T124 & T124X agreements. During the two world wars, many passenger ships were requisitioned by the Admiralty and commissioned as warships under the command of a naval officer. They were partly manned by naval officers and ratings, and flew the white ensign. In many cases Merchant Service officers and ratings already serving in these and other ships taken over by the Navy, and if not already in the naval reserve, remained on board and signed special agreements for the duration of their time in the ship. These 'articles', known as T124 & T124X agreements, often resulted in some friction between the merchant seamen and the naval contingent on board because of pay disparity, the former being on higher Merchant Service rates of pay.

Home Trade voyage (HT). Any voyage within Home Trade Limits was referred to as a Home Trade voyage.

Foreign-going voyage (FG). The term used for a voyage beyond Home Trade Limits.

The Pool. (Official term – **Merchant Navy Establishment**). Unless a company chose to engage its crews on a more regular basis, the employment of seamen was a casual affair until the Pool was established to give seamen greater certainty. When they left a ship they were off pay until they were able to find further employment and even if their ship was sunk by enemy action their pay stopped from that time. Once The Pool was introduced in 1941 (it was reorganised in 1947) a seaman, not being contracted to a particular shipping company, could find employment by offering his services at the *Shipping Office. His engagement usually came about by being present when a master (or his deputy, usually the mate) was there to engage a new crew who would then be *signed on for the voyage. Occasionally a master might require only one or two new men and, rather than attend in person, would inform the *shipping master who would sign them on and give instructions to report on board.

Pool man. As the name suggests, a seamen who joined The Pool and was available at the Shipping Office for employment on a regular basis.

Unestablished seamen. Those wishing to keep their employment on a casual basis, becoming available only when and if it suited them, were known by this name. (They could decline two appointments but were obliged to accept a third when offered.)

Company man. A Seaman with a contract with a shipping company on a more permanent basis than simply the articles for a voyage only. He tended to be a better type with a reputation for competence and good conduct, and was pleased to have more secure employment, usually in ships of a good standard.

Picking up. A crew was said to be 'picked-up' when seamen were called forward by the Shipping Master (or his deputy) to accept an instruction to join a ship and sign *articles. (New Zealand seamen were picked up **on the corner**.)

Indenture. A contract binding an apprentice to his master. An *apprentice was originally a seaman (i.e. deckhand apprentice) and not an officer apprentice until well into the 19th century. Some tramp companies retained the 'seaman' description until post-WW2 although it was expected that in due course the apprentice would seek an officer's berth.

A lad was apprenticed to a shipping company for four years unless previous attendance at an approved nautical school earned him some remission of sea time. This was often for six months but not more than a year. As a general rule apprentices did not sign *articles as they were already 'bound' to their master by their indenture. (Note that 'master' here refers to the shipowner to whom the apprentice was bound although, for most of his time, it was the shipmaster, as the shipowner's agent or assign, to whom the apprentice was directly answerable.)

The last indentured British apprentice completed his apprenticeship in the early 1970s and the final vestiges of the system had been swept away by 1980. Many indentures contained fascinating, legalistic language. A typical example included, '... and will not embezzle or waste the Goods of his Master, or his Assigns, nor give or lend the same to others without his or their licence; nor frequent Taverns or Alehouses unless upon his or their business, nor play at unlawful games...'.

An apprentice was, in effect, a cadet. Some shipping companies carried only cadets who were technically not apprentices as they were not indentured to the company but signed the *Articles of Agreement for each voyage. (Apprentices signed articles on some occasions but this was unusual and possibly in error.) One or two companies, the best known being Blue Funnel Line, referred to their apprentices as **midshipmen.** (Apprentices of the Union Steam Ship Company of New Zealand were referred to as Apprenticed Cadets during its latter years.)

In practice Apprentices/Midshipmen/Cadets were all the same as far as their type of uniform, training, and overall duties were concerned. They were aspiring officers under training. However, not all shipping companies treated them alike. Some treated them almost as junior officers, spending a good deal of their time on the bridge. Others gave them some junior officer privileges but employed them more on deck as seamen, giving them good training and experience, often working apart from the rest of the deck crew but on similar types of work.

Some companies took little or no interest in their training and used apprentices simply as additional deck crew. They were used as little more than cheap labour and given very little bridge experience.

Serving his time. After an *apprentice signed his *indentures he began to 'serve his time', i.e. the time required to complete the contract which bound him to his master. This was the principal use of the term but occasionally others on board were required to fulfil a time obligation and were also said to be serving their time, e.g. a seaman who obtained his sea time for a certificate of competency to become an officer might be said to have 'served his time in the fo'c's'le'.)

Distressed British Seaman (DBS). A British seaman who, for some reason such as hospitalisation overseas, loss of ship or other event, found himself outside the UK without a ship and requiring a passage home.

A DBS was often placed by a Mercantile Marine or Consular Office for repatriation aboard a British merchant ship having a spare berth.

Remuneration:

Allotment Note. (Generally simply Allotment.) A sum of money which a seaman could elect to have deducted from his wages for payment to a nominated person (usually a mother, wife or other next-of-kin) or to a bank, on a regular basis (usually monthly) while he was away. Arrangements for this were made at the time of *signing on.

Note on owners. An advance note for a small sum to be cashed at the *Shipping Office after the ship had sailed. It was intended for the seaman's wife to provide her with some money until the first allotment arrived.

Portage Bill. The master's accounts of the crew's earnings during the voyage; it was required by the *shipping master at *pay-off.

Pay Off Slip. The Account of Wages form - Form F; the final statement of wages given to a seaman when he *signed off. It detailed his pay still due to him as shown in the *portage bill after deducting money withdrawn for various purposes during the voyage.

War risk bonus. During WW2, and for a short time after, ships' crews, being civilians and not members of the armed forces, earned extra pay as compensation for the exceptional dangers they ran in an industry of vital importance to their country. Introduced at £3 it later changed to £5 per month for the first year of employment and £10 per month for subsequent years. It was commonly, but unofficially, referred to as **danger money.** It came to an end shortly after WW2 when a new scale of seamen's renumeration was introduced.

Sundays at sea. During the latter part of the review period some crew members, depending upon the terms of their engagement, received extra pay or an extra day's leave on pay for every Sunday spent at sea. This was later extended to provide extra pay for Saturdays at sea, and in some cases for other duties.

The dole. Officially the **Unemployment Benefit** – the weekly sum available to seamen who could not obtain employment.

(Amongst those grateful for the benefits of queuing outside the Labour Exchange on a Friday afternoon were also apprentices and cadets studying for their Second Mates' Certificates; most were unpaid by the companies with whom they had served their time and therefore were unemployed.)

Salvage awards. In exceptional situations a merchant ship's crew which voluntarily assists in saving another ship from peril may be awarded a sum of money in relation to the value of the property salved, and other considerations. It is paid on a scale depending upon rank. Efforts to save one's own vessel do not qualify unless the ship has been lawfully abandoned upon the master's orders.

A famous case of this involved the tanker *San Dometrio* abandoned in the North Atlantic during WW2 when some of the crew returned under the command of the second officer and brought her into a UK port.

While the above terms were the official ones concerning remuneration the following were in common use during the period:

White stocking day. The day a seaman's allotment was paid to his nominated beneficiary. The probable origin of the expresion lies in the practice of seamen's and firemen's wives dressing up to collect their money at the company's office; white stockings being de rigeur and the height of fashion at the time

Sub. A payment of part of the wages earned but not already drawn by a seaman or made as an allotment. Shortly before arrival in a foreign port where there would be shore leave, the purser or chief steward (or the master when not carried) sent around a sub list on which the ratings would request the amount of cash required.

Channel Money. A small cash advance on wages (a form of *sub) paid shortly before docking at the port where the seaman were to pay off or, where no cash was held on board, it was paid shortly after arrival. As pay-off time was often not until the next day this enabled the seaman to have some cash, often spent in the pub to celebrate the end of the voyage.

To flog a dead horse. Upon *signing on, a seaman often received an advance of a month's wages and was rarely prepared to do any extra work until he had worked off his debt to the shipowner. At the end of the 'dead' period when he began to earn again, a stuffed effigy of a horse was paraded around the deck before being hoisted to the yardarm and cut adrift to fall into the sea. (This ceremony refers principally to the sailing ship era and to the days before overtime was paid for extra hours worked.)

Documents:

Seamans' Identity Card. After 1 January 1943, every seaman was issued with an identity card containing his photo and

A British Seaman's Identity Card

fingerprints. Rarely needed after the war, it was revived by a resolution of the General Conference of International Labour Organisation on 13 May 1958. (With the introduction of the ISPS Code, brought about to counter terrorism after 9/11, the introduction of a biometric ID card is now being considered.) **Discharge book.** The 1850 Merchant Shipping Act (MSA) provided for a **paper discharge** (the information was contained on a single sheet of paper to be issued to a seaman on paying off.) In 1900 a small booklet was introduced, officially known as a **Certificate of Continuous Discharge** by which each seaman was allocated a unique number prefixed by the capital letter 'R' providing identification for official purposes e.g. R337943. It was an important document, accepted throughout

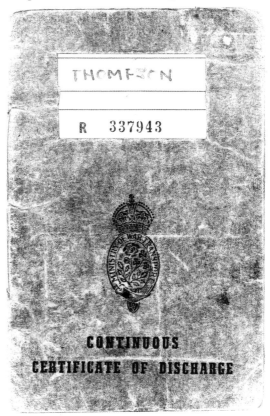

The Discharge Book contained details of the seaman's service and reports.

the world in lieu of a passport. It recorded the dates of engagement and discharge from a vessel, her name and official number, the trade in which she was engaged and the master's signature with a very basic report on the seaman's conduct. The report detail was also recorded in the *ship's articles when the seaman *paid off.

The discharge book contained two columns for the master to report on 'Conduct' and 'Ability' respectively. The following initials were used to indicate a seaman's conduct and ability until the system was abolished by the 1970 Merchant Shipping Act.

VG – Very Good, i.e. satisfactory.

G – Good, i.e. acceptable.

DR – Decline to Report, i.e. unsatisfactory.

VNC – Voyage Not Completed, e.g. where a seaman failed to complete his contract, usually by *jumping ship.

'Failed to join', which rarely occurred, was used where applicable.

In most cases a seaman would get a VG for both conduct and ability or just occasionally G for one or the other. (In practice the word very did not necessarily denote anything much more than satisfactory – there was no provision for a seaman being above average.)

MN Clothing coupons. During WW2 when clothing was rationed in Britain a similar constraint was placed upon seamen buying clothing in the United Kingdom. A book of coupons, each having the MN badge printed on it, was issued to a seaman by the *Mercantile Marine Office on joining the Merchant Service and again from time to time. (See opposite.)

Log books. While the above comprised the seaman's personal documents the ship required several of her own, among the most important being the Official Log Book (OLB), the Deck Log and the Engine Room Log.

Deck and Engine Room Logs were primarily operational records. The Deck Log covered navigation, ship employment

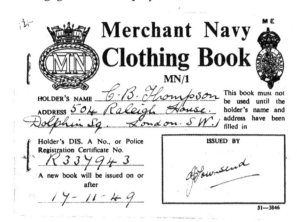

A Merchant Navy Clothing Book issued shortly after the end of WW2.

and cargo working, while the Engine Room Log covered machinery performance and maintenance. Of vital importance as evidence in any official enquiry into casualties involving the ship, most log entries were made by the OOW or EOW, at the end of his watch, or as soon as possible after events occurred. They were later countersigned by the master.

Official Log Book (OLB). Quite separate from the Deck and Engine Room logs, it recorded the compliance of the ship and her crew with statutory provisions such as the vessel's freeboard

Clothing coupons which had to be surrendered when buying clothes.

arriving at and departing each port, the master's inspection of food and accommodation, the execution of prescribed fire and boat drills, and matters concerning *discipline. It was usually kept by the master but in some ships this duty was delegated to the mate (or staff captain) who would present the signed entry for the master's counter-signature.

Discipline:

Logging. The master, whose authority was derived from the Merchant Shipping Act, had considerably fewer disciplinary remedies for misconduct than the Naval Disciplinary Act conferred on the commanding officer of a naval vessel. Very minor offences would usually result in admonition by a seaman's *Head of Department but in more serious cases he would be 'logged'.

If a seaman breached the statutory code of discipline on board he was usually summoned before the master who made an entry in the *Official Log Book describing the offence and any disciplinary action taken. In some ships, the logging was carried out by the mate (or staff captain) acting on the master's delegated authority, normally with the seaman's *Head of Department present. The punishment usually consisted of fining the seaman one or two days' pay.

In extreme cases the master could order a seaman to be restrained and handed over to the police at the next port, but generally discipline was limited either to placing a seaman off duty or fining him for an offence. Although there were provisions in the Merchant Shipping Acts over the years for the commanding officer of an H.M. ship to convene a Naval Court if requested by a master or others in a British merchant ship, this very rarely occurred.

A bad discharge. The commission of a serious offence, or repeated lesser misconduct leading to multiple loggings, would result in a seaman being given a DR under 'Conduct' in his *discharge book at the end of the voyage. A DR could be given for either conduct or ability although later was uncommon.

Paying off with a bad discharge significantly reduced a seaman's chances of obtaining another job, particularly with a favoured shipping company. As a general rule a master would never engage a seaman without inspecting his discharge book to check his record.

A single DR or **a double DR.** These terms referred to the master's report in the *ship's articles and the seaman's *discharge book, the former applying to a DR for either conduct or ability and the latter to a DR in both categories. A 'double DR' would make a seaman almost unemployable while a 'single DR', although of concern, might be overlooked by a benevolent master, particularly if he was desperate to complete his ship's manning when short-handed.

A burndown. The colloquial term for a bad discharge used principally by Liverpuddlian seamen.

Jump ship. It was common for seamen, particularly in the years immediately after WW2, to desert their ship in countries where they felt they would enjoy a better lifestyle than in Britain, or frequently where they had met a woman to whom they had become romantically attached. This principally occurred in Canada, Australia and New Zealand. Although 'deserted overseas' was probably the proper term, it was usual to say that a seaman had **jumped ship.** His *discharge book was then annotated 'Voyage not completed' and handed over to a *Shipping Master. Also, **Skin out.**

Miscellaneous terms relating to a seaman's employment and voyages

Ship out. A seaman was said to have 'shipped out' of a port or 'shipped aboard' a ship when he had sailed from that port or joined that ship.

Pierhead jump. An expression for joining a ship at the last moment, with little notice or time to prepare for the voyage, and usually because of a last-minute appointment. Occasionally a seaman might join his ship as late as a few minutes before she departed her berth, while she was in the lock or even later when the pilot boat, as a courtesy, might put him aboard as it went alongside to disembark the pilot just outside the port.

Run-crew. Crew for a short trip, usually between two UK ports.

Run-job. Employment solely for a voyage of short duration from one port to another, usually between the UK ports. The short duration contract was referred to as **Run articles.** Typically, a run-job might follow discharge of cargo in one port with a requirement for the ship to go to another for repairs, survey or other purpose. As the voyage was likely to be very short and the opportunity to earn much money thereby denied, **run money** (in effect, a bonus) was sometimes paid, usually with a rail fare home at the end.

Fly-out job. Today, when flying is common for seamen joining and leaving ships abroad, the term has little significance. However, when the practice was in its infancy and cause for comment, a seaman would use the term when he had to fly overseas to join a ship.

Delivery voyage. Similar in meaning to run-job but suggesting a voyage of longer duration, probably involving a new vessel or one sold to new owners intending her for an established service elsewhere. In the early post-WW2 era many Union Steam Ship Company vessels, after being built in the UK, were delivered to New Zealand for the company's coastal and Trans-Tasman service largely by seamen seeking a one-way passage to settle in New Zealand.

Deck chair job. Sometimes said of a run-job or delivery voyage where the crew have little more to do than get the ship from A to B with no responsibility for anything else.

Double-header. A second outward voyage after arriving in a UK or home port from a previous voyage without being relieved or able to take any leave, i.e. two voyages, one following the other without a break. The term was sometimes also used to describe a voyage in which a ship repeated part of a voyage before returning to a UK or home port, e.g. a voyage from the UK to North America and Australia, then back to North

America and to Australia again before returning to a UK port and *paying off.

Working-by. An officer, and sometimes a reliable rating, might remain aboard for a time after the crew had been *paid-off at the end of a voyage and before the next crew joined and *articles being opened prior to sailing. Before going on leave, and usually only if not sailing on the next voyage, the person working-by would attend to whatever might be required for the vessel's safety and essential day-to-day requirements while the ship was discharging and preparing for the forthcoming voyage. He was then said to be working-by the ship. Some liner companies had members of their sea staff temporarily employed ashore in their home port, and at least one company referred to them as **dock staff.** Other companies permanently employed ex-seafarers more permanently in a **shore gang** to perform the same function.

The home port. When used with the definite article this usually referred to the port where the company's head office was situated – often the port where the company's ships spent most of their time when in the UK. If a ship rarely returned to the UK but was based on an overseas port to which she returned from time to time, this might be considered her home port. It was sometimes said of the port where the ship was registered which was frequently, but certainly not always, the port where the company had its head office. More correctly such a port would be referred to as her **Port of Registry.**

A home port. When preceded by the indefinite article, 'a home port' often referred to any port in a vessel's home country – any UK port was 'a home port' for a UK based ship.

Deep-sea. Beyond the coastal waters normally plied by coasters. UK based cargo liners often started a voyage by loading in the North European ports (this portion of the voyage being referred to as the **coastal voyage**) and then departed for more distant ports requiring an ocean passage to reach them. The crew would often then refer to 'going deep-sea'.

Run. A vessel in the liner trades was said to be 'on a run' when she was plying her trade between ports and countries at which she regularly called, e.g. 'on the New York run' or 'on the South American run'.

Trip. A round voyage was often referred to as 'a trip', as in, 'It was a good trip' or, 'I am not signing on for the next trip'. But sometimes the term might be used to refer to a specific part of a voyage as in, 'The trip across the Bay was a rough one.'

An 'eleven trip man'. A seaman who made one round voyage only – One (1) trip out and one (1) trip home (i.e. 11).

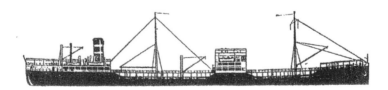

An oil tanker built between WW1 and WW2.

CHAPTER TWO

Deck Crew
Officers & Ratings

The hundred years between 1875 to 1975 saw many changes in the manning of merchant ships. As ships grew in size, so did the need for them to be manned by larger crews, many with new skills.

There was a high demand for British seamen who enjoyed an excellent reputation for their seamanship and navigation skills, but the sheer size of the British merchant fleet meant that they had to be supplemented by seamen from elsewhere. As a result many ratings were recruited from around the ports of the British Empire and later, the Commonwealth, notably India, Hong Kong, West Africa and the West Indies.

Traditionally many merchant ships, particularly sailing ships, had carried a master and two mates but with the advent of steam and the growth in the size of ships, it was not long before the majority of cargo vessels carried a third mate. The larger passenger ships commonly carried two certificated mates for each deck watch, and often a staff captain too.

Steam ships required engineers and their number steadily increased as ships grew in size. Most cargo ships soon had to carry three or four engineers but as the size and complexity of ships escalated there was an increasing need for engineers with skills others than those pertaining to the main propelling machinery. Some needed specialised knowledge to operate and maintain electrical and refrigeration equipment.

Where a small passenger ship had once required no more than a clerk and a few stewards to look after the passengers, the growth of this type of ship called for more crew to provide for passengers increasingly sophisticated demands.

No longer was the business and crew management by the master a simple matter and a more complex administration became necessary, with the crew divided into three main departments. Each had a Head of Department directly responsible to the master; the Deck Department discussed below, another concerned with her propulsion and other machinery, while the third was needed to provide the food and, in passenger ships, other hotel services.

THE DECK DEPARTMENT

Concerned with navigation, seamanship, maintenance of the ship's structure and cargo operations, the chief officer (the mate) was its Head of Departmment and responsible for it. He was accountable on board direct to the master for the administration and performance of the deck officers and ratings but ashore to the marine superintendent in head office, a position once almost exclusively the appointment of a senior master but now, if the company manages its own ships, often of an ex-seagoing engineer.

In cargo ships those concerned with radio and medical matters were usually also included in the Deck Department for administrative purposes but in large passenger ships they were more often considered as being separate Radio and Medical Departments.

The Master. A master's training and experience was as a deck officer and in some companies he was still regarded as one, but in most ships he was seen as non-departmental as befits one who is responsible overall for the performance of all the departments. Under the Merchant Shipping Act, The Master was the official name for **the captain.** A master was the captain of his ship but, as a form of address, Captain was strictly a courtesy title, e.g. Captain Smith. (In the Royal Navy, Captain is more than a title – it is a substantive rank but a naval officer of junior rank could still be the captain of a ship if in command of her.)

The master's station (place of work) when arriving or leaving a port was on the bridge while, in the ordinary course of a voyage it could be anywhere that required his presence to ensure the ship was running efficiently.

He had a number of nicknames among the officers and crew. The most common was, **The Old Man** and sometimes **Father.** Both were used no matter how young a captain might be. **The Skipper** was another but this was a less favoured and was more properly used only when referring to the master of a fishing vessel. Also, rarely and rather disrespectfully, **Slippery Flipper.**

In a cargo ship making long ocean passages the master's life could be very lonely. To some of his officers he was 'God' but often he was simply seen as a tyrant to others of his crew. The chief engineer was often the only one aboard who could drop in for a chat with him although the mate might occasionally be invited to his cabin for a drink. He usually kept himself well apart from his officers and, with relatively few duties each day, had time on his hands. It was not unusual for a captain to become a keen carpenter or take up some other time-absorbing hobby. Too many took to the bottle.

The life of a passenger ship's captain was very different and most were sociable and good ambassadors for the ship's owners. Their life was generally busy with official duties, including daily inspections of various parts of the ship, holding meetings with senior officers and, as far as their navigation duties would allow, entertaining passengers.

Some ships carried a **Staff Captain** or **Deputy Captain** but this position had no official status under the MSA although usually the second in command. He was usually nicknamed **Staffie** or **Staff.**

Commander. In some companies, among them for many years P & O and B.I., this term was used in place of captain and, in some passenger ships, for the Staff Captain – as **Staff Commander.** It was a legacy from the days of the Honourable East India Company and is still used by *Trinity House for the captains of its ships. Marketing departments, so concerned today with the importance of the company's image, have been responsible for the title being dropped in most cases in favour of 'captain'.

Deck officers. There were many forms of address and nicknames or abbreviations for the other deck officers who were sometimes collectively referred to as **the navigating officers.** Legally, under the MSA, they were **the mates.** In some companies, particularly the liner companies, the officers were often referred to as officers rather than as mates. (e.g. The second mate was referred to as 'the second officer') but to the Board of Trade and its successors, the second mate was th proper term.

OFFICERS' DUTIES

A brief outline of their principal duties follows. It is by no means a complete inventory of their duties which could vary slightly from ship to ship.

The Mate. The official title of the **chief officer**, normally second in command except in some passenger ships, and the person upon whom certain statutory duties were imposed under the MSA. Often referred to as the chief mate in the days of sail (and still in American ships) the word 'chief' was usually dropped later in steam ships, although occasionally used, particularly by shore officials and stevedores. The **first mate** was sometimes also used but this could lead to confusion in passenger ships which carried a first officer as well as a chief officer who was his senior. Sometimes addressed by the more respectful European crew as 'Sir' (**Sahib** by Indian crew – as all officers were addressed) the mate was more often addressed by the crew as 'Mr Mate' or by his name as 'Mr so-and-so'. The position had a number of nicknames among the crew including,
Harry Tate.

Ship maintenance, the running of the deck crew and usually the planning of the cargo stowage were his principal responsibilities. At sea he usually kept the 4-8 watch (unless additional certificated deck officers were carried) and his *station when arriving and leaving a port was traditionally on the *fo'c's'le. In a few companies his station was on the bridge and the rationale for this change was simply that the mate would be better equipped there, rather than if on the fo'c's'le, for his later ship-handling responsibilities when promoted to command if he had a closer opportunity to observe and understudy the master.

Other deck officers. The **second** and **third** officer (and, where carried, a first, fourth and fifth, and occasionally sixth) were sometimes addressed or referred to by the crew simply as second or third etc. but these terms were more often reserved for the engineers of equivalent rank. Deck officers were often addressed or spoken of as '**Two-O**' and '**Three-O**' etc. because their ranks were writen as: '2/O, 3/O' etc. (There were sometimes more than one officer of similar rank e.g. junior second officer, and in at least one company 'junior' was replaced by 'supenumerary' – he was known as 'the super-second officer'.)

The Second Mate was the navigator and usually kept the 12-4 watch at sea. He was generally directly responsible to the master for maintaining the charts and most other navigation equipment. His traditional berthing and un-berthing station in port was at the stern, caring for the after mooring ropes and the ropes or wires to any tug employed aft. (If the mate was stationed on the bridge the second mate would go to the fo'c's'le and the third mate aft. Although the second mate was likely to be less experienced than the mate when confronted with anchoring, his performance could at least be clearly observed from the bridge.)

The Third Mate kept the 8-12 watch, closely supervised by the master if lacking in experience. He was usually responsible directly to the master for keeping the *deck log-book and to the mate for care of the lifeboats and their equipment. Except in the varied pattern for the mate and second mates as explained above, his port entry and departure station was on the bridge with the master where he kept the *log and *bell book. Liverpool crews, with their distinctive accent, would often give additional emphasis when referring to the third mate as the **turd mate.**

The roles explained above were the customary ones in almost all cargo ships which carried only three mates. This applied in almost all tramp ships. Many of the liner companies carried four mates in their cargo ships and the fourth mate's station for entering and leaving port was on the bridge with the master. In many passenger ships there were additional officers, often with a variation in the customary pattern.

A gangway station was a common addition and an important one as numerous customs, port, Post Office and agency personnel eagerly waited for the ship to be alongside when they then swarmed aboard in droves.

The Radio Officer(s) (R/Os). In a few cases shipping companies employed their own radio officers. However, generally they were not directly employed but were employees of three companies specialising in servicing radio equipment and supplying staff. The best known of these companies was The **Marconi Company** which serviced the majority of British ships. The other two main companies were **Siemens** and **International Marine Radio.**

Cargo ships normally carried only one radio officer but in wartime there was a need to keep a continuous radio watch and most foreign-going ships then carried three R/Os. Passenger ships usually carried at least three. (The *Queen Mary* and *Queen Elizabeth* carried 12, necessitated by the volume of passenger radio traffic that was generated in these ships.)

Apart from maintenance of the radio equipment there was little other work normally required by the R/Os in port. Particularly if they were shipping company employees, as distinct from those contracted through Marconi or other radio

A cartoon by Beuttler early in the 20th Century
depicting the officers' responsibilities.

companies, R/Os sometimes assisted the mates with cargo work, or if no chief steward was carried, they assisted the master with his official correspondence and catering accounts. (In the New Zealand Shipping Company the R/O was responsible for checking and issuing books from the ship's library, running weekly film shows for officers and crew, and setting up and operating the public address system for ship-board parties. In Blue Funnel Line the Chief R/O was in effect the purser and did most of the paperwork, while the second R/O kept the radio watches.)

In addition to the care and operation of the main radio installation, the R/O was usually also responsible for the Radio Direction Finder (RDF), the lifeboat radios and, after its invention, the radar.

As the years went by R/Os became more involved with all the electronic equipment fitted to ships and in many companies became known as **electronic technical officers** (ETOs). Subsequently the improved reliability of radar and other electronic equipment, together with the development of long-range radio telephone and the advent of the **Global Maritime Distress and Safety System** (GMDSS) has meant that there is no longer a need for radio officers. (With the simplification of emergency communications this equipment is now operated on the bridge by the deck officers. R/Os are almost only found today in passenger ships, oil rigs and oil rig supply vessels.

It is perhaps an anomaly that R/Os were the only officers who actually signed the ship's *Articles of Agreement with the title 'Officer' (the deck and engineer officers being signed on as 'mates' and 'engineers'). For most administrative purposes they were usually considered part of the Deck Department although strictly they formed a department of their own, responsible for their duties directly to the captain.

Sparks or Sparkie. The name by which the radio officer was known on board. He was **Marconi Sahib** (regardless of his actual employee) to Indian crews.

Apprentices/Cadets. (See also Chapter 1) The former were indentured and the latter were not. Otherwise they were really indistinguishable one from the other. Both were, in effect, junior officers under training and members of the Deck Department. (Towards the end of the review period engineer cadets were also carried.) Apart from training ships actively engaged in commercial trading where a large number were carried, many passenger and cargo ships carried from two to four, sometimes six, of these young men often jocularly referred to as **'the lowest form of marine life'** – they were likened to barnacles, shipworm and other troublesome creatures. Sometimes also known also as **Gadgets, Gophers** (ordered to 'go for' this and that) or gannets (on account of their propensity to consume large quantities of food.) Occasionally even referred to vulgarly as **Shitehawks.**

Brassbounder. An occasional name for an *apprentice which had become largely outdated by mid-twentieth century. The Oxford Companion to Ships and the Sea suggests it is possibly derived from a thin gold lace binding on earlier apprentices' caps.

OTHER TERMS RELATING TO DECK OFFICERS

Fo'c's'le man. The term was applied to an officer who, having served at least four years as a deck hand, was promoted after successfully completing the examination for a Second Mates' Certificate of Competency. (*Up through the hawsepipe).

A China coaster or an **old China hand.** Usually said of an officer, particularly a master, who served for years in ships based on the coast of China especially during the 1920s and 1930s.

Royal Naval Reserve. A few officers, principally those of the larger liner companies, were encouraged to become naval reserve officers and were commissioned into the Royal Naval Reserve. They held the same ranks as regular naval officers but replaced the letters RN after their names with RNR, e.g. Lieutenant Commander J.R.Black RNR. (Engineers and pursers were also recruited into the RNR in small numbers.)

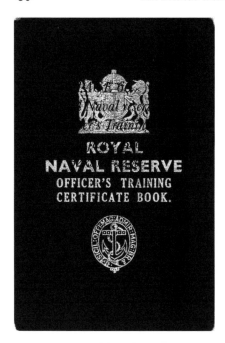

*Training record for an officer
of the Royal Naval Reserve.*

Reserve Decoration (RD). After fifteen years satisfactory service in the RNR (war service in the Navy counted as double time), an officer was eligible for the Reserve Decoration which earned him the letters RD after his name, e.g. Commander John Smith RD RNR.) A long-serving officer might earn a second RD referred to as a 'Bar to the RD' which was denoted by an asterisk after RD. A similar decoration was awarded to RNVR officers who were disparagingly referred to as **week-end sailors,** being part-time naval officers whose principal employment was in non-seagoing professions. Their decoration, now the **Volunteer Reserve Decoration** (VRD) was originally simply, 'the Volunteer Decoration' (VD) which suggested a sexual social disease but, particularly when accompanied by a 'bar', the combination was even worse, acquiring the unfortunate nickname of 'VD and Scar'. Some recipients of both decorations, in moments of undue modesty, may refer totheir awards as being earned for '15 years undetected crime'.

'P' Courses. Following the restructuring of the RNR after WW2, and the re-opening of entry in the early 1950s, special courses for new-entry reserve officers were again instituted by the Navy. As each was organised it was given a successive number prefixed with the letter 'P'. They were known as P Courses.

Skipper RNR. Although Merchant Service officers holding a commission in the RNR held the same ranks as Royal Navy officers, a fishing vessel skipper joining the RNR was the exception, holding the special rank of 'skipper' which was usually accompanied by command of a naval trawler or small minesweeper.

RATINGS

In the Merchant Service the senior ratings have never been as clearly defined by an official title as in the Royal Navy where they are referred to as chief petty officers or petty officers. However, for most practical purposes the most senior ratings are usually referred to in merchant ships as petty officers (POs) and rightly enjoy privileges not available to more junior ratings. (The rank of petty officer does not appear in the Merchant Shipping Acts, although the *Uniform Regulations in the December 1921 Order in Council refers to the dress of petty officers.)

The *carpenter, the *bosun and the *lamp trimmer, were the usual three POs in most cargo ships but in passenger ships there was usually a *plumber; all except the lamp trimmer often had an assistant, a more junior PO. Many passenger ships also had a senior rating concerned with mail when carried as cargo, the *yeoman of mails or some such name, and another, the *master-at-arms, was in a category of his own. The bosun and carpenter, both day-workers, were occasionally referred to as the idlers, the name a hang-over from the days of sail when the sail-maker was also included. (Many early steamers also had sails).

Carpenter. Usually a time-served shipwright, the carpenter was regarded as the senior petty officer. Nicknamed **Chippie** or **Chips**, his principal role was inadequately suggested by his title, as he was the handyman and 'Mr Fix-it', but he also had responsibility for sounding (checking the quantity) of the fresh and ballast water tanks, and replenishing the fresh water in port. Another important duty was to care for and operate the windlass and anchoring equipment, and maintain all openings and moveable items on the weather deck except cargo winches. (Engineers' responsibility).

Bosun (an abbreviation of **Boatswain**). The 'foreman' of the deck ratings having earned his position from his years as an able seaman. He was responsible to the mate for the work of the deck crew which principally involved external maintenance of the ship, her cargo gear and the cargo holds. He had several nicknames; among them were **Bose** (pronounced with a long 'O' as in Dose) **Bo-Bo, Boss, Sheriff** or **Cruncher.** (The latter was used in New Zealand ships and is not to be confused with the similar term, 'crusher' used in the Royal Navy for a member of the Regulating Branch, the equivalent of the Army's Military police.) **Gunner Sahib** was the name used by an Indin crew for a Caucasian bosun and was used without the suffix when being referred to by another Caucasian.

Lamp trimmer. Although effectively the bosun's mate his principal role was as the **deck storekeeper** responsible for the bosun's stores. By the mid-1960s the name became rather outmoded as the only kerosene lamps on board were the emergency navigation lights. (In Australian ships he was known as the storekeeper and in some Brirtish ships he was later renamed assistant bosun.) Nickname: **Lamps** or **Lampie.**

Plumber (and **second plumber**). Usually time-served tradesmen, they were kept busy in passenger ships, often with hundreds of basins, toilets and service pipes requiring attention.

Yeoman of mails (YOM). In passenger ships whose owners had Post Office mail contracts, a petty officer, with this title in P&O but others elsewhere, was the mail officer's assistant. When not specifically involved with mail he acted as a **bosun's mate**.

Master at Arms (MAA). A senior petty officer in passenger ships, particularly those with white crew. The MAA was usually responsible to the staff captain or chief officer for discipline and was the ship's policeman.

Quartermasters.(QMs) Usually carried in passenger ships and in some cargo ships of liner companies, most of these deck ratings fulfilled two primary roles. As watch-keepers at sea they were the helmsmen and when the ship was in port they were the gangway watchmen. Quartermasters usually wore a uniform similar to that of the traditional naval rating and tended to fall into a category of their own between the senior ratings and the rest of the deck crew.

Day-work *quartermasters. The term appears to contradict the definition above about quartermasters being watch-keepers but some ships carried an additional quartermaster or two who were day-workers. They were sometimes permanent day-workers, or day-workers by rotation with the watch-keepers, and were assigned special sailorising duties such as canvas work, making lifeboat boat covers and awnings.

Sports *quartermasters. Passenger ships often carried day-work quartermasters whose special role was to care for sports equipment and assist with organising passengers sports, e.g. deck tennis, quoits and horse racing.

Able seaman (AB). The most experienced of the deck crew with the exception of the petty officers and possibly the quartermasters. (More fully explained in Chapter 3 under Deck Ratings for training and qualifications.)

Efficient deck hand (EDH). A qualified deck rating with less sea time and experience than that required for rating as an AB (More fully explained in chapter 3 under Deck Ratings.) Sometimes nicknamed **Educated Deck Hand.**

Ordinary Seaman (OS). The deck rating between deck boy and EDH or AB. There were usually two grades of ordinary seaman, Junior Ordinary Seaman (JOS) and Senior Ordinary Seaman (SOS), the difference between them being experience rather than qualification. (The term **Bucko** was used in

Australian and New Zealand ships.)

Deck boy. The entry level for a lad wishing to serve in a merchant ship on deck as a rating. He had usually spent a short time at a pre-sea school before joining his first ship.

White crews. Many ships were manned solely by Caucasian officers and ratings. In British ships they were mostly from the United Kngdom but there was often a sprinkling of Caucasians from throughout the Empire (later Commonwealth). A seaman from Scandanavia, the Continent of Europe and even the USA would also be found occasionally in a British ship.

A white crew(ed) ship. A ship almost entirely manned with Caucasian officers and ratings.

Native crews. During the period 1875 – 1975 many of Britain's most respected shipping companies employed ratings from various parts of the British Empire (later Commonwealth), in particular from the Indian sub-continent – India, Pakistan, Bangladesh, Sri Lanka (then Ceylon) and Goa – and from West Africa, the West Indies and Hong Kong. The areas from which the Indian crews were recruited, and their port of engagement, depended largely on the parts of the sub-continent to which the ships traded. These crew were principally Moslem and Hindu but sometimes a Christian might be included. A small number of Indian nationals were employed as officers in some British companies, particularly those with ships trading largely on the Indian Coast.

Native crew(ed) ship. British ships usually carried British officers but the remainder of the crew comprised ratings from the Indian sub-continent. They were referred to occasionally as 'Asian crew' ships but usually as 'native crew' or 'native crewed' ships. It was more common to refer to ships with crews from other specific areas as West African, West Indian or Chinese-crewed.

INDIAN DECK RATINGS

Lascars. Seamen from the Indian Sub-Continent. As they served in large numbers in British ships, the Hindustani name of the various ranks is shown below. They were generally good seamen but, particularly around the times of their religious festivals their prior fasting left them lacking the physical strength of white crews. Discipline was usually good and they were respectful and cooperative with their officers who generally treated them well, showing genuine concern for their welfare and respect for their religious beliefs. Their language, Urdu was commonly referred to as Hindustani and sometimes as Lascari. Lascars referred to the Captain as the **Captain Sahib** and to deck officers, as the **Malim Sahibs.** When referring specifically to one of the deck officers they prefixed 'Malim Sahib' with a number to indicate rank, (e.g. the fourth officer was **Char Malim Sahib** or more briefly **Char Sahib.**) The exception was the chief officer who was **Burra** (chief) **Malim Sahib.** A junior officer, if not referred to by rank, was a **Chota Sahib.**

Many ships under flags of convenience, and of course Indian ships, today employ Indian sub-continent crews but the names of their ranks, once so familiar to officers of the British companies previously employing them, have now largely disappeared. They were:

Deck serang. Bosun.

Burra tindal. Bosun's Mate.

Mistri. Carpenter, (a European Carpenter was a Mistri Sahib.)

Cassab. Storekeeper.

Paniwalla. Waterman. (The carpenter's mate whose principal role in port was to look after the receipt of fresh water (pani) into the ship's tanks.)

Winchwalla. He looked after the oiling of the winches. (Also a carpenter's mate.)

Sukunni. Quartermaster.

Kalassi. Lascar seaman.

Topas. Sweeper/cleaner, usually referred to as 'jacki'.

Bandari. Native cook. It was usual for there to be a bandari for the deck crew and another for the engine room crew.

(The above terms are as recalled by the author who was familiar with crews who joined in Bombay (now Mumbai) from the local area, but different shipping companies employed native crews from many other parts of the sub-continent, resulting in variations in the terms used.)

Other terms relating principally to white deck ratings:

Peggy. A messman, usually a deck boy in a *white crew ship. Both deck and engine room crew had a peggy who collected the food from the galley and cleaned up afterwards. In the deck department there was sometimes one peggy for the POs (the bosun's peggy) and another for the deck hands (sailors' peggy). There are two suggested origins of the name which may, or may not have any substance, one being that it was an old name for a messenger. The other is that an injured seamen, often with a 'peg leg' but still ambulant and able to combine light duties with that of messman, was employed; hence 'Peggy'. Sometimes referred to as housemaids with bollocks.

Royal. Long time crew or the mate's favourite.

Fo'c's'le hand. The term was sometimes applied to a deck hand.

A Scalieback. A seaman.

The crowd. Collectively the deck crew were often referred to by this name as in, 'It's time for the crowd to turn-to.'

Dock Street brigade. Seamen signed on at the Prescott Street labour pool adjacent to Dock Street in London. Also Dock Street Fusileers.

Painter. While all deck crew would be expected to paint, the quality of their work varied considerably. Ben Line ships, whose steel deckhouses were painted to resemble dark wood with a prominent grain, carried a skilled Chinese painter, one of whose special roles was attending to this exacting work.

Kinker out. Usually a deck boy who assisted the seaman handling the hose when washing down the decks. His role was to make sure no kinks occurred in the hose which might stop the water flow and damage the pump supplying it. Also **The kink.**

Dip-stick. The AB in New Zealand ships responsible, in lieu of a carpenter, for taking the routine tank soundings to check their remains.

Blue water man. A sailor with a strong preference for serving in ships trading to warm tropical areas rather than to those nearer home. More often than not they were bachelors who were happy with longer voyages and were not concerned about spending more time closer to their wives and families.

Deep sea man. Although without official status, this term was often used to describe a seaman who had spent most of his seafaring years in foreign-going, rather than home trade ships. When in company with seamen from the latter they described themselves, often with an air of superiority, as 'deep sea men'.

A passenger liner of the India-Australia run
before and after WW2.

CHAPTER THREE

Deck Training and Qualifications

For many years there was no special requirement for those joining the Merchant Service to have pre-sea training and for most it simply became a case of learning on the job.

Few deck ratings had more than a very elementary introduction to life at sea. For some this might be as orphans, and for others more voluntarily, with schooling in one of the once numerous quasi-nautical establishments in Britain. It was not uncommon for those with no nautical background at all simply to run away to sea.

Some aspiring officers and ratings had their first introduction as Sea Scouts or, when a little older, as Sea Cadets but many had no pre-sea training at all and joined their first ship as green as grass.

Perhaps surprisingly many *apprentices and *cadets often had little serious pre-sea training although there were more opportunities for a lad wishing to become an officer whose parents could afford to send them to one of the officers' training establishments.

In due course the value of pre-sea training was given fuller recognition and it became more necessary as a prelude to life at sea. In particular the *Shipping Federation realised its value for ratings and initiated short introductory courses which gave them insights into the new life they had chosen. For prospective officers nautical establishments developed to provide shorter and less costly opportunities than those offered at the three principal Merchant Service officers' training establishments.

Nevertheless, it was often suggested that attendance at one of the training establishments did little in the long term to make these youngsters more competent seamen although the knowledge and experience gained at them undoubtedly helped in the short term. It made them more useful members of the crew when they joined their first ship and even if they gained little else these youngsters at least learnt to live and work together.

DECK OFFICERS

Training and qualifications:

Pre-sea training. Although the proportion may have been relatively small, many joining the Merchant Service as deck officer *cadets and *apprentices attended pre-sea training ships or establishments, generally for one, two or more years. The time usually qualified as double time up to a maximum of one year's remission of sea time. Having satisfactorily completed their course they received a certificate, accepted by the Board of Trade, as evidence of qualifying sea time. These young men then went to sea and *served their time for between three and four years (depending on their remission) before sitting their first examinations for a *Certificate of Competency as Second Mate. (During WW2 the qualifying time was reduced by a year to allow them to sit for a temporary certificate, the shortfall then being made up before they sat for their *Mates' Certificate.) Discipline was often very strict in pre-sea schools and a beating with a cane, occasionally even a fencing foil, was a common punishment. (On the *Conway* a rope's end, known as a **teaser**, was used.) In some nautical schools, lesser breaches of discipline could require a boy to write out in full 8Article 9 of the International Regulations for the Prevention of Collisions at Sea in place of the customary schoolboy punishment of writing a hundred times, I must be a good boy. (Under the 1910 Regulations the individually numbered rules were called **Articles** but were renamed **Rules** when the 1954 Regulations were introduced.)

Article 9 covered the lights and day signals to be shown by vessels fishing and was by far the longest of them all. It ran into hundreds of words. Depending on the severity of the misdemeanour, writing a single copy or sometimes a repeated writing, of Article 9 provided a time-consuming and tedious punishment but it did have some practical learning value.

Training at sea. The quality of the training received by *apprentices or *cadets at sea depended almost entirely on the attitude of the shipping company in which they served; in some they were treated as a source of cheap labour when the mate was reluctant to use the deck crew. They often learnt little navigation, spending minimum time on bridge watch-keeping, and acquired their seamanship knowledge almost entirely on deck as day-workers, often under the charge of the bosun. However, a few companies gave them a first-class, all-round training, which fully prepared them for their later duties as deck officers, often far exceeding the requirements of the Merchant Navy Training Board. Some companies even appointed one of the junior officers to be directly responsible for their training.

Mid-apprenticeship release. Towards the end of the review period significant changes were made to the system of training cadets after joining their first ship and involved a study period or periods ashore at approved nautical schools in lieu of some actual sea time.

The Merchant Navy Training Board (MNTB) provided a syllabus and course material for *cadets and *apprentices during their time at sea and monitored their progress as they studied for the second mates' certificate.

Home Trade (HT) and **Foreign-Going** (FG) Certificates. For those serving at sea in Home Trade passenger ships there were two HT certificates – Mate and Master – and three for foreign-going ships – Second Mate, Mate, and Master. (Also *Extra Master but see below).

Until the 1970s there was no requirement for certificates in HT cargo ships although many officers held the passenger ship certificates. Almost all obtaining HT certificates had served as ratings, often in quite small vessels, and usually without pre-sea training. The seafarers who obtained FG certificates had generally served either as deck apprentices, some with at least twelve month's pre-sea training, or as deck ratings although their number was much smaller.

Second Mates' Certificate. This was the first certificate of competency for a lad wishing to become an officer in a FG ship. As its name implies it qualified him to sail as a second mate but, except in some tramp ships, it was more likely that he would first obtain a berth as a third mate (or junior) for a year or two while gaining watch-keeping experience. Uncertificated third mates were common in tramp ships but in the liner companies the requirement for a third mate's berth was usually a Second Mates' Certificate or higher. For a second mate's berth, a Mates' or even a Masters' Certificate was often needed. A number of ABs, intent upon getting out of the fo'c's'le and sufficiently confident of their ability to become officers, successfully sat the examination.

Mates' and Masters' Certificates. The two principal subsequent certificates were for qualification as mate and master. With the manning scale for a particular ship requiring a certificated officer in those ranks, an officer could serve in them only if he was appropriately qualified. As with second mates, the liner companies in particular required further experience before making such appointments. (See page 72 for an illustration of a Master's certificate.)

Extra Masters' Certificate. Now abolished and largely replaced by university examinations at degree level, this was the superior certificate for deck officers. Apart from covering the more theoretical aspects of subjects, such as mathematics and physics, it required a greater understanding of ship construction, hydrographic surveying and several other subjects than was required for a Master's Certificate. It was of a significantly higher academic standard but did little to increase

CERTIFICATE OF COMPETENCY

AS

MASTER

OF A FOREIGN-GOING STEAMSHIP   No. 74502.

To *Cecil Barrington Thompson.*

WHEREAS you have been found duly qualified to fulfil the duties of
Master of a Foreign-going Steamship in the Merchant Service, the Minister of Transport
and Civil Aviation, in exercise of his powers under the Merchant Shipping Acts and of all other
powers enabling him in that behalf, hereby grants you this Certificate of Competency.

SIGNED BY AUTHORITY OF THE MINISTER OF TRANSPORT and CIVIL AVIATION and
dated this .... 19th .... day of .... **April,** .... 19 55.

Countersigned

Registrar General

A Deputy Secretary of the
Ministry of Transport and
Civil Aviation.

REGISTERED AT THE OFFICE OF THE REGISTRAR GENERAL OF SHIPPING AND SEAMEN.

Certificate of Competency for a Master of a Steam Ship (ForeignGoing).

a shipmaster's essential knowledge, being studied largely by officers wishing to teach in nautical schools or join the Board of Trade (and its successors) as surveyors and examiners. There was no legal requirement for it at sea and consequently it was rarely held by seagoing officers.

Special proficiency certificates and re-validated certificates. From about the 1950s and 1960s a requirement was introduced for officers to attend a number of specialist courses to qualify for special proficiency certificates, e.g. **Fire fighting, Radar observer, R/T operator** etc. Later a number of other important proficiency certificates were introduced and holders of certificates of competency were required to re-validate them by further sea experience, or by attending a nautical college to up-date their proficiency.

A square-rig endorsement was available to those holding certificates of competency for service in steam ships (this included motor ships) if they had served the prescribed time in square-rigged sailing ships and had been examined in the appropriate skills. This endorsement was abolished towards the end of the period and about the same time the whole of the certificate structure underwent a major overhaul.

Certificate of Service. Suitably qualified naval officers, following their service in the Royal Navy, could apply for this certificate which often enabled them to obtain a berth as an officer in a merchant ship.

PMG Certificates. Radio officers were also required to be qualified shortly after radio became an established medium of communication at sea. During much of the period there were First Class and Second Class PMG Certificates. (PMG referred to Postmaster General.)

Study for the Second Mate's examination. Having completed the requisite sea-time, almost without exception *cadets and *apprentices underwent a short period of intensive study at a nautical school to prepare them for sitting their Second Mate's Certificate. Similar opportunities were available to deck ratings who wished to study and sit this examination but their study time was likely to be longer since they usually lacked the same opportunities for study while at sea.

Study for subsequent examinations. Having obtained a *Second Mate's Certificate and gained the necessary sea time, officers studied at a similar institution before sitting the examinations for Mate and, later, for Master. In the mid-twentieth century the study time averaged about two and three months respectively although the more academically inclined would often sit their examinations after a shorter period of study. As the content of the examinations became more complex towards the end of the period, the study times, particularly for the *Masters' Certificate, increased. For the *Extra Masters' Certificate a twelve-month study period was common.

Examiners and Surveyors. The Board of Trade employed ex-seafarers to examine candidates for certificates of competency and carry out ship surveys to ensure compliance with statutory regulations. The Examiners of Masters & Mates were master mariners, usually those who had been in command at sea and held an *Extra Masters' Certificate, some being exclusively engaged in examining and others alternating the role with that of surveying. (The engineer examiners and engineer surveyors were mostly ex-chief engineers, in many cases also holding the superior certificate of *Extra Chief Engineer.)

THE OFFICERS' TRAINING ESTABLISHMENTS

The three principal institutions in Britain:

HMS Conway. Initially situated in an old 'wooden wall', (a typical warship of the era of the Napoleonic Wars) this college, the oldest of the three, was strongly supported by the Mercantile Marine Service Association and encouraged by Liverpool shipowners, notably Alfred Holt & Co. Founded in 1859 the college remained based in a vessel moored in the River Mersey, near Rock Ferry pier, until 1941 when she was towed to North Wales and berthed at Bangor Pier, previously occupied by the reformatory ship *Clio*. The Conway was wrecked in the Menai Straits while under tow back to Liverpool for a refit in 1953. A shore establishment then carried on with the work until the college was closed in 1974.

HMS Worcester. Also originally a 'wooden wall', she was moored as a training ship in the River Thames, latterly at Greenhithe between the Royal and Tilbury Docks. Founded in 1862, the college received good support from London shipowners, P & O being one of its most ardent supporters who recruited many of its cadets from this establishment. In 1938 the ex-tea clipper *Cutty Sark,* then recently returned to the British flag, was presented to the college and moored for many years close to the Worcester and used in conjunction with her for cadet training. Later, as the Thames Nautical Training College, the training facilities of the Worcester were transferred ashore to nearby Ingress Abbey. The establishment finally closed in 1968.

Pangbourne Nautical College. (The Devitt & Moore

Nautical College Ltd.) The college was founded in 1917 as a nautical shore establishment on the River Thames, a few miles upstream from Reading, in Berkshire. Established by the Devitt & Moore shipping company, renowned for the excellence of training in its sailing cadet ships, the college continued the tradition briefly with the topsail-schooner yacht *St George,* converted into a sail-training vessel.

Often referred to as '**the public school in uniform'**, Pangbourne's students, like those of *Conway and *Worcester, enjoyed the privilege of wearing the uniform of RNR cadets. Some of its nautical training, carried out in naval gigs and whalers on the Thames, at Pangbourne, lacked the quality of the salt-water boat-work of *Conway and *Worcester whose cadets referred to Pangbourne, scornfully and quite unjustly, as **the ranch up the river.** With the steady decline in the number going to sea for a career, Pangbourne changed course in 1969. It raised its academic standards, dropped its nautical training but has survived most successfully, simply as Pangbourne College. It has managed to avoid the demise which befell its two sister training establishments.

Royal Navy entry. While all three of these establishments were principally set up to train officers for the Merchant Service, entry from them into the Royal Navy was also possible for the more academically inclined. This corresponded with the 'Special Entry' scheme available to others from public schools.

Other officer training establishments

School of Navigation, Warsash. Now a part of the recently established Southampton Solent University, the present Warsash Maritime Centre, situated in buildings at Warsash on the River Hamble, was established in the early 1930s by Captain G.W. Wakeford at Southampton. It moved to Warsash in 1946. A year at the school, which trained exclusively for the Merchant Service, also earned remission of sea time towards a second mates' certificate.

General Botha. Many South African officers trained for the Merchant Service in the General Botha, the majority serving in UK-based shipping companies. She was a converted British 2nd Class cruiser moored off Simon's Town, Cape Province until the establishment moved shore during WW2. When South Africa left the Commonwealth in 1961 the Botha lost an outlet for many of its cadets and closed in the 1980s. Past trainees are known as Bothie Boys.

Dufferin. Another training ship based in a retired warship hull, built in 1904, *Dufferin* was moored at Bombay, India (now Mumbai). It trained deck cadets from 1927 and engineering cadets from 1935, until 1949. Many Indian officers trained in her for the Merchant Service between the two world wars and later, with the growth of the Indian and decline in the British shipping industries, more and more cadets joined Indian companies. *Dufferin* was decommissioned in 1972 after being replaced by a purpose built training-ship affiliated to the University of Bombay, and was retired in favour of a shore establishment in 1993.

Several of the schools and colleges discussed later under the heading of 'The principal pre-examination study establishments' also ran pre-sea training courses enabling trainees to go to sea as *apprentices.

Cadet/School ships

A number of shipping companies operated one or two of their cargo ships as cadet ships, carrying a large numbers of deck *cadets (in many cases actually indentured *apprentices) who replaced the majority of the deck rating. A similar arrangement existed later in some ships after the introduction of engineer cadets. The cadets were involved in all aspects of the ship's operation and their training, both theoretical and practical, was invariably of a high standard. Sometimes known as school ships, these cargo ships were employed in normal trading and usually carried an extra officer whose specific role was as schoolmaster. Some of the best-known cadet ships during the review period, and their operating companies (with figures in brackets indicating the number of cadet ships they operated over the years) were:

Sailing ships.

Harbinger, Hesperus, Macquarie, Illawarra, Port Jackson and *Medway* – Devitt & Moore.

Dartford – Union Steam Ship Company of New Zealand

Mersey – White Star Line

Steam or motor ships.

Devon, Durham, Rakaia, Otaio – New Zealand Shipping Company/Federal Line (12)

Chantala, Chindwara – British India (13)

Calchas, Diomed – Alfred Holt (2)

Obuasi, Fourah Bay – Elder Dempster (2)

City of Lucknow – Ellerman (1)

Clan Line, South American Saint Line and Shell also ran cadet ships for a time.

Nautical establishments for study courses:

In the heyday of the British Merchant Service there were numerous schools and colleges in many ports of the United Kingdom providing tuition for aspiring second mates and often for higher qualifications. In most cases they were run by enterprising mariners with a scholarly bent and usually holding *Extra Masters' Certificates. There was one notable college whose joint principals had never been to sea but had an exceptional ability to understand and impart the knowledge without practical seagoing experience. The success rate of their pupils was very high.

In due course many of the private schools fell by the wayside or were absorbed into technical colleges as more and more government-funded institutions included nautical subjects. Then, as the numbers of British seafarers declined so did the number of nautical schools until today there are only a handful remaining.

Some of the best-remembered schools:

King Edward VII Nautical School took over from the Chapman & Nichols Academy and was situated in the headquarters of The British Sailors' Society at 680 Commercial Road near the docks at Poplar in the East End of London. This school, which for a time had a pre-sea school attached to it, saw many study for their Second Mate's Certificates and the name of Captain Chase will be long-remembered as its highly respected principal after WW2. The school's nickname was **King Ted's** or **KE VII.**

Sir John Cass College. This Aldgate, London, technical college, which during the 1940s also provided pre-sea training, had a navigation department at which numerous London-based officers studied for their Mate's and Masters' Certificates. In 1969 it merged with the King Edward VII Nautical School and moved to a new building at Tower Hill. It was usually known simply as **Cass's.**

Liverpool Nautical College. Founded by the City Council in 1892 at the request of seafarers, this college gradually took over from the various private schools, becoming part of Liverpool Technical College. Later a part of Liverpool Polytechnic, it is now a department of Liverpool's John Mores University. In the 1960s it became a leading centre for degree courses for mariners.

Nellist's Marine School. For many years, this private nautical school at Tyneside prepared students for the Second Mates' examination. It was started by a shipmaster but later run by two brothers who had never been to sea; nevertheless, they were particularly successful. The school gets a special mention for its outstanding reputation for students' successes in passing the examination at their first attempt.

School of Navigation, Warsash. Already mentioned as a pre-sea cadet training establishment, it also had a highly respected senior department, which provided teaching for all grades of certificates of competency for deck officers from Second Mate to Extra Master.

Some others of note:
School of Navigation, Royal Technical College. Glasgow.
The Nautical College. Leith.
Nautical College Department, Central Technical School. Liverpool.
LCC School of Engineering, Poplar. London.
Navigation School, Plymouth.
Marine School, South Shields.
Trinity House School (Adult Section), Hull.
The Smith Junior Nautical School. (Set up at Cardiff in 1921 with funds raised by Sir William Reardon Smith, the renowned local tramp ship owner.)

With the vast changes that have taken place in recent years in nautical education, the trend has been for the few nautical establishments that have survived to become the Navigation Departments of universities in the major port cities of the UK, where they provide courses for both certificates of competency and nautical science degrees. They generally also cater for cadet courses but these have become less pre-sea courses and now have more emphasis on shore-based education at intervals during a sea-going cadetship.

TERMS FOR OFFICERS' QUALIFICATIONS

Ticket. The term is frequently, albeit incorrectly, used to refer to an officer's certificate of competency. When used by those ashore, or even by seafarers not possessing a certificate, its use is seen by some qualified officers as belittling the status of the certificate. Nevertheless the term is in general use even amongst those who hold certificates of competency. The name originates from early regulations referring to the chit provided to a successful candidate by the Mercantile Marine Office as soon as candidates passed the exam and before receiving the properly engrossed certificate.

Curry & Rice ticket. Slang for an officer's certificate of competency issued in India, and sometimes also in Hong Kong or Singapore. It was a British certificate although the term was used in a slightly derogatory sense suggesting its inferiority to one issued in the United Kingdom. During the days of the British Raj many British ships traded to India and their officers often spent long periods on the Indian Coast or based in the Far East. If these officers had sufficient sea-time to qualify for their certificates of competency, their companies would sometimes give them the opportunity to sit their examinations locally rather than return to the UK. Naturally, many Indian officers also obtained these certificates.

Up for his ticket. Said of any seaman, but more often an ex-apprentice or junior officer, who was ashore studying for a certificate of competency (*ticket).

Wetting one's ticket. This expression conveyed the elation with which many successful candidates celebrated in the local pub when they passed their examinations.

No salt water on his ticket. Said of a candidate who, having just received his *Second Mate's Certificate, had yet to secure a berth in a ship as an officer.

The ink's hardly dry on his ticket. A slightly derogatory expression used to explain an unwise practice by an officer and suggesting he has only recently passed his examinations to obtain a certificate of competency – usually Second Mates'. Also, **There's not much salt water on his ticket yet.**

Certificate of Watch-keeping and Conduct. The name of the prescribed form completed and signed by each master under whom a junior officer served. It was required to prove the exact nature and extent of the officer's qualifying sea-time required for their *Mates' or Masters' Certificates. It was similar to the naval 'Flimsy'.

The standard seamanship textbooks. (See Chapter 16 for navigation textbooks.) The principal seamanship and general nautical text book, a copy of which was to be found in the kit of almost every officer under training, and of a good many seamen too, was *Nichol's Guide to Seamanship and Nautical Knowledge* (Brown Son & Ferguson, Glasgow). Another well-respected

IFICATE OF WATCH-KEEPING SERVICE.

For a First Mate's or Master's Certificate.

his is to Certify that Mr *C.B.Thompson*

served on the ss. *Strathmore*

ı *22nd May 1951* to *3rd December 19 ͘*

...........................,in the capacity of *(1st) (2nd)*

ı) Watch-keeping Officer.   During this time

C.B.Thompson

an officer in ——*(full)*—— charge of a watch for

ıt hours out of every twenty-four hours at sea,

ıpt as stated below.

√atches were not doubled at any time during the

ıage.†

√atches were doubled between the following

ı and at no other times ....

ıny this time Mr.

ıd as the *(senior)* of two Bridge-keeping

ıers.§

ıa entry to this effect has been made in the Mate's

ıgnature of Master. *W. Pallitt*

Date *2nd Dec 1951*

ıtrike out the words that do not apply.

Effective charge of a watch" means responsibility for the watch, con-
by an entry to this effect in the Mate's log, but it does not preclude
ıonal Supervision by a Senior Officer, provided that that Senior Officer
ıot take charge of the watch at any time.

ıelete this paragraph if watches were doubled at any time during the
ıe.

ıelete this paragraph if watches were not doubled at any time during
ıoyage.

CERTIFICATE OF SERVICE AND CONDUCT.

This is to certify that

Mr. *C.B.Thompson*

has served as *Second Mate*

in ss. *Perim*

under my command from *7th June 1942*

.... to *24th December 1942*.

during which period he has conducted himself*

*To my entire satisfaction.
He has conducted himself with
zeal and sobriety.*

John Peace Master.

ss. *Perim*

Date *December 24th 1942*

* Here the Master is to insert in his own handwriting his remarks on the
conduct, ability and sobriety of the officer.

Certificates of Watch-keeping and Conduct

seamanship book often found in a seaman's kit was *The Bosun's Manual* by the same publisher, but there were several others.

DECK RATINGS

Training. In many cases ratings in British ships simply learnt the hard way without any formal training, although as conditions improved most received some pre-sea training on board a training ship or at a shore-based institution. The colloquial name for any pre-sea training school for deck ratings was sailor factory. In due course a system was introduced where those serving on deck were required to pass qualifying examinations, and the regulations provided a scale of manning to ensure that sufficient qualified seamen were carried in every ship. Further, to ensure that ships carried sufficient crew competent in lifeboats, they were trained for the **Lifeboat Certificate** issued after a basic examination. This certificate was not confined to deck ratings and, to ensure the requisite number of certificated lifeboatmen in passenger ships, members of the Engine Room and Catering Departments also obtained them.

Able Seaman (AB). The most experienced of the deck crew with the exception of the petty officers. The manning scale required a specified number of ABs to carried in almost all ships; in some cases senior apprentices could be carried as substitutes. Qualification, by sea-time (originally four years but later reduced to three) and examination, were the principal requirements and a pre-requisite for advancement to *Bosun.

Efficient Deck Hand (EDH). This grade of deck rating, less experienced than AB, was introduced into British ships in 1936 to overcome a shortage of ABs. Seamen at least 19 years of age who achieved a useful standard of competence on deck, including a **Steering Certificate** and a **Lifeboatman's Certificate,** could sit the examination to become EDHs. This was a stepping-stone to becoming ABs. and required further sea time before they could be upgraded. (Another later, temporary provision was the introduction in the mid-1950s of **Deck Hand Uncertificated** (DHU). The certificate for a rating lacking sufficient seas-time to qualify for EDH or AB, but too old or experienced to serve as a deck-boy. Towards the end of WW2 and during the post-war period of National Training many young men joined the Merchant Service as an acceptable alternative to compulsory service in the armed forces, but some left as soon as permitted. They often obtained their EDH certificates but had insufficient sea-time to be rated as ABs.

The principal ratings training establishments

Between 1856 and 1986, apart from HMS *Conway* & *Worcester*, a number of other obsolete wooden warships hulls were moored in harbours and rivers around Britain and used as training ships. Except for the *Conway* and the *Worcester* most of these old wooden hulls were originally established to provide further education and nautical training to boys who had left school with a wish to become ratings but were often not old enough to enlist in the Royal Navy or obtain employment in the Merchant Service. Some organisations charged a fee, others were subsidised by ship-owners and a few were run by charitable societies for the benefit of paupers and orphans. Local authorities operated others for juvenile delinquents. Not all the vessels so used were ex-naval vessels and a small number of ex-merchant sailing ships also became respected training establishments or were run in conjunction with them. Many thousands of young lads from these training ships and institutions joined the two sea services as ratings, a number achieving officer rank and some becoming senior officers of distinction.

The Marine Society.   Established in 1756, this organisation has been at the forefront of training for the sea. It has run several training ships; *Warspite*, moored off Grays in the River Thames in 1929, was particularly well known between the two world wars until closed as a training ship in 1939. Associated with the *Seafarers' Education Service and *College of the Sea which had absorbed the *British Ship Adoption Society, the Society had earlier taken over the *London School of Nautical Cookery, established in 1893 and the first school to train ships' cooks. It ran other small training ships for a while and has recently amalgamated with the *Sea Cadet Corps.

The Navy League has been responsible, in various ways, for supporting the training of boys for the sea for more than one hundred years. The Liverpool Branch of its *Sea Cadet Corps formed **The Lancashire Sea Training Home for Boys** at Wallasey in 1896. After a name change to T**he Lancashire and National Sea Training Homes** the organization merged with the training ship **Indefatigable* in 1945. (**Now the Marine Society and Sea Cadet Corps.**)

Gravesend Sea School. As the *Shipping Federation's training school established at Gravesend on the Thames after WW1, this school trained deck boys and firemen, the latter being later replaced by stewards. It closed on the outbreak of war in 1939 but its training ship * *Vindicatrix* was towed to Sharpness near Gloucester, to continue the work. In 1945 the school reopened again at Gravesend as a shore establishment.

The Watts Naval Training School. Formally opened in 1906 this school, a branch of Dr Barnado's Homes, trained a number of boys for the Merchant Service although many more went in to the Royal Navy. It was closed in 1949 as a nautical school, the boys being transferred to **Parkstone Sea Training School** in Dorset. Dr Barnardo's also had another school, **The Russell Coates Nautical School.**

The Prince of Wales Sea Trainig School. Founded in 1921 in Limehouse, London, this respected school which received support from the Royal Family, trained almost 5,000 ratings for the Merchant Service. It moved to Stalham in 1940 and later to Dover, closing its door in 1976.

Indefatigable. (The Liverpool Sea Training School for Boys.) This establishment was founded in 1864 with an obsolete sailing frigate loaned by the Admiralty, the second ship of the name, moored in the River Mersey. She trained boys for many years and was merged in 1945 with the *Lancashire and National Sea Training Homes.

Arethusa. A training establishment founded in 1866, the Shaftesbury Homes' last ship of the name was moored at Upnor on the River Medway, opposite Chatham Dockyard. She trained boys for the sea until after WW2 when the old ship was towed to New York and is exhibited there today as a museum ship restored to her original appearance as the 4-masted barque *Peking.*

Foudroyant. Originally the frigate HMS *Trincomalee,* built in 1817 and recently restored at Hartlepool as a museum ship, she was a training ship through much of the 20th century until retired in 1986.

Mercury. Another permanently moored old warship, now

restored to her original state as HMS *Gannet*. She became a familiar sight on the River Hamble for many years where her predecessor had begun sea-training late in the nineteenth century. She was closed down as a training vessel in 1968. The English cricketer Captain C.B. Fry R.N. commanded her for many years and a significant proportion of *Mercury* trainees went to sea as officers.

Exmouth. Established when the Admiralty lent the first HMS *Exmouth* to the Metropolitan Asylums Board in 1876 for use as a Poor Law Training School, she was anchored in the River Thames at Grays. Many of her trainees entered either the Royal Navy or the Merchant Service. The establishment closed in 1939 but a successor bearing the same name, built in 1905 as a training ship, later became the replacement HMS *Worcester* in 1945.

Vindicatrix. *The Gravesend Sea School's training ship, an old 3-masted merchant square-rigger, was towed away from the Thames in 1939 and permanently moored just inside the Sharpness Canal near Gloucester where she carried on the school's valuable work. The ship remained until 1966 at Sharpness and was broken up the following year. By the time *Vindicatrix* closed, in 1966, 70,000 boys, many becoming officers, had trained for a life at sea. They later became known as Vindy Boys and now have a strong Association.

The Outward Bound Sea School at Aberdovey, Wales. This unique school was founded during WW2 by the combined efforts of the educationist Dr. Kurt Kahn, who founded Gordonstoun School on the Moray Firth, and the Liverpool shipowner, Lawrence Holt. It provided for both future officers and ratings with the substantial support of the Blue Funnel Line and the training ship *HMS *Conway*, arising from a desire by its founders to toughen-up younger seamen. This was essential to help in saving their lives and making them more resourceful to survive the privations of life in open lifeboats after the sinking of their ships by U-Boats. Continuing to use its founding principles to present challenges in close association with the sea, it dropped its 'sea' prefix after the War but continued as the forerunner of the Outward Bound movement now established in many other countries which use the alternative challenge of the hills and the mountains.

The decline in the British Merchant Service towards the end of the second half of the 20th century saw the officers' and ratings' colleges and schools decline to such an extent that most have disappeared completely, only a very few having adapted successfully.

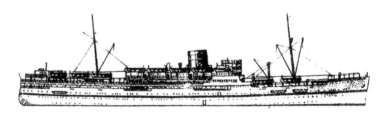

A full-time troopship of the pre-war and post-WW2 era.

CHAPTER FOUR

Engineers and the Engine Room

When sail began to give way to steam, not only was there significant change in ship design and equipment but there was also a major change in their manning. For some time a *donkeyman had been carried to look after the simple *donkey-engine and boiler in the later sailing ships but now engineers and their assistants were required in ever increasing numbers. As a result a whole new department grew up in ships and by the time the large transatlantic liners were built, the Engineers' Department far outweighed the Deck Department in numbers.

For many years the captain and the mates had been the only officers, but when skilled engineers came upon the scene they too were accorded officer status. Although the Board of Trade referred to them as engineers, just as it referred to mates as their counterparts on deck, they were engineer officers in the same way that mates, particularly in the liner companies, were often referred to as deck officers. In practice it has been customary to refer to them simply as 'engineers' except on formal occasions when 'officer' is added. (The abbreviated, common name, prefixed with their order of ranking where appropriate, is used throughout this book.)

During most of the review period marine engineers trained by serving their time as apprentices in shore-based industries. Many obtained steam experience in the railway workshops at Swindon, Derby, Crewe and elsewhere, while ship builders and marine engine manufacturers were another prolific source of training. But, as the number of those with an interest in going to sea began to dwindle, engineers began to be recruited from lighter industries and their sea time to qualify for their first certificate of competency was increased. During the early post-WW2 period some junior engineers went to sea with university engineering degrees and opted for four-years sea time in the Merchant Service instead of the then mandatory two years compulsory National Service. With the number of shipyards in Scotland and the North East Coast of England at that time it is not surprising that many engineers were Scotsmen and *Geordies.

The Engine Room Department was the responsibility of the chief engineer. It included almost all mechanical aspects of the ship's operation, extending beyond the main propulsion alone to include auxiliary machinery; in sophisticated ships towards the end of the review period this also encompassed electrical and refrigeration machinery, air-conditioning equipment and a variety of equipment required for a ship's hotel services.

Engineers' Certificates of Competency covered either steam or motor or, in some cases both. An engineer, having qualified in one, could obtain an endorsement for the other after gaining sufficient sea-time and passing a further examination. The two principal qualifications for engineers were First Class Engineer (usually referred to as **Chiefs**) and **Second Class Engineer** (**Seconds**), with endorsements for service in steam and/or motor ships. An engineer qualified in both steam and motor at first class level was known as holding a **Combined Chiefs** or **Double-headed Chiefs.** (In Australia and New Zealand there was an extra qualification level -- **Third Marine.**) For those wishing to demonstrate a higher academic knowledge, often to enable them to join the Board of Trade as engineer surveyors and examiners, there was an **Extra First Class Engineer** certificate.

Many *electrical and *refrigeration engineers were technically unqualified although time-served, but some did hold Ordinary or Higher National Certificates.

Unlike many deck officers, engineers did not attend pre-sea

schools and, surprisingly perhaps, it was not until as late as 1960 that a seagoing apprenticeship scheme was introduced for engineers. Before sitting their examinations most engineers attended appropriate schools in the principal UK ports.

ENGINEER OFFICERS

The Chief Engineer. The senior engineer and nominally in charge of the 8-12 watch. In practice this watch was usually covered by the fourth engineer as the chief rarely kept a watch. His role was partly practical but largely administrative and in technical matters he was responsible to the engineer superintendent in the company's head office but with immediate operational responsibility to the master. Nickname: **Roast Beef** or **Bully Beef.**

Second Engineer. Much of the practical day-to-day work in the engine room was left to the second engineer who, depending on the size of the vessel, might be either a day-worker or a watch-keeper. If not on day work he was usually in charge of the 4-8 watch and was the engineering counterpart of the mate. In some ships (usually steam) the title of **Junior Second Engineer** was used to denote a certificated motor engineer (quite often at chief's level) undertaking steam time towards his endorsement. This practice became more prevalent as the number of steam ships dwindled and the opportunity to gain steam time became more difficult. Also **The Deucer.**

The other engineers. Numbered in descending rank they were usually referred to as:

The Third Engineer. (Whether simply because of the Liverpool accent or more deliberately, this became **The Turd.**) **The Fourth Engineer** (Fourth), the **Fifth Engineer** (The Fiver) and the **Sixth Engineer** (The Sixer). They were mostly watch-keepers, one of the juniors being a day-worker. The third engineer usually looked after the 12-4 watch and in many ships there would often be more than one engineer keeping the same watch. When this occurred the senior engineer, referred to as the **Engineer-of-the-Watch** (EOW) was stationed in the engine room and was in overall charge. The junior, his assistant, was usually responsible for the boiler room in a steam ship. In writing, the engineers were abbreviated: C/E, 2/E, 3/E, 4/E, 5/E and 6/E.

Boilermaker. A large steam ship often also carried a boilermaker, known as **Boils** or **Boilers.** (The author once sailed in a ship whose boilermaker's actual surname was Boyle, the plumber's, Plumb and the second plumber's, Plumbley – a rare coincidence.)

Electrical Engineers. One or more were carried as electricity took the place of steam for auxiliary machinery and ships became more sophisticated. Often referred to as **Leckies,** the **First** or **Second Lecky** was sometimes nicknamed **the light bulb mechanic** by his engineering colleagues and if no electrical engineer was carried the third engineer usually had this additional responsibility.

Refrigeration Engineers. Ships with holds fitted for refrigerated cargoes (* reefer ships) carried a refrigeration engineer, and more than one if the ship was large. They were referred to as the **Chief Freezer** or **Second Freezer.** Occasionally a senior engineer joining a ship in which he was to take over as chief engineer would make a voyage as a refrigeration engineer for ship familiarisation.

Gingerbeers. The name by which the engineers were frequently known by the deck officers. Cockney rhyming slag, it was not intended as a derogatory term and its use was not confined to ships with London crews. In some ships they were also nicknamed, in a rather derogatory manner, **Pig Iron Polishers** or **Blackfeet.**

Professional Third. A term sometimes used for an uncertificated third engineer who did not aspire to higher rank and responsibility.

ENGINE ROOM RATINGS

Unlike their counterparts on deck there was very little formal shore training for engine room ratings although for a brief period there were short training courses for firemen. By and large they learnt on the job.

Donkeyman. The senior engine room rating whose status was comparable with the deck department petty officers. He was responsible for the *donkey-engine (when one was fitted) and for the *donkey-boiler, the auxiliary boiler still fitted in most ships long after the donkey-engine has been replaced by a number of other items of deck machinery. Also **Donks** or **Donkey.**

Pumpman. Another senior engine room rating who, in an oil tanker, maintained and generally cared for the cargo pumps and their operation during loading and discharging cargo.

Greasers. Responsible to the EOW for lubricating parts of the machinery such as shaft bearings, crank pins, piston rods, guides, bearings and all the numerous moving parts. Day-work greasers were generally worked on maintenance in the engine room.

Wipers. Greaser's assistants – the lowest rank in the engine room.

Firemen (stokers) and **Trimmers.** In the old coal-burners the steaming coal received at the bunkering ports was stored in compartments known as *coal bunkers. During the bunkering operation the coal had to be trimmed into the wings by trimmers to allow the maximum amount of bunkers to be taken. As coal was later consumed at sea, the coal in the bunkers was transferred from the more remote parts to those adjacent to the boiler room from which the firemen (stokers) could shovel it into the boilers. Firemen and trimmers comprised a large part of the engine room crew in coal-burning ships and were also carried in smaller numbers in oil burning steam ships where they were required to clean the burners, fit different size nozzles to suit the steam demand and watch the water level which could change rapidly in a water tube boiler. (Before conversion to oil-burning the old North Atlantic liner *Mauretania* of 1907 consumed 1,000 tons of coal per day.)

Coal lumpers. Shore labourers who carried the coal bags and baskets on their shoulders,
dumping the coal into the bunker chutes.

F.W.T . Firemen/Water tenders. In some ships the firemen had a dual role.

Ag Wallas. Many ships carried crews from the Indian sub-continent and Ag Wallas were Indian engine room ratings, who, like their counterparts on deck, were mostly very loyal servants of their companies. They signed British articles at the ports where they joined, principally Bombay and Calcutta, many of the former being Pathans from the area of the North West Frontier, or Punjabis from the plains further south. They were from what is now Pakistan and were nearly all Muslim.

Shortly after the partition of India in 1947, a revealing story was told about the loyalty of the many deck and engine room ratings. When asked whether he was now an Indian or a Pakistani, one rating, especially loyal to his company, is said to have replied, 'Sahib, I'm still P & O'.

As in the Deck Department, the engine room ratings had a *Serang in charge; the **Ag Walla Serang.** His assistants were the **Ag Walla Tindals.** Others were, **Paniwallas** (Watermen), **Talwallas** (Greasers) and the **Battiwalla**, a rating who generally worked with the Electrical Officer (**the Batti Sahib.**) The engine room ratings had their own **Bandari** (Cook) and a Topas (cleaner/sweeper) separate from those who served the deck ratings.

PARTS, EQUIPMENT AND TERMS

In steam ships, principally coal-burners:

Boiler room. The area adjacent to the engine room in both coal and oil burning steamers in which the boilers were situated. It was also referred to as the stokehold in coal-burners where it was usually larger than in oil-fired ships as extra space was required for the firemen to stoke the boilers manually.

Black Gang. Collective term for the *firemen and *trimmers in a coal-burning steamer. Also **Black Squad** and **Black Watch.**

Ash hoist. A ship burning coal had to regularly dispose of the resultant clinker and ash. After being raked from the boilers, this was hoisted up to the main deck and disposed of over the ship's side.

Ash chute. The ash and clinker was dumped over the side via a metal chute on the main deck fitted adjacent to the top of the *ash hoist. A similar chute was often fitted to the ship's side for galley and other waste.)

Ash Bags or **Ash Buckets.** Receptacles for the ash from the boilers requiring to be dumped.

Bunkers. The steaming coal was stowed in the bunkers and accessible through the side bunkers alongside the stokehold. Ships had bunkering hatches above the bunkers on the port and starboard sides of the main deck, and most coal-burners also had a **cross-bunker** running athwartships, usually forward of the funnel, also with a hatch on deck. The coal in the cross bunker usually ran down into the side bunkers as they were emptied and there was often access to it from the 'tween deck of an adjacent cargo hold, one end of which could be boarded off from the rest of the cargo space to provide extra bunker capacity. This cargo space was usually the first to be worked out by the trimmers before the permanent bunkers were emptied. Bunkers was also the generic term for all coal, fuel oil or diesel oil required for propelling a ship.

Fiddley. Casing over the top of the engine room, boilers and stokehold on which the funnel and boiler room ventilators stood, part of it consisting of an iron grating.

On the blood. In *coal-fired steamers the quality of the coal, the condition of the boilers, the seawater temperature and the skill and effort of the firemen had a significant influence on the amount of steam available to drive the ship. Ideally, and with a favourable combination of these factors, the steam pressure rose almost to the maximum before the safety valve released the excess pressure. This maximum was indicated by a red line on the pressure gauge and when reached gave rise to the expression, 'she's on the blood'. Good steaming coal was not found in all places where coal was mined and only some bunkering ports enjoyed a good reputation for providing high calorific coal which significantly affected the ship's speed.

Blowing off. Once the maximum safe pressure was exceeded and the pressure valve lifted, the boilers were said to be blowing off as they released their excess steam through a pipe running up inside the funnel.

Steam is stiff. Said when difficulty was experienced in getting the steam *on the blood.

Slice, Rake & Pitch. The slice, the rake and the shovel were three of the most important fireman's tools and from them arose the term for three essential operations performed by a fireman in maintaining the steam pressure. The burnt coal in the boiler, often comprising little more than clinker, frequently had to be sliced to free it from the furnace and brought to its door for removal. The fire then had to be raked over and prepared to receive fresh coal, which was pitched into it.

Banjo. A fireman's shovel.

An old man. A large, awkward lump of coal, difficult to handle by a fireman in the stokehold.

Fire bar. An often-replaced part of the firebox in a boiler. Old fire bars were used as weights for various shipboard purposes, among them weighting the canvas body bag (shroud) used for burial at sea.

Coaling ship. The process of filling a ship's bunkers with coal through the **bunker hatches** on deck. The more sophisticated ports had mechanical means, often employing towers on the quayside, which could lift, tip and empty entire railway wagons of coal. At the other end of the scale were the ports with very basic facilities, employing native labour to carry sacks of coal aboard and tip the coal into the bunkers. Somewhere between was a system of coaling which used *baskets lifted on board by a *derrick.

Coaling ship was always a filthy process and, depending on the weather and the method used, it could be almost impossible to keep the coal dust from permeating just about every nook and cranny on board, no matter what precautions were taken. (The author has a lasting memory of a hot day in Montevideo Harbour when coaling ship while a tramp steamer, anchored to windward, discharged her coal cargo through open chutes into lighters. The chutes ended many feet (metres) above the lighters and clouds of coal dust were carried down to leeward by the wind. This, together with his own ship's coal dust from her own bunkering, was most unpleasant and left the crew with a major clean-up after sailing.)

Coaling baskets. Normally supplied by the coaling company rather than the ship (which might carry a few of them) these woven rattan cane baskets were attached by rope to a ring and lifted from the quayside or coaling lighter by a small crane or ship's *derrick.

Buckle-at-the-back boys. The name used in some ships for the *firemen who often wore
their belts back to front. They did this to avoid a metal buckle worn in front becoming unpleasantly hot from the direct heat of the furnace.

Firemen's badges. The permanent bruises on the shoulders of firemen who, when previously still *coal trimmers, had repeatedly struck the steel structure of the bunkers as the ship rolled.

Blowing tubes. Particularly in an oil-fired boiler the fire tubes became clogged with carbon soot as a result of the oil combustion. The tubes had to be cleaned out, usually once a watch, by steam injected under pressure which blew the carbon out through the funnel. Before doing this the *EOW was required to inform the OOW so that the ship's course could be altered if necessary to ensure the wind carried the soot clear of the ship on the beam or quarter. Failure to do so with a following wind could result in all the soot landing on the deck – an extremely unpopular result with the mate and passengers alike!

Punching tubes. The term used if vacuum was lost when turbine condenser tubes become blocked with sand and shell in shallow water, requiring the debris to be punched out with steel rods and hammers. It was done in an emergency only.

Blowing the glass. During each watch the contents of the boiler gauge glasses were blown out to ensure that they were indicating the correct level.

Lumpy oil. Boiler fuel oil when too cold. It was one of the causes of black smoke which usually raised an urgent request from the bridge to stop making smoke.

Swab brush. The brush used on high pressure rods of a triple expansion steam engine to lubricate them with a mixture of cylinder oil and graphite using an action similar to the thrust and parry of a swordsman.

Slinging his own fat. Some small coastal vessels carried only three engineers and the third engineer had the dubious distinction of slinging his own fat – no greaser was carried in the ship and the engineer had to oil around himself.

In motor ships:

A Doxford accent. Companies whose ships were powered by Doxford diesels ideally engaged engineers familiar with these engines. A result was that many who served in these ships came from Weirside, the home of the Doxford engine manufacturers, and spoke with the local dialect.

A Suck-squeeze-bang-blow engine. Nickname for a four-stroke diesel marine engine.

MAVIS. (Main Air Valve Is Shut.) This was written on the main engine manoeuvring platform of a motor ship when all was ready for departure and awaiting 'stand-by' being rung on the engine room telegraph from the bridge. It was a reminder that the main air-starting valve was still closed.

In most engine rooms

Nerve Centre. A term used by engineers for the engine room particularly when speaking to deck officers.

Pit. The engine room, Also **Mechanical garden, Disneyland** and **The Fiery dance hall** (particularly in a steam ship).

Shed. Engine Control Room.

Field Day. Watch-keeping engineers were sometimes required to turn out during their watch below to undertake essential maintenance or repairs but, as officers, they did not earn extra pay for overtime and referred to this as 'working a field day'. The term was also applied to ratings both on deck and in the engine room in a similar situation but with the payment of overtime in the latter years of the review period, the imposition of extra work during their watch below was of less significance, sometimes even welcomed for its financial benefits.

Paddy's (or **Irish**) **Watch.** More than a field day, the term was used when there was a major emergency in the engine room – a total blackout, loss of all propulsion or a fire – and every engineer was called below to work until the job was completed. It particularly arose in motor ships and all the engineers were then on Paddy's Watch.

Mickey Mouse. A term for something not working properly. Although this term is in common usage ashore, marine engineers claim a special ownership of the term, contending that it comes from Glaswegian engineers, who will tell you, 'it dis ney work' – hence it is Mickey Mouse!

A Ding. The engineer designated to answer the bridge to *engine room telegraph when the ship is being manoeuvred.

Donkey engine. A steam engine on the deck of a sailing ship used for lifting and heaving gear, particularly for working cargo in port. It took the donkey-work out of the task.

Donkey-boiler. The general purpose boiler, not a main propulsion boiler, originally so named as it provided steam for the donkey-engine. The term was retained for the boiler which generated steam for a number of purposes including driving the steam windlass and cargo winches and providing heat and power when the main boilers were shut down.

A Three-legged engine. A three-cylinder steam engine with high, medium and low pressure cylinders.

Bauer-Wach turbine. There were a number of items of specialist machinery designed to improve the efficiency of boilers and propelling machinery. These included the Bauer-Wach turbine – an exhaust turbine fitted in some ships with reciprocating engines to improve fuel consumption. Economies of about 20% were said to have been achieved with them.

On the plates. The steel plates or gratings, which form the engine room floor.

8-12 Pimp. The most junior engineer on the 8-12 watch at night in a passenger ship. So named because this engineer, who called the next watch at 2345, delivered the girls to the party cabin for those coming off watch at midnight.

Prince of Darkness. Any engineer who successfully, and unpopularly, blacks out a vessel so that all the electrical power fails.

Lamp Tramp. The greaser who has the special and popular task of replacing lamp bulbs around the ship.

Feeling her over. An expression referring to the monitoring and lubricating of the machinery carried out by the greasers under the supervision of the *EOW.

Underground Savage. An engine room rating on a ferry where the engine room is below the car deck and therefore below the waterline.

Greenhouse. Engineers' uncomplimentary name for the bridge. So called because it has lots of windows and is full of vegetables (deck officers).

Rock dodgers. Engineers name for deck officers. Also, slightly derogatory, **Window lickers** and **Deck ornaments.**

Department of approximation. Another slightly derogatory engineers' name for the deck department.

Powerhouse to shite house. An engineer's crude greeting when telephoning the bridge.

Flash up the .... An instruction from the bridge to the engine room in small vessels such as rig tenders and supply vessels to start main engines, thrusters or other machinery. It can be an instruction relating to starting any machinery.

AC/DC. Referring to either alternating current or direct current, it was applied to a person whose sexual orientation was in question.

Steaming Bonnet. Uniform cap, only worn by engineers at boat drill.

A WW2 'Liberty' ship

CHAPTER FIVE

Hotel Services, Catering Staff and Food

The largest of the three major departments in a passenger ship was usually **The Purser's Department** which was principally concerned with accommodating, entertaining and feeding the passengers. Feeding the crew and administering the officers and ratings in this department was also its responsibility.

As the name suggests **the purser** was Head of Department. He was responsible to the master when a voyage commenced but at the end of it he reported to a superintendent in the company's head office. Where large numbers of passengers and crew were carried, the department was often subdivided; one part was concerned with passenger services and accommodation, the other with the galley and stores. The duties of those involved were essentially 'in house', whether involved with administration (**the pursers**), entertainment (**the entertainment officers**) cooking (**the galley staff**) or passengers (**the barmen and stewards**).

In the regular mail and passenger services to North America, sailing mainly from Glasgow, Liverpool and Southampton, those in the department were mainly British although many in the dining saloon also from Continental Europe. In some *white crew passenger ships sailing principally from London to the Far East, Australia and New Zealand, the cooks and stewards were generally British but the *Indian crew ships had a mix of British and Goanese (from Goa, Portuguese India). Those trading elsewhere often had an ethnic mix from Britain or countries to which they were trading.

Cargo ships were usually similarly manned but the department was commonly referred to as the *Catering Department and headed by the **chief steward** (in some ships he was a purser/ chief steward.) He sometimes had a **second steward** as his assistant and the cook, another important member of the crew, was also responsible to him. Often a qualified cook himself, many a chief steward has had to take on that role in *white crewed cargo ships when the cook *jumped ship, but few cargo ships have a chief steward today.

Ranks. The pursers were officers and in some companies the chief steward was also accorded officer rank. Senior ratings – **cooks, second/third stewards, head waiters,** senior **barmen, writers** and the like – were generally referred to as leading hands and were, in some respects, comparable with the petty officers in the deck and engine room departments.

Food. In First Class the food for passengers was invariably of a high standard in both quality and quantity– indeed passengers sometimes complained that there was too much food for their waistlines. Second (named Tourist in some ships) and Third Class passengers expected a lower standard but it was usually quite adequate and commensurate with the fare paid, the standard being almost entirely within the control of the shipping company. However, the cleanliness and suitability of galleys and storerooms was subject to Government regulations and inspection. In **emigrant ships,** and **troopships,** the Government had a far greater responsibility, laying down ration scales and checking that they were observed, and the food adequately prepared and cooked.

There were few considerations of more importance than food to the crew. During the 19th century, the *Board of Trade introduced a scale of provisions and some companies kept to the bare minimum while others were more generous. The *liner companies generally provided better food than the tramp companies but there were exceptions and the quality and quantity sometimes varied between ships of the same company.

The skill of the cooks made a significant difference and good ones would often contribute significantly to the success of a voyage. The reverse was equally true. The honesty of the master and the chief steward also had a major bearing on the standard of feeding in many cargo ships; quite often the two were in cahoots depriving the crew and lining their own pockets. However, some chief stewards did their utmost to feed the crew as best they could on the company's feeding allowance, even gaining a reputation for kindness. Others were mean and more than one was discovered attaching a lump of putty on the bottom of scale pan.

A series of Merchant Shipping Acts and their amendments through the latter half of the 19th century and early part of the 20th century made steady improvement to the scale of provisions for merchant seamen. The 1844 Act required masters to state in the *Articles of Agreement the scale of victuals provided, the official proviso being *sufficient without waste. The 1854 Act recommended a scale as published by the Liverpool Mercantile Marine Association and became known as the **Liverpool Scale**, adding a requirement for weighing scales on board for the crew to check that they were getting their due. In 1894 the *Shipping Federation recommended further improvements which formed the basis of the 1906 Act, providing for the first time a compulsory scale that became known as the **Lloyd George Scale.** Under this legislation ships were, at last, required to carry a qualified cook. This scale remained in force until 1940 when cheese was added, but it was 1957 before frozen or fresh fruit eventually joined the list and the milk allowance was then increased. Refrigeration allowed considerable improvements to be made and in the second half of the 20th century there was no longer any reason why shipowners should not provide fresh food where dried and preserved food had been necessary earlier.

Company practices varied but in passenger ships the catering was often the responsibility of the deputy purser in association with the chef; in cargo ships the chief steward was invariably responsible.

The above provision scales were for *white crew ships and were different for ships

with a *native crew who required their customary national or religious fare. It was not unusual for the native crew, if in port at the time of their religious festivals, to be provided with, or to buy, live animals which they slaughtered and cooked as their custom dictated. These ships had separate crew galleys and their own cooks to prepare the food.

Meals. Normally three meals a day were provided for the crew at the company's expense. For many years these were eaten by the seamen in their fo'c's'le accommodation which doubled as their mess room and sleeping quarters. But, as the conditions on some ships improved between the two World Wars, and particularly after it, separate mess-rooms were provided.

In cargo ships the officers, both deck and engineer, usually had their meals in the dining saloon amidships with the captain. In some large passenger ships the junior officers had a separate mess-room but in many they dined at a separate junior officers' table in the main dining saloon where the passengers had their meals. (Towards the end of the period passenger ship Saloons were often renamed Restaurants.)

In most ships there was also a duty mess-room where a lower standard of dress was acceptable for officers, mostly engineers, in working rig. In many companies the apprentices dined with the officers but in some tramp companies they too had their own mess-room.

Generally in passenger ships the senior officers, and particularly the captain, had their own tables in the dining saloon at which passengers were also seated. Part of their duty was the entertaining of passengers, the extent of which varied as each company had its own policy. Except in port it was customary to dress for dinner which usually required passengers to wear evening dress and ship's officers their *mess kit.

Meal times. In companies owning cargo ships almost exclusively, whether tramp
ships or cargo liners, breakfast at sea for the watch going on duty at 0800 was usually at *one bell (0720) and lunch also at one bell (1120) although in some ships officers would take over their watch and then be relieved a little later. The evening meal was normally at 1700 or 1730 which, in the case of those on watch, necessitated a meal relief during the course of the watch.

In the cargo liners of companies owning passenger ships, and also in their passenger ships,
breakfast for officers and passengers was often at 0830, lunch at 1230 and dinner at the more sociable time of 1900. This required the OOW to be relieved, although in passenger ships where the meal service often extended to two sitting, the 4-8 watch-keeping officers would usually dine after 2000 when they came off duty.

The meal times were usually much the same in port as at sea although occasionally they might be varied slightly to fit conveniently with cargo working hours – an 0715 breakfast for example, before the stevedores started at 0800 – and there was a similar time adjustment when a port arrival or departure coincided with a normal meal time.

In port, for those wishing to go ashore for the evening, the practice in *white crew cargo ships of an evening meal at 1700 was welcomed; for those staying aboard, particularly if on duty, this was considered inconveniently early but there was no alternative as the cook and steward wasted no time before going off duty as soon as this meal was finished. For officers in cargo ships with a *native crew the evening meal was often later.

Those on duty at night when working cargo or maintaining a gangway or engine room watch usually received a **duty-watch meal** which, in cargo ships, they would have to cook for themselves.

The summons to meal times was often by means of a gong but in passenger ships, where dinner was an important occasion, a recording of 'Roast beef of Old England' was often played over the public address system, or a bell boy would go around the passenger accommodation with a small xylophone playing a welcoming tune.

Menus. In the saloons of passenger ships the menus were extensive, particularly for lunch and dinner when the menu cards were frequently quite elaborate with a coloured picture on the front. Inside was printed the name of every available dish together with some recommended wines to accompany them.

In cargo ships the menus were much less elaborate but the chief steward frequently managed at least to type a much simpler menu card which usually had the shipping company's name and logo, or its house flag, printed at the top. It never ceased to amuse the officers how cargo ship menus so often carried the same name local place names for the dishes regardless of where in the world the stores had been taken during a long voyage. The roast lamb was usually saddle of Southdown (or Canterbury) lamb, the ducks invariably from Aylesbury, the bacon from Wiltshire and the turkeys from Norfolk – or so the menu said.

Even in cargo ships where the fare was often quite plain, chief stewards invariably managed to include some sophisticated name on the menus for quite simple food. 'Kromeskies á la Russe' was a common description for a meat or fish croquette, and potato crisps were often 'Saratoga potatoes'.

For the seamen there were no menus and rarely more than a few mumbled words from the *peggy as he carried the food into the mess room telling them in words of one syllable what fare had been provided for the meal. Most of the dishes had a nickname which he would usually use, preceded by an expletive or two.

A number of terms and expressions relating to food came from cooks and stewards in passenger liners and many appear to have originated in the Cunard Line. Others came largely from tramp ships where the food was often very inadequate and a constant subject of complaint.

Among this department's quoloquial terms were:

Grocer. A European chief steward, his position sometimes elevated in name to Purser/Chief Steward. In an Indian crew ship he was **Chief Steward Sahib** while the Hindustani term for an Indian chief steward, carried in some cargo ships in lieu of a European, was **Butla.** Nicknames in a *white crew ship were, **The Boss, Bunch-o-Moss, Chief Grub Spoiler** & **Thief Steward**. In some ships he was seen as the Captain's 'Grass'.

Baby grocer. The Chief Steward's deputy, usually the Second Steward or Storekeeper

The Doctor. The Cook. Also **Babbling Brook** (Cockney rhyming slang), **Butcher's Hook** and **Tucker Fucker.** (An Australian coast term).

Bricklayer. The Second Cook/Baker in a cargo ship was sometimes referred to by this name. Also **Galley Bosun.**

Pants. A Pantryman.

Galley rat. Galley Boy. Also **Spud Barber.**

Kitchen Porter (KP) The galley drudge, particularly in passenger ships.

Scull. A sculleryman.

Glory hole steward. The stewards' *peggy in a white crew passenger ship.

Bells. The bellboys, often the youngest lads on the ship.

Captain's Tiger. The captain's steward. He attended to the captain's requirements in his cabin and often worked in the pantry serving meals when the captain dined in the Saloon. In some tramp ships the second steward combined his other duties with that of captain's steward. A captain's tiger needed to be particularly discrete as he was likely to become privy to confidential information from time to time and enjoyed a privileged position of trust. One possible explanation for this unusual term is that in Nelson's time sailors wore shirts with red, blue and white stripes. The captain's steward is said to have also performed menial tasks on deck and to mark him out as not being a sailor he wore a shirt of black and yellow stripes.

Baggage Master. Different companies had different names for this member of the Purser's Department. He was responsible for looking after baggage stowed in the **baggage room** intended for access by passengers during the voyage. (**Hold baggage**, stowed away in a cargo hold and inaccessible to passengers until arrival at destination, was usually the responsibility of the Deck Department.)

A jacket man. A waiter in charge of the silver, glass or crockery locker. This duty came as a privilege and a jacket man was excused menial tasks such as the daily scrub-out of the alleyways. A silver steward was known as the Silver King.

Boots n' bath. Nickname for a bathroom steward who also cleaned the shoes left outside cabins at night and ran baths for passengers.

Commis (or **Commy**) **Waiter.** A steward who had gained enough experience to serve passengers.

Winger. Table waiter

Piss pot jerker. A cabin steward. Also **Po juggler.**

Hash slinger. A saloon steward.

Disc jockey. Plate washer.

Steam Queen. A female worker in the ship's laundry.

Barberon. A female barber.

Cowboy. In passenger ships this term was often applied to the lower grade of stewards and relatively unskilled members of the Catering Department. It could also be used to describe any incompetent and inefficient members of the crew.

Fruit. A homosexual. Gays generally gave very good service in the Catering Department but it was rare to find them in the Deck or Engine Room Department. Also **Pineapple.**

Geraldo's navy. A collective, 1950s term for the musicians who played in a liner's orchestra.

Bloods. A steward's name for passengers, to be bled for tips.

Dropsy. Bribes, sometimes tips.

Nightrider. A passenger who disembarks without tipping.

A gannet. A glutton.

Spud locker. Although a potato locker situated in fresh air on deck was common in many cargo ships the term was also applied to the vegetable preparation area in some passenger ships.

Topside. First Class passenger accommodation.

Benders. Knees put to hard work when scrubbing passenger alleyways.

Cunard socks. Bare feet.

Cunard feet. Splay feet derived from many years carrying trays of food on rolling decks. Whether the name came about simply because Cunard was a leading liner company on the North Atlantic where the problem was particularly prevalent, or was derived from 'he cun-ardly walk', as some suggest, is uncertain.

Strap-up. Washing and clearing the cutlery and dishes after a meal.

Cunard strap-up. This term was used when stewards 'accidentally' dropped the dirty plates and cutlery over the side after passengers had meals served on deck. In large liners the stewards were required to carry dirty utensils a long way down to the scullery for washing up and sometimes saved themselves the trouble.

Hot half-crown. A small tip from a Third Class passenger.

Demmy Tassie. A steward's name for a small coffee cup, from the French demi tasse.

Growler. Empty jam or fruit tin to which was added a wire handle for coffee brewed on the galley stove.

To bull the growler. A term for extending the life of a brew of tea when half consumed by adding water to the teapot or *growler.

Kit. A round metal container in which *peggies drew food for the deck and engine room ratings for carrying to their mess-rooms.

Scran. A general term for food.

Chew and spew. A sailor's comment on poor food.

Stewards' breakfast. A cigarette and a spew.

Bullion. A steward's name for the thin soup served to passengers mid-morning, a term derived from the French.

Tea. The name for the evening meal when served at 1700 in cargo ships. It was usually less elaborate than dinner.

Board of Trade whack. A scale of victuals as laid down by the BOT, it varied from time to time and was detailed in the *Articles of Agreement. In 1860 the allowance included nine items only and lacked important diet items such as citrus (vitamin C for scurvy), fresh greens (iron for the blood), milk (calcium) and carrots (Vitamin A for eyesight). By 1960 it contained 30 items but the quantity of some of the original items was reduced.

Pound & Pint. This term was also used to describe the minimum ration scale which the BOT required to be supplied on British ships.

Bare whack. The term applied when a ship provided only the minimum BOT scale of rations with no extras.

Full & plenty & no waste. Said of well-provisioned ships.

As hungry as a nun's cunt. A vulgar expression conveying a ravenous appetite.

Blackpan. Often cooked in a black frying pan, a fry-up left in the galley, usually for cooking by the 12-4 watch-keepers coming off at 0400, as they would later be sleeping through breakfast, or in some ships at 2000 by the 4-8 engine room watch which had missed their 1700 tea. In the old *coal-burners it was seen as a gesture by the cook to the firemen for keeping the galley supplied with coal.

Lifeboat rations. During WW2, in anticipation of lengthy periods in the lifeboats after abandoning ship, sustaining and concentrated food was required to be carried in them. These included Horlicks tablets, chocolate, pemmican, barley sugar, condensed milk and fresh water. The practice continued for some years after the war but lifeboat rations were then reduced, commensurate with the lessened risk. Provisioning the lifeboats was often an *apprentices' job to whom disposal of the old chocolate was a particularly welcome task.

Lime juice. Concentrated, rather bitter, lime juice was a requirement under the BOT scale of provisions to prevent scurvy due to lack of vitamin 'C' from fresh green vegetables. In ships with a sufficient supply of fresh vegetables and adequate refrigerated storerooms there was no need to issue the crew with lime juice and the requirement for it was eventually dropped. (It was later discovered that lemons were a more prolific source of Vitamin 'C' than limes.)

Bonded stores. Wines, spirits, beer, cigarettes, cigars and tobacco at duty free prices carried by ships for use when beyond the custom's regulated boundaries of countries to which they were trading.

Master's bond. In many cargo ships the master kept a supply of *bonded stores for the crew to purchase by deduction from their wages. The risk and the profit were the captain's concern. Needless to say the less scrupulous masters made very certain that the profit more than compensated for the risk.

Ship's bond. In many cargo ships of the *liner companies, and in passenger ships where these items and other liquor was available to the passengers, it was usual for the shipowner, rather than the master, to make these bonded items available to the crew.

Bond issue. The issue of duty free cigarettes and beer made at sea at regular intervals
for purchase by the ratings. Officers usually had more frequent access.

Nicknames for various dishes:

Many dishes prepared with the minimum of good ingredients and lacking imagination were sometimes given the prefix, Board of Trade, (or its initials) e.g. *BOT salad, but they sometimes took the alternative prefix of the shipping company's name, e.g. Clan Line pie.

Board of Trade centipede. Chicken, usually only served on Sundays. This mythical creature was credited with a dozen legs and more wings than a triplane, the crew invariably believing that only the captain and chief steward, eating alone in their cabins, received the breast.

Board of Trade salad. Salads made from beetroot and onion covered in vinegar appeared in some ships when the fresh items like lettuce had passed their 'use by date' and replaced the fresh salads enjoyed for a few days after leaving port. Also known as **Deep sea salad.**

Honeymoon salad. Lettuce (let-us) alone.

Board of Trade strawberries. Prunes. Also **Texas strawberries.** (In some Australian ships prunes were known as Howard Smith strawberries.)

Board of Trade Duff. Occasionally served on Sunday as a luxury in some ships, this consisted of a boiled, suet pudding such as plum pudding. Also, **Plum duff.**

Duff. A general term for almost anything provided as the sweet course following the main dish. It was duff whether an actual pudding or not. Even tinned fruit could be referred to as duff.

Adam and Eve on a raft. Two fried eggs on a piece of toast.

Sharks on a Raft. Sardines on Toast.

Sailors' revenge. Bacon & eggs – presumably because the seaman felt he was getting back at the shipowner at last.

Harriet Lane. Canned, corned beef. Allegedly, a young woman of this name went missing in the vicinity of a packing plant in London in the early 1900s and was never seen again.

A Pot of Shackles. A rough weather stew.

Scouse. Liverpool hot pot made from meat and vegetables. Without the meat it was known as **Blind Scouse.**

Babies' head. Steak and kidney pudding.

Colonial goose. A meat dish served in ships of the Union S.S. Company (NZ) which had certainly never been near a goose.

Sealed orders. Pasties. The cook and chief steward alone knew what left-overs from previous meals was being put into the pasties, so they were likened to sealed orders, which remained secret until opened.

Woolly Dog. Lamb.

Bungalow duff. Cottage Pie.

Wounded Cow. Steak. A very rare luxury indeed in many tramp ships.

BITS. Brains In Tomato Sauce.

Dogs' Vomit. Mince meat.

Underground Chicken. Rabbit.

Lickers, flickers and tickers. Ox tongue, tail and heart.

Corned dog. Corned beef.

Stornoway steaks. Kippers. (Stornoway in Scotland's Western Isles is a major fishing port.)

Duck shit and Hailstones. Curry and Rice.

Argentine chicken. Tinned corned beef.

Piss filters. Kidneys.

Slum gullion. Preserved potato mixed with tinned meat. (Sailing ship era.)

Chutney locker lids. Oxtails.

Shirt flap lifter. Pea soup.

Thick & Thin. Cream soup and clear soup.

Jessie's Dream. White sauce.

Jipo. Gravy.

Driftwood. Chips.

Doorstep. A sandwich.

Sarny. A sandwich. (Liverpuddlian).

Jam Butty. A jam sandwich. (Liverpuddlian).

Banjo. A large sandwich.

Bunghole. Cheese.

Train smash. Tinned tomatoes.

Apple daddy. A pie made with dried apples.

Burgoo. Porridge. In the days of sail it was not strictly porridge alone and comprised a gruel of boiled oatmeal seasoned with salt, sugar and butter.

Chinese wedding cake. Rice pudding, a cheap, standard sweet at dinnertime. Also, **Japanese wedding cake.**

Napoleon's retreat. Rice pudding with sultanas.

Tea & tabnabs. In the better-provisioned ships the cook would sometimes bake scones or rock cakes which the crew had with their afternoon 'smoko' cup of tea. The combination was then known as tea & tabnabs.

Connie onnie. Tinned, sweetened condensed milk. It had a long shelf life and was principally used to make cocoa. Usually two small holes were punched in the top which could be closed with matchsticks to keep out cockroaches. The arrival of UHT milk was a great leap forward in that it displaced conny onnie which so often had already spent many months in a lifeboat until replaced with new before the old was given to the crew.

Shaky. Unsweetened condensed milk frequently of the I'deal' brand.

The slush cask. An empty cask with a square hole cut in one end, which was turned uppermost and provided with a lid, into which all the fat trimmed from the meat was placed by the cook. (Sailing ship era).

Dandy funk. Hard ship's biscuit placed in a small canvas ditty bag, pounded with a belaying pin and the powder mixed with molasses and water. (Sailing ship era).

Cracker hash. Powdered ship's biscuit mixed with grease from the cook's slush cask. (Sailing ship era).

Dog's body. Broken ship's biscuit soaked in water and covered with scraps of beef or pork fat and baked. (Sailing ship era).

Sea pie. Although the recipe varied to accommodate whatever was available it consisted primarily of layers of salt meat, vegetables and fish, separated by 'pastry' made from bread crusts and crushed biscuits. It was a sailing ship dish but the name has been preserved by the Southampton Master Mariners Club, *The Cachalots. Their famous Annual Sea Pie Supper, held at the Southampton Guildhall and to which shipping dignitaries are invited, is an important event in the port's calendar.

Cockney ryming slang

When crews were signed on in London they were often mostly cockneys and the use of cockney rhyming slang was inevitable

for some of the food on board, including:
Nobby Clark. Shark.
Ruby Murray. Curry.
Lilian Gish. Fish.
Loop the loop. Soup.
Jack the Ripper. Kipper.
Kate & Sydney. Steak & Kidney.
Rosy Lea or **You & Me.** Tea.
Stammer & Stutter. Butter.
Stand at Ease. Cheese.
Uncle Fred. Bread.
Crash. Sausage & Mash.
Army & Navy. Gravy.

CHAPTER SIX

Uniform & Dress

Unlike the Royal Navy, where the wearing of a uniform by all the ship's company is decreed by the Admiralty, there is no comparable situation in the Merchant Service. There, the wearing of a uniform is a matter for individual employers, the shipowners, to decide and though invariable referred to as a uniform, it might more correctly be referred to as 'the company's livery'.

The wearing of uniforms by officers on duty was a necessity in most companies, some attaching considerable importance to their officers' appearance, especially in passenger ships. Many cargo *liner companies had high expectations of their officers too, but off duty the wearing of uniform was usually relaxed although expected for meals in the saloon while the ship was at sea. But the practice varied considerably and many companies accepted a much lower standard.

At sea in wartime, if they did not wear uniform, officers were at risk; if captured, at best they might not be accorded the usual treatment as officers or, at worst, might be shot as spies.

A uniform for ratings, except in some *native crew ships, was uncommon in tramp ships and many other cargo ships, but in some cargo liners and most passenger ships, uniforms for deck ratings and stewards, was normal. Again there were exceptions: commonly, blue trousers and a blue jacket (deck petty officers); blue trousers and blue sweater (for other deck ratings); blue trousers and a white jacket for stewards.

Over the years, as was to be expected, the style of uniforms tended to follow changes in civilian dress.

OFFICERS

Standard Merchant Navy uniform. (See illustration on page 118.) It was always intended that the Standard Merchant Navy uniform, approved by an Order in Council of 1918, would replace the many different liveries of the shipping companies, but this never quite happened. Although many officers did wear the new uniform, and the companies did not discourage it, the new uniform never replaced the liveries of some of the larger companies.

A standard pattern of blue uniform, comprising the same type of cap, double-breasted jacket and trousers as worn in the RN, but with MN buttons and cuff braid to indicate rank, was specified. Apart from a different cap badge and rank markings it was very similar to the naval uniform although originally the ornamentation on the peak of the cap for masters, a row of laurel leaves, was different form that of commanders and above in the RN who had oak leaves. But in time this distinction disappeared and the MN adopted the naval pattern. (Not restricted solely to the MN, the colloquial term for the peak adornment was **scrambled eggs.**)

(The term **'dress uniform'** tended to be used for both the ordinary uniform jacket, sometimes referred to as a reefer coat, and the mess-dress uniform. This distinguished it from the more casual battle-dress and tropical uniforms.)

Uniform caps were rarely worn with uniform except in one or two of the top *liner companies where its omission was seen, as in the RN, as a failure to wear the uniform correctly.

Merchant Navy cap badge. The Standard Merchant Navy Uniform Regulations included provision for officers to wear the new MN cap badge as an alternative to the many individual company cap badges, or where no company badge existed. The badge consisted of a silver anchor (without cable) on a red velvet cushion with a gold rope rim, surmounted by a gold naval crown, surrounded below and at the sides by gold oak leaves and acorns.

Bombay Cap badge. On the standard MN cap badge, the oak-leaf wreath was smaller than the laurel-leaf wreath on the cap badge of RN officers. An unofficial, modified MN badge, rather more impressive with a wreath similar to the RN badge, was preferred by some officers. It was produced by skilled gold lace workers in Bombay and was known as **The Bombay Rose.**

Standard Merchant Navy rank markings. Apart from their configuration, the stripes of gold lace under the new regulations were similar to those worn by naval officers except that they were generally reduced in width although in practice this reduction was sometimes ignored. The regulations provided that on dress uniforms for certificated officers the straight gold stripes on the cuff, one to four from third mate to master or junior engineer to chief engineer (with maroon between the stripes) were to be accompanied by a diamond shape worked into the braid. Pursers, (white between the stripe) and surgeons (red between the stripes), followed the same pattern except that the senior rank in these departments had only three stripes. Chief radio officers had two wavy stripes, diamond between, and a second radio officer had a single wavy stripe with a diamond.

Wartime rank markings. As a wartime economy, sleeve braid was worn only on the outer part of the cuff and did not extend right around the sleeve, almost halving the quantity required.

Company Uniforms. Many shipping companies had their own uniforms, and their different insignia often engendered a great sense of pride among their officers. The pattern of the uniform varied little but a company's insignia on the cap badge was unique although it usually followed a well-established pattern.

It comprised the company's house flag largely surrounded by a gold wreath, and a few companies surmounted it with a Royal or naval crown.(For a time, the wreath of the Brocklebank and Orient Line cap badges was blue, similar to that of naval chaplains.) A notable exception to the conventional type of

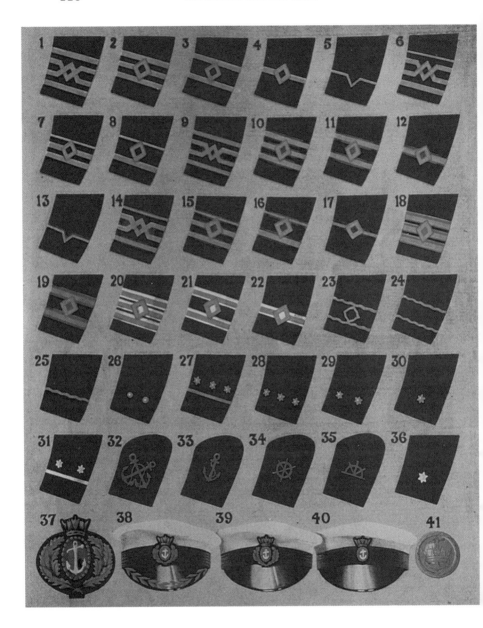

Rank markings and caps of the Standard Merchant Navy uniform. (Details, by number, opposite.)

RANK MARKINGS (OPPOSITE).

Certificated Deck & Engineer Officers, Surgeons and Pursers have full diamonds and their gold lace (or black mohair) was originally of 1/4in. width but was later increased to 3/8in. Uncertificated Officers have half diamonds with 1/4in. gold lace (or mohair) later increased to 3/8in. & Radio Operators 1/4in. Russian braid or black braid, also later increased to 3/8 inches..

(In later years, although not officially sanctioned, there has been a tendency for the more senior officers in particular to increase the width of the gold lace more in line with that worn by Royal Navy officers.)

Deck Officers – 1. Master 2. Chief Officer 3. Second Officer 4. Third & Junior Officer 5. Uncertificated Junior Officer 6. Second Master. 7. First Officer 8. Junior Second Officer

Engineers – (Purple beside the stripes) 9. Chief Engineer 10. Second Engineer & Chief Refrig. Engineer 11. Third Engineer & Second Refrig. Engineer

12. Fourth & Junior Engineer 13. Junior Engineer 14. Second Chief Engineer 15. Junior Second Engineer 16. Junior Third Engineer 17. Junior Fourth Engineer

Medical – (Scarlet beside the stripes) 18. Surgeon 19. Assistant Surgeon Pursers (White beside the stripes) 20. Senior Purser (where more than three are carried) 21. Purser 22. Assistant Purser

Wireless Operators – 23. First Wireless Operator 24. Second Wireless Operator 25. Third Wireless Operator

26. Cadets & Apprentices (Two buttons on the cuff)

Stewards – 27. Chief Steward on a passenger ship 28. Assistant Chief Steward 29. Steward– 30. Assistant Steward 31. Steward on a cargo ship

32. Petty Officers – Bosun 33. Bosun's Mate

Quartermasters – 34. Quartermaster 35. Quartermaster's Mate Galley – 36. Cook

37. Caps & badges – Officers' Cap badge 38. Peak of Master's Cap 39. Peak of cap of other officers 40. Petty Officer's cap badge 41. Coat Button

badge until the late 1960s was that of the P & O which comprised a rising sun for all but the deck officers who were distinguished by having the addition of a slewed anchor beneath it. This changed to the contentioal pattern in the late 1960s.

Buttons usually bore a similar insignia to the cap badge, but many shipping companies used the standard Merchant Navy button.

Company rank markings. While in many cases conforming closely to the Standard Merchant Navy cuff braid, officer's rank in some companies was often indicated in quite a different style. In most cases the gold lace was worn on the cuff, but occasionally on the shoulder. Some interesting variations included:

(i) British Tanker Company, Clan Line, Ben Line and Trinder Anderson – braid similar to that of the RN with a curl above the top stripe rather than incorporation of the diamond within the design.

(ii) Royal Fleet Auxiliary, British Antarctic Survey and South African Railways (which operated the port tugs) – the diamond above the top stripe.

(iii) Cunard and B.I. – without the curl or diamond.

(iv) Orient Line (Captains and Staff Commanders only) and Royal Mail Lines – large inverted chevrons on the cuff.

(v) Canadian Pacific – Similar to the Standard MN braid but with minor variations and with a maple leaf in the diamond. (The leaves on the cap peaks of captains, staff captains, chief engineers and staff chief engineers were maple leaves in lieu of oak leaves.)

(vi) The New Zealand Shipping Company wore shoulder braid on its dress uniform similar to that worn with tropical rig, but with straight stripes and no diamond or curl.

(vii) P & O uniform rank markings until about the middle of the 1960s, was most unusual. While also having braid on the shoulder for all except engineers, it did so in a very different manner – deck officers, surgeons and pursers (and later radio officers) had narrow shoulder straps, referred to by the naval outfitters, Gieves Ltd. as 'P & O binders'. These binders, sewn across the shoulder adjacent to the join with the sleeve, carried the braid for the senior officers in a 'fore & aft' direction across the shoulder. For other officers the binders were similarly fitted but the braid was at right angles to them in an 'athwartships' direction along the shoulder. Chief officers had a single 'fore and aft' broad gold shoulder stripe on the right shoulder and **staff commanders had one on each. ** Commanders had the same as staff commanders but with a rising sun above the stripe. The coloured braid between the surgeons' and pursers' braid (scarlet & white respectively) followed the convention but all P & O deck officers had royal blue between the stripes, or as an edging in the case of the commander and staff commander. (Pale blue between the stripes was used in some companies for radio officers and electricians, and in B.I. by matrons, but when P & O acquired its own radio officers, they then had green.) Until 1947 the shoulder braid, except for commanders and staff commanders, was worn on one shoulder only – on the right for deck officers and the left for others.) P & O engineers followed the convention of colour (maroon) but with straight stripes without a curl, on the cuff.

(viii) Apprentices and cadets in most companies wore a small gilt button and a twist of gold Russian braid beneath it on each collar of their jacket. In Blue Funnel Line, which referred to its apprentices as 'midshipmen', in Port Line and a few other companies, they wore three buttons on the cuff as was once customary for naval midshipmen.

Tropical dress. Most cargo ship officers wore a white cotton, open-neck shirt with white shorts and long white stockings with black (sometimes white) shoes. Rank markings were worn on the shoulder.

Some companies allowed the wearing of the same tropical dress in their passenger ships but many required their officers to wear the RN pattern comprising a single-breasted jacket,

** In the late 1950s the term 'Commander' was replaced by 'Captain'.

with company's buttons buttoning to the neck – often known as a **choker** – with long white trousers and white shoes. A different type of jacket was worn by P & O officers comprising a conventionally styled single-breasted white jacket with a white shirt and black tie.

Khakis. For officers in many cargo ships an alternative to white tropical rig was one comprising khaki shirts, shorts (or trousers) and long khaki socks; khaki was more practical and easier to keep smart for longer. (In Esso tankers, khaki shirts and trousers were worn with a standard blue uniform jacket as a winter dress and deck officers had the option of wearing company suppled baseball caps without a badge.)

Mess dress. In passenger ships it was customary for the officers to dress for dinner. They then wore a navy-blue monkey jacket and waistcoat, similar to the RN pattern, usually with the company's buttons, a white dress shirt with a black bow tie and navy-blue trousers. When 'in whites' the waistcoat was dispensed with and a white, cotton monkey jacket replaced the heavier navy-blue one, with a blue cummerbund wound around the waist to conceal the belt and trouser top. This dress was usually referred to as **mess kit** in the MN and mess undress in the RN.

Red Sea Rig consisted of a white open-neck tropical shirt with navy-blue trousers, a black cummerbund, black shoes and socks. (For a time at least one company's Red Sea rig substituted white trousers for blue.) It provided a cooler and less formal tropical dress than mess dress for evening wear and was worn in some ships in hot weather, particularly in cargo ships where the rig was often worn as a slightly more formal dress for evenings.

Bum freezer. The name by which the short monkey jacket, worn as part of an officer's mess kit, was sometimes known.

Frock coats. Some shipping companies required their masters to wear naval pattern frock coats for formal occasions until shortly after WW1.

Swords. Except for a short time in the early days of the P & O, the ceremonial naval sword has not formed a part of the dress of Merchant Service officers. This did not stop P & O officers, for a long time after they had ceased to wear them, becoming the butt of some relatively good humoured chiding by officers in rival companies. There were many caustic comments about 'wooden swords' and a supposed refusal by the Admiralty to allow them to wear 'proper' swords. Another version of the story is that the Admiralty gave its permission so long as the sword was worn on the opposite side of that for officers in the RN. (No evidence of this alleged slight is documented to the best of the author's knowledge.)

A 'proper' P & O sword was a fact; it was identical to that in the RN except that the crown on the blade was replaced by the rising sun from the crest of the Company's Coat of Arms. One or two examples remain to prove the point.

Twin Screw Tie. A slang term for a bow tie as worn with mess kit.

White cap cover. Until shortly after WW2 the crown of the cap was of blue cloth. Until then, when the crown was replaced with white, it had been customary in warm climates, including summer in the UK, to fit a temporary white, linen cover over the blue crown. White plastic covers were sometimes worn in lieu of cotton ones.

Plastic and paper collars. Many officers wore white plastic, rather than cotton, collars on shirts with detachable collars. Plastic collars could be easily cleaned with a soapy cloth thereby extending the interval between shirt washes. Collars made of good quality, glazed, heavy-duty paper, could also be bought by the dozen from naval outfitters and were worn by officers in many cargo ships, but they could not be wiped clean and were discarded when dirty. Both types disappeared when shirts with attached collars became the norm.

Battle dress. During the war the formality attached to the wearing of uniforms was relaxed and much of the time the traditional dress was not worn. Instead, many officers wore a single-breasted jacket of a coarse woollen material, similar to that worn in the Army but dyed dark blue, and usually worn with Merchant Navy 'brass' buttons. Trousers were of the same colour and material. Battle dress continued for some years after WW2 as a practical working rig on cargo ships.

Patrol jacket. The 1918 Order in Council which gave official approval for the MN uniform also prescribed a working uniform for officers. Worn in some companies, it consisted of a single-breasted jacket of dark blue cotton, with patch pockets and buttoning to the neck, with MN 'brass' buttons. Known as a patrol jacket, it was worn with similar cotton trousers as a practical every-day dress in cargo ships where little or no formality was expected of the officers. Rank markings were originally of black mohair on shoulder straps but later the mohair gave way to gold braid.

Woolly Pully. A navy blue, long sleeve woollen pullover, RN pattern, with rank markings on the shoulder. It was worn with blue trousers as an everyday rig in some ships. Making its appearance around the end of the review period it was a practical alternative to the slightly more formal uniform of reefer jacket and trousers.

Duffel coat. During WW2 the fawn-coloured, hooded duffel coat made from a thick, warm fabric, fastened with wooden toggles into rope beckets, was popular. It was worn principally by officers and became an acceptable, practical item of their cold weather working uniform, even in the RN. Duffel coats later became fashion garments in several colours for civilian use.

Boiler suit. Officers undertaking dirty work, both deck and engineer, usually wore a white boiler suit. In some companies, particularly those with passenger ships, an officer was expected to wear a uniform cap with it whenever practical. The cap badge was then the only indication that the wearer was an officer. Safer, more visible colours, like fluorescent orange, later became common and were sometimes worn with a baseball type of cap, occasionally with the Company's logo on it.

PETTY OFFICERS, QUARTERMASTERS, RATINGS

Although reference has been made above only to officers' uniforms, POs and QMs, principally in the *liner companies, frequently wore a similar uniform to that of their counterparts in the RN. POs wore standard MN or company petty officers' cap badges, marks of rank and buttons with a reefer coat. QMs wore the naval seaman's dress with a jumper and collar but with the ship's or company's name on the cap ribbon. The term **square rig** was sometimes applied to this rig.

European deck ratings dress. Almost anything was acceptable in tramp ships and as a working rig in many other ships too. Smarter ratings wore a blue shirt and *dungarees but generally any coloured shirt or T-shirt was worn with dungarees or other old trousers. For headwear they wore a flat, felt hat, a woolly hat, a trilby, a beret or even a white cap cover. Many made their own special type of hat known as a *revi. In cargo ships of the *liner companies and in passenger ships, a blue jersey, often with the company's or ship's name on the chest, sometimes accompanied by the house flag, was worn with blue trousers. This was a requirement whenever in the public eye.

Monowai blues. In the Union Steam Ship Company deck ratings in the passenger ships and passenger/cargo ships on overseas voyages wore a light cotton, blue working rig known as Monowai blues named after a company's passenger ship on the Trans-Tasman run. (*Monowai* ex-*Razmak* from P & O 's Aden/Bombay service).

Lascar seamen's dress. There were numerous Indian seamen in British ships ranging from passenger ships of the P & O and B. I. to cargo ships of many of the smaller and less familiar companies. Their dress varied considerably but the following was worn by many crews from the Bombay region:

A cargo ship rig consisted of blue dungarees and shirt with a round, brimless canvas, and a hat (**topi.**) In passenger ships, particularly when in the public eye, the crew's dress was more colourful with the topi having a red riband around it. The plain shirt and trousers was replaced with a knee length, embroidered cotton tunic (**lalchi**) having, around the waist, a folded red kerchief (**rhumal**) knotted in front, and white pantaloons. The lalchis of the serangs and tindals were even more elaborately embroidered, while their topies, with fancy designs painted on top, had a Bengal tartan riband around them. The authoritative appearance of these senior Indian ratings was further enhanced with a bosun's call (whistle) on a silver chain around the neck.

GENERAL

Civilian clothes. In many ships in the UK coastal trade, in most sailing ships and in some tramp ships, officers often did not wear uniform even on duty, although on days of arrival or departure some effort might be made to present a more professional appearance. Sometimes part civilian dress and part uniform was an acceptable rig; even the sight of the master wearing an old sports jacket and grey trousers was not uncommon, although a reefer coat and uniform cap might be kept in his wardrobe for special occasions.

Except for a special ceremonial event, even in wartime MN officers rarely wore uniform ashore. It was always considered not the done thing unless, of course, they were intent upon impressing the ladies.

MN lapel badge. This silver coloured badge, worn on the lapel of a jacket, consisted of the letters MN surrounded by a rope, its ends tied beneath with a reef knot, and surmounted by a naval crown. It was first authorised in 1939 to be worn by seamen when ashore in civilian clothes to indicate they were in the MN and to avoid being mistaken for draft dodgers or pacifists. In spite of this precaution more than one young merchant seaman was given a white feather.

Tanker trained. Slang name for the appearance of an officer's cap with the crown pulled hard back and the peak pulled down so that the badge stood well apart from the rest of the cap.

Revi. Seamen's working hats, worn on deck for protection from the sun. They were usually homemade from off-cuts of white duck canvas with a peak sewn into them but were sometimes a rather shapeless, blue denim cap.

Steaming Revy. Slang term for a well-used cap

Dungarees. Working trousers, often made of denim. The denim versions later became fashion garments commonly referred to as jeans. Also **Dungys.**

Oilskins. Unlike the reliable, modern weatherproof outer garment made of plasticised materials, oilskins were originally made of cotton cloth treated with a drying oil to make it waterproof. This could become sticky in hot weather and sailors often coated them with their own concoctions consisting of copal varnish, fish oil and linseed oil in the right proportions.

Sou'wester. Waterproof hat worn with an oilskin and made of similar materials. It is no longer used, as most modern 'oilskins', made of synthetic fabrics, have an attached hood.

Body and soul lashings. Rope lashings around the waist, the bottom of oilskin legs and sleeves. They contributed to safety, the former providing something for a fellow seaman to grab in the event of a shipmate needing support. They also helped to keep the weather out and the term was especially relevant in sailing ships on whose yards seamen were required to furl sail in heavy weather and work on open decks often swept by heavy seas.

Sweat rag. A cotton neckcloth, like an uncoloured, open-weave kitchen dishcloth, was sometimes worn by seamen to absorb perspiration but principally by firemen, trimmers and greaser whose working place was often exceedingly hot and caused excessive sweating.

Slop chest. The small amounts of clothing and other items such as soap and matches carried by some ships and sold to the crew with a deduction from their wages. Some slop chests were quite comprehensive, carrying more gear and clothing.

Board of Trade shoelaces. Sail twine or rope yarn as replacements for worn out shoelaces.

Bottom ends. Firemen's shoes

Parish or **schooner rigged.** Parish rigged was the term originally applied to needy or ill-clothed men sent to sea by the parish. This, and schooner rigged, were commonly later said of ships or sailors provided with minimum gear and equipment and justified their use in a derogatory sense. (The origin of schooner rigged lay in the schooner carrying many fewer sails than a square-rigger.)

Dunnage. The term a seaman would sometimes use for his kit. In some cases it was said to consist of, '53 articles – a pack of cards and a clean sweat rag'.

Empire Builders. Large, baggy shorts often seen in the East. Also *Bombay bloomers.

Lungi. An Indian loincloth worn hanging from the waist. It was quite common for seamen, particularly officers, to wear a lungi rather than pyjamas as night attire in native crew ships.

Japanese seaboots. Simple rubber sandals commonly known as 'Flip flops'. Also **Abadan seaboots, Bombay wellies** and **Jesus boots**.

Bombay lace. The ragged edges of clothing that had become worn and badly frayed at the cuffs or trouser legs. Also **Maltese lace.** (This was a little unfair to Malta where some very fine lace was produced.)

Uniform outfitters:

Supplying officers with uniforms and the other gear required on joining a ship provided naval outfitters with good business. There were several well-known firms, some with branches around the country, including:

Gieves Ltd. This old established firm (1785) with branches in several UK ports, Gibraltar & Malta, boasted that it supplied uniforms to Admiral Lord Nelson. It was the principal outfitter to officers in the RN but it also kitted-out a small number of Merchant Service officers who, in many cases, had been wooed when still cadets at Pangbourne Nautical College. With the decline in the number of officers, both RN & MN, Gieves eventually amalgamated with the famous military tailors, Hawkes who claim to have made uniforms for the Duke of Wellington. They now trade as 'Gieves & Hawkes, of Saville Row'. Gieves, a relatively expensive firm of naval outfitters, was nicknamed **Thieves.**

Miller, Raynor & Haysom Ltd. Primarily a Merchant Service outfitter, this well-established company had branches around the country and was favoured by a number of shipping companies. It was nicknamed **Miller, Rayner and Paysome.**

S.W. Silver & Co. at one time Silver & Edgington, had its premises in London's Eastcheap. Silvers was another well-established outfitter principally supplying uniforms and other seagoing gear to Merchant Service officers. P & O officers were well looked after by this firm and many of its officers would have first become acquainted with Silvers as cadets on HMS *Worcester.*

Baker & Co had premises in London, Southampton and Liverpool. This firm catered for officers in the smaller shipping companies to whom the quality of their uniforms was of less importance.

Gardner & Co in High Street, Whitechapel was another London outfitters at the cheaper end of the market. Another was **Harvey's.**

Changes to uniform dress. A study of the outfit list for a cadet joining *Pangbourne Nautical College in the 1930s shows how clothing has changed over the years. Although the College's cadets wore the uniform of the Royal Naval Reserve the requirement was not very different from that of the larger British shipping companies at the time. It comprised:

1 Uniform jacket, superfine cloth

1 Trousers, superfine cloth ('Superfine', often known as 'doeskin', is rarely worn in the Merchant Service today

1 Uniform jacket, tweed (presumably we would refer to this today as serge.)

2 Trousers, tweed

2 Caps, peak turned down

4 Cap covers

1 Regulation watch coat

8 Shirts, of which 4 are to be without collars, (As a gracious gesture the compiler of the outfit list did note that '... where a cadet has been accustomed to wearing white flannel shirts in winter, the use of these may be continued until worn out.' The list goes on to say that 'silk and artificial shirts and underwear do not conform to the College outfit requirements and must not be supplied.)

6 white regulation collars, stiff, and 8 soft. (These were the days of front and back studs with detachable collars.)

6 vests – 3 thin, 3 thick

3 pairs cellular cotton drawers (Short underpants) for summer

3 pairs thick drawers (underpants) for winter

Neck ties, black (silk) of uniform pattern

2 pairs of braces (belts were not approved items in those days)

An oilskin coat. (This was referred to as a 'pegamoid'.)

1 pair of glacé leather shoes

2 or more pairs of strong laced boots with soles at least 3/8 inch thick. (These had to be plain-fronted without the toecaps which were fashionable in civilian clothes at that period, but definitely not approved with uniform.)

To convey his 'outfit' to the College, the new cadet was required to provide:

1 trunk or box of oblong shape size approx. 2 ft 6 in. by 1 ft 6 in. by 1 ft'. (This was still the era of passengers' hold and cabin trunks.)

CHAPTER SEVEN

Recreation and Social Behaviour

Generally very little entertainment was provided on board for the officers or ratings.

In most ships they were expected to make their own. Reading was a common past-time and in later years a crew library was often supplied, particularly after the birth of the *Seafarers Education Service under the aegis of the *Marine Society.

In older ships with the ratings' accommodation in the fo'c's'le or poop, there was often little privacy, plenty of movement in rough weather and little comfort so that sleeping (when possible), playing cards and reading were about the only means of relaxation. In the 1937 regulations applying to crew accommodation, all new ships were required to be built with accommodation amidships and the crew had to be provided with proper washrooms, but it was many more years before the crew were given double and single berth cabins.

At sea, in cargo ships, a wood and canvas swimming pool was sometimes erected on deck and as weather conditions improved, a film show, usually also on deck, might be arranged on a Saturday or Sunday night at sea.

Even in passenger ships the entertainment situation was little different for many although the larger numbers of crew made it possible for the ratings and stewards to organise their own social club and arrange some entertainment. This would sometimes constitute a concert organised by the crew and presented to the passengers, usually near the end of a voyage.

Shipping companies were obliged to lay down fairly strict rules regarding the social relationship between the crew and the passengers. Generally, all ratings were forbidden to associate with passengers except strictly as required in carrying out their duties.

Only officers could take part in passenger entertainments. The extent to which they were permitted to socialise with passengers varied between companies, with junior officers rarely being allowed this privilege until about the middle of the 20th century and then only on a limited scale as approved by the captain.

Senior officers were generally expected to show some interest as a public relations exercise. This often consisted of hosting a group of passengers at their table – similarly to 'The Captain's Table' – and sometimes senior officers would invite groups of passengers to their cabins for a pre-dinner drinks, or join them in public rooms and bars for a drink and coffee. Dancing and other evening entertainment was often encouraged for those not watch-keeping during the night.

Needless to say there was usually a very strict regulation that 'No officer may invite a lady to his cabin on her own'. This did not mean that it never happened. Although in the ordinary course of events many officers did not shut their cabin door at sea and relied upon a curtain drawn across for privacy, there was an unwritten law that if an officer's door was shut it meant, 'Do not enter', as the occupant might be entertaining a lady.

In port the seafarer was generally left entirely to his own devices. For some, a night ashore might consist of a visit to the *Mission to Seamen but for many the attraction was the bright lights, the bars and the ladies of questionable repute. From their social contact with the latter, several commonly used expressions among seafarers have arisen and the activities often had unpleasant results later. (See Chapter 8, Medical.)

Captains of sailing ships often took their wives and families to sea with them but with the advent of the steam ship and its generally shorter voyages this practice largely came to an end. It was revived again in many shipping companies about the middle of the 20th century and often extended to other officers, at least for short voyages or parts of longer ones where international travel was relatively easy to arrange. This privilege was rarely offered to other members of the crew and inevitably arrival home, at least for most of the married men, was a very special event.

Contrary to a commonly held belief shipmasters have no legal powers to marry people in British registered ships. However, some countries do permit the marriage ceremony to be conducted by the master on board their ships, and some also provide for marriages by registered marriage celebrants (who may sometimes be also shipmasters) within their territorial waters, provided a licence has been issued for that particular situation. (British law does not permit this because a wedding must take place at a 'permanent and identifiable' place and clearly a ship does not provide the former of these requirements.)

SOCIAL BEHAVIOUR

Miscellaneous Terms:

While away at sea the generally monastic life of the seafarer inevitably led to his thoughts and actions being directed strongly towards the female sex. Many, often vulgar, expressions reflected this yearning.

Spliced. Married, as in 'getting spliced' or 'already spliced'.

Taking the plunge. Getting married.

Getting married 'Board of Trade'. Marriage in the lesser formality of a registry office rather than a church.

On Aussie Articles. Invoking the concept of seamen signed on Australian *Articles of Agreement, this term was sometimes used for unmarried life-partnerships.

In the lee of bum island. At home in bed with the wife on a stormy night. A sailor's favourite 'anchorage'.

Shore bosun. A dominating oversize woman.

Bunks. A seaman's bunk played an important part in his life at sea as a means of passing the hours of his watch-below or as an essential means of recuperation; consequently a number of expressions related to it:

Scratcher. A Bunk. The term was an allusion to bedbugs once prevalent in many fo'c's'les of older ships, but by the middle of the period they were rare. Also **Pit, Cart, Chariot**, or **Wagon.**

To Kip. To sleep. Also, **To Crash. To turn in.**

Egyptian PT. Another term for a sleep, often a short nap.

Carpentry. Putting a head and two legs on a bunk, for a rest.

Battened down. Asleep in one's bunk.

All parts taking an equal strain. Resting on one's bunk.

To have a caulk. Strictly, to sleep on deck but the term was also used for other occasions when a seaman had a sleep. It is said to have originated because lying on the deck was emulating the caulking in the deck.

Carrying out a deck-head survey. The prelude to having a sleep, because counting the number of rivets in a deck-head above his bunk when trying to sleep was a seaman's alternative to counting sheep.

Poodle-faking. This term was use used to convey a shipmate's pursuit of the opposite sex, more often than not as an affair of the heart rather than for purely lustful sex.

Brothel creepers. A pair of suede or other stylish shoes usually fitted with a rubber or other soft, quiet sole.

Bagging off. Going ashore for a woman.

Up the rags. Ashore to visit the brothels.

Get your end away. As in, 'Did you get your end away?' Which meant, 'Did you get a whore?' – or at least 'Did you get a one night's stand?'

Meat Boat. A sampan in Hong Kong that brought prostitutes to a ship.

Jungle bunnies. Young, and some not-so-young, women who inhabited the crew accommodation for their 'entertainment' while ships were principally in Australian or New Zealand ports, sometimes travelling illegally on the ship from port to port, or overland to rejoin at the next port. Also **Coastal hostesses, wharf rats** and **wharf angels.**

Ringbolt. 'To ringbolt' meant to travel illegally in New Zealand coastal ships between ports as a non-fare paying passenger. Usually concealed by the crew on their own initiative, or sometimes as part of a well-organised illegal operation with their acquiescence, the term was also used as a noun.

Donkey Rigged. Referring to a crew member with a large penis.

The man in the boat. The female clitoris.

Dip his wick. A expression for a seaman engaging in sexual intercourse.

Greasing his fid. A similar expression to that above. (A fid was a wooden instrument used in rope splicing and bears some similarity with the male genital organ.)

No lead in his pencil. An expression referring to a shipmate considered unable to satisfy a woman sexually.

Having a bit of black velvet. Sex with a coloured woman.

Jiggy-jiggy. A multi-lingual word for sexual intercourse, understood in just about all countries. It was often the seafarer's greeting by the local pimps or prostitutes as he walked out of the dock gate in search of female company.

Port Said bibles. Explicitly written sex books readily obtainable in this port.

Downtown to lunch. Cunnilingus.

A sixty-niner. A graphic description for the position adopted by a couple for simultaneous cunnilingus and fellatio.

Madame Judgaprix. The manageress of a brothel.

A Leg Opener or LOM (Leg Opening Mixture.) A relatively innocuous drink laced with an alcoholic spirit, usually vodka which is difficult to detect, and offered to a young lady with a view to loosening up her moral inclinations when she professed not to drink alcohol, or to drink very little.

Two blocks. An expression indicating the maximum penetration of a female during sexual intercourse. (It is derived from the seamanship expression for a tackle – a system of ropes and pulleys – when hove hard up with one part of the system jammed hard up against the other.)

Using a Portuguese hand pump. Masturbating.

Short time. Intercourse with a woman with no longer-term commitment. Also in similar vein, a seaman going ashore for a woman might content himself with a knee trembler or quickie.

Homosexuality. Although homosexual behaviour was rare in cargo ships many of those in the Purser's Department in passenger ships, principally stewards, cooks and barmen, were gay. They led a very different life on board from the majority of the deck and engine room crew who were mostly heterosexual. Some, principally around mid 20th century, were the source of a different language and associated behaviour at sea which arose because of their sexual orientation.

This language, **Polari,** was a secret language used, although not exclusively, by gay seafarers and flourished in the 1950s, but by the end of the period it had declined in use. For many gay seafarers, Polari was a part of their everyday lives, a form of language that they took for granted. According to Dr Paul Baker and Dr Jo Stanley in their book, *Hello sailor: The Hidden History of Gay Life at Sea,* Longman 2003, gay seafarers who had learnt Polari could while away hours, gossiping about who they fancied, who was doing what with whom, and who was the most well-endowed man on board. Also spelt **Palare, Palari** or **Parlaree.**

This language of gay seamen and a long-established attitude of heterosexual seamen towards homosexuality, gave rise to some terms and expressions:

Sea queen. An effeminate gay seafarer, usually in the Purser's Department of passenger ships.

Queen Bee. Leader of the gays in the Purser's Department.

Balmoral. Cabins recognised as gay territory – 'Balmoral' because the Queen spent time there.

Fruit locker. A cabin full of sea queens; a 'fruit' being a gay man.

Brown Hatter. A homosexual

Glory hole. The accommodation occupied by a number of the Purser's Department personnel (see also Chapter 11.) According to Drs. Paul Baker & Jo Stanley, the term was also applied to the circular hole cut in the internal bulkhead (wall) through which gay men had sex.

Whose turn in the barrel? Usually said in jest by heterosexuals during a lengthy sea pssage without any contact with women. This expression referred to homosexuality.

RECREATION AND ENTERTAINMENT

Shiplover. Ships hold a fascination for many and real enthusiasts derive great pleasure simply from seeing ships and discussing various aspects of them with others. Perhaps surprisingly this interest often seems strongest in those who had no professional association with ships and although there were exceptions, many professional seamen wished to have little more than a purely working association with them. They often used the term shiplover in a derogatory sense as though there is something slightly odd about a person with such a keen interest.

Crossing the Line. The ceremony for initiating those who have not previously crossed into the other hemisphere. Occasionally in cargo ships, but especially in passenger ships, the ceremony was performed with enthusiasm as a welcome entertainment - except by those who were on the receiving end of the banter and high-jinks, which could sometimes be rather overwhelming, even rough. The older hands took the part of King Neptune, his Queen, the Barber and the Doctor, with others performing as policemen, bears and members of the King's retinue assisting the initiation of new entrants into Neptune's Realm. It was not unknown for the celebrants to be well fuelled with alcohol.

Alcohol and Tobacco contributed to relaxation at sea and was usually purchased at duty-free prices. Spirits were rarely available to ratings who were restricted to beer in their cabin or mess-room, and on deck in hot weather, but officers could usually purchase spirits. Some companies had special contracts for their supply; Burne & Turner's gin label proudly stated Specially bottled for P & O. In some, principally tramp ships, drunken masters were all too common and excess consumption could be a problem, but most officers drank responsibly at sea and there was no legal limit until about the end of the 20th century when some companies and nations introduced a 'dry ship' policy. Shortly after WW2, duty-free gin cost an officer as little as four shillings and six pence (23p) a bottle and whisky six shillings (30p.) In some companies where officers were encouraged or required to entertain passengers, an entertainment allowance was provided to cover the expense.

(The author particularly recalls that as a naïve first-trip apprentice he witnessed a *slops issue shortly after leaving Liverpool, and was amazed at the number of blue tins of what he believed to be Brasso – a well-known brand of metal polish – were being issued to the ratings. Little did he realise until later, with a very red face, that this was the crew's issue of Barclay's beer, in tins of very similar size and appearance.)

Plug tobacco, cigarette tobacco and 'roll your own' papers, and 'tailor made' cigarettes were readily available to all on board. Cigarettes, frequently Players or Churchman brand, were packed in tins of 50, either flat with a cellophane seal, or round and sealed in the tin with a cutter in the lid. At the same period they sold for about two shillings (10p) for 50.

In port, alcohol presented a major problem for the master of many a *white crew cargo ship. At the first opportunity some of his crew would be ashore to the nearest pub and, many beers later, were fighting one another or worse, picking a fight with the locals. It was not uncommon for the master or mate to attend the local Court next day with the ship's agent to bail out a member of the crew. Fights ashore were common but sometimes, when they broke out after a return on board, they could be of more concern. More than one mate or second engineer had to defend himself against a knife attack by a disgruntled member of the crew. Particularly at sailing time the master could be presented with the problem of shortage of crew and this required his officers to bring them back from the pub, albeit often too drunk to be of any use before they had slept it off.

Wardroom. Officers often drank in their cabins but many ships had a comfortable lounge in which to relax. In some ships, fitted with a bar, it was known as The Wardroom, a favoured place of social gathering. A merchant ship's wardroom differed from a warship's as most officers dined in the saloon and did not need an adjoining ante-room to serve as their mess-room as in a naval vessel.

The Pig & Whistle. The crew bar and recreation room in a passenger ship; often known simply as **The Pig.**

Sunday beer. At one time in Shell Tankers there was an issue of a free bottle of beer for every officer on Sundays. This was paid from a fund, the origin of which was a gesture by Queen Wilhemina of the Netherlands after WW2, as an appreciation for Shell tanker crews' war service. This arose because the Dutch Royal Family were major shareholders in the Royal Dutch Shell Group of which Anglo-Saxon Petroleum (later renamed Shell Tankers) was a part.

Stopping his tap. For officers, the purchase of spirits was usually allowed, but abuse of the use of alcohol resulted in the privilege of any alcohol purchase being withdrawn. When the master did this it was referred to as stopping his tap.

Docking bottle. Although in most ships spirits were not available to the ratings, an exception was sometimes made shortly before arrival home at a UK port. They might then be allowed to buy a bottle of spirits for taking ashore when they paid off. Many seamen took advantage of this concession as the UK Customs regulations permitted the landing of a part bottle of spirits, duty free. Known as the docking bottle, the owner had to break the seal and take the top off to satisfy the Customs but sometimes the drop in level did not stop there and the master might be left regretting the concession when the privilege was abused long before the bottle found its way ashore.

Top end spanner. A beer bottle opener.

Cape smoke. South African brandy. Relatively cheap, it was popular with seamen when on the South African coast and many had reason to regret the extent to which they imbibed it.

Tarpaulin muster. This could refer to a cash collection for a shipmate but often referred to the pooling of money, usually small denomination notes and loose change, before sailing when one man was sent ashore to buy beer for the benefit of all the donors. It was called a tarpaulin muster because each man threw his money onto a hatch tarpaulin where it was counted. Underlying this was its significance in demonstrating the bond between them all. (The hatch immediately adjacent to the deck and engine room ratings' accommodation was a popular place to gather on social occasions.)

Six o'clock swill. This was not a nautical term but one well known to seamen visiting ports in Australia and New Zealand for many years until the 1960s. Seamen often became a part of the drunken scenes in the streets after the unseemly scramble for booze in the pubs whose closing time was then as early as 1800 hours. (Introduced in New Zealand in 1917, it was abolished in 1967.)

CHAPTER EIGHT

Medical

The majority of cargo ships did not carry a doctor and the master was responsible for the health of his crew although this duty was usually delegated to the mate. In some ships he, in turn, delegated most of the day-to-day work to the third mate, but officers were little trained in medical matters beyond holding a first aid certificate. They relied heavily upon excellent guidance in the standard work, **The Ship Captain's Medical Guide**, an essential part of a ship's medical equipment required by the Board of Trade.

Cargo ships with less than 100 crew and passengers, provided the latter did not exceed 12 (the number doubled during WW2), were not subject to the stricter passenger ship regulations and were not required to carry a doctor. However, a number of them, principally those in the liner trades, often carried a doctor although rarely one who was a regular company employee. Frequently a young, recently qualified practitioner overseas was granted a free passage to the UK to continue medical studies at a British university or to return home afterwards. The doctor became temporarily a member of the crew and signed the *ship's articles, being *paid off at the end of the outward or homeward voyage. He (some doctors were female when their husbands were also passengers) received a **shilling a month** for his services. (A payment, in this case a very nominal one, was necessary to fulfil one of the legal requirements of a contract of employment. Tradition had it that this 'payment' was not claimed but was donated to seamen's charities.)

Passenger ships were required to carry doctors, usually referred to as **surgeons,** and many also carried other medical staff, including **nursing sisters,** a **dispenser** and sometimes others with medical experience. It was usual for the **senior surgeon(s)** to look after the passengers and the **junior surgeon(s)** the crew, although the latter were also assisted by passengers when required in an emergency. Senior surgeons were usually long-term company employees and were often kept busy with passengers' real or imagined ailments for which a charge was made for each consultation.

Seamen were afflicted by many of the same medical complaints as in any community ashore. Coughs, rashes and stomach disorders were common and unless they became serious were readily manageable on board. They were treated with standard medicines and ointments provided to all ships under a Board of Trade scale of medical supplies. Copious quantities of cough and stomach mixture were doled out and third mates soon learnt to sort out the *lead swingers from the genuinely afflicted. Venereal diseases were common and a few days after leaving port it was not unusual to see a queue outside the sick bay/surgery.

In a cargo ship anything more than relatively minor complaints often called for more medical expertise than was available from a deck officer. This could be provided after arrival in port but at sea the master was dependent upon advice by radio which, in the United Kingdom, was readily available from Portishead Radio whose close links with medical practitioners were readily available. There was also a well-respected organisation in Rome which assisted with medical information by radio and sometimes advice could also be obtained from a doctor in another ship within radio range. When there was a passenger ship in the vicinity it was often possible to arrange a meeting at sea and transfer a doctor by boat; in serious cases requiring longer-term treatment, the patient would sometimes be transferred to the better-equipped ship.

In cases of death at sea, particularly if no doctor was carried, it was common in ships with ample refrigerated storerooms, to keep the corpse until arrival in port. If **burial at sea** was necessary, the corpse was first sewn into a canvas shroud and then laid on a *hatch board with the national flag draped over it. Traditionally, the last stitch passed through the nose and it is said that this was a precaution to ensure that the victim really was dead. The crew member who did the work, commonly the bosun, received a bottle of rum for his efforts.

With the hatch board perched over a shipside rail and the engines stopped, several ship's officers usually assembled to accompany any family on board while the master read a prayer. At the appropriate moment the body was then slid off the hatch board and committed to the deep, the ship's position being noted in the *deck and official log books.

COMMONLY USED TERMS AND EXPRESSIONS

Black draught. The common name for medicine for constipation. It was a 'cure-all' laxative prescribed by the 'doctor' at the drop of a hat. Often referred to as **a dose of No. 11s.**

Cement mixture. Common name for medicine to alleviate diarrhoea.

Short arm inspection. Doctors' inspection for VD, particularly in the USA.

Dreadnoughts. Anti-VD kits issued to the crew in ports where venereal disease was particularly rife and brothels received little regulatory attention.

A dose. A general term for one of the varieties of venereal diseases.

Cop out. To catch VD.

The galloping knob rot. Any form of VD. Also, **a load.**

A dose of clap. Gonorrhoea. Also **The Drip.**

The pox. Syphilis.

A full house. Both Gonorrhoea and Syphilis.

Andy McNabs. Crabs. Pubic lice.

A dose of crabs. A case of pubic lice.

Blue butter. Mercurial ointment for crabs.

Do not sit on this seat, the crabs here can jump six feet. A shipmate with crabs was morally bound to warn his shipmates when he used the communal heads (toilets.) Not wishing to reveal his identity he would place a notice so worded on the door.

Dobi itch. Insufficient rinsing following the use of cheap soap powders by native laundries and *dhobi wallas, particularly in hot weather, could produced an unpleasant rash. Also **Dobi rash.**

Prickly heat. An unpleasant, itchy rash associated with heavy sweating in the tropics accompanied by inadequate ventilation. This was common before the fitting of air conditioning in ships.

Salt tablets. For many years seamen were advised to take regular doses of salt in the tropics. This was usually administered in the form of tablets. (Current medical opinion cautions against taking too much salt in the diet.)

Gyppo gut. Diarrhoea. Also **Bombay Crud** and **A dose of the squitters.**

The Quack. A medical doctor, either on board or ashore.

Rose Cottage. A port clinic for the treatment of venereal diseases.

Dreadnought Hospital. The name of the seamen's hospital at Greenwich.

Dry-docked for repairs (or for a survey). Said of a person in hospital for treatment (or for a check-up).

CHAPTER NINE

People Associated With Ships

Apart from the crew there were many people associated with ships in one way or another. The shipping industry employed a large number of people with a variety of skills and they all contributed in their own way to its success and wellbeing.

Employees comprised both *Sea Staff and *Shore Staff; the word **'staff'** generally applying to permanent employees to distinguish them from those engaged on a casual basis. The sea and shore staff often had little association with one another and, perhaps with this contributing to misunderstandings, there was often animosity between them; each was critical of the other's alleged failure to work more harmoniously with the other.

Many of the shore staff comprised the usual employees required to operate any major business but shipping companies also needed specialist departments whose staff were experienced in ship operations, ship design, sales and purchase, marine engineering, freight brokering, and marine insurance, among others.

The diagram on the next page 146 outlines a typical shipping company's head office structure. It did not apply to all and there were many variations but the example gives a good indication of the customary requirements where shipowners took care of, or at least responsibility for, the company's day to day operation.

In many traditional shipping companies it was common for one or more directors to be actively involved. They would regularly visit the ships when in their *home port and in some companies the chairman would invite the master to dine with him at the end of a voyage to discuss any problems. This is very different from today where many so-called shipowners are little more than finance companies owning a single vessel. These companies rely almost entirely on other independent, specialist companies to handle almost all of their ship's operation, including the vital one of manning. Many of today's shipowners have little regard for those who man their vessels and quite often few in their offices have any knowledge of ships.

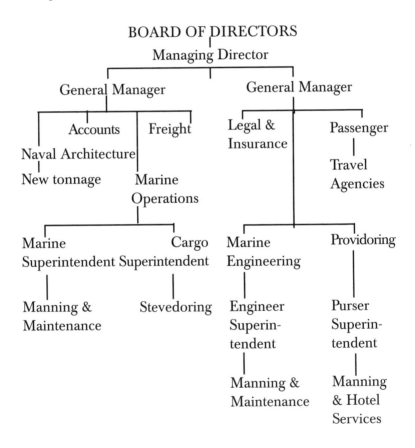

A typical head office organisation chart .

Some of those involved in various aspects of a company's operation:

The Super. A company's superintendent. Usually drawn from the ranks of seagoing officers appointed to the position in head office, the title was generally prefixed with the superintendent's specialist skill, e.g. Marine, Cargo, Engineer, Medical, Purser, or Catering. In the larger *liner companies there might also be a superintendent in another port or country to which its ships regularly traded.

A Super Cargo. A shipping company's or charterer's employee who supervised cargo planning and handling. Not a member of the normal crew, he might remain on board a ship for a while, often travelling around the coast to other ports where the ship engaged in cargo operations. **Loadmaster** in the USA.

Dock staff. In a home port, and sometimes at other ports where a company's ships called regularly and spent substantial time, there might be a **Dock Superintendent** with a supporting office and technical staff.

Shore Gunner. At least one prominent British shipping company running cargo and passenger ships to the Far East had a long-serving bosun, referred to as the shore gunner (from the Hindustani name for a European Bosun) permanently based in Hong Kong. He had wide-ranging responsibilities but principally those concerned with the ship's berthing arrangements, stores, maintenance and other work carried out on board by contracted local labour in that port.

Shore gang. Shipping companies employed seamen and riggers, usually only in their home port, to work their ships after the crew had paid off and left at the end of a voyage. Their role was to carry out any necessary work on deck or with cargo operations.

Gulls. Shore gang used by mud pilpots to run the lines and moor the ships. (Liverpool).

Office wallah. This Indian term refers to anyone employed in an office. It was commonly used by seafarers, usually disparagingly, particularly when referring to their own company's office personnel.

Other operating peronnel:

A shipowner needed to engage or contract others to support their ship operations, particularly when away from their home port.

Provedore. A firm supplying ships' provisions and stores. The term was sometimes used for the firm's employee who acted as liaison with the ships while in port.

Ship's Agent. Shipping companies appointed agents, usually local companies but sometimes individuals, to act for them in ports to which their ships traded. Their role was to look after the ship's interests in their port, assist masters with local knowledge and arrangements, and often also to act as cargo brokers.

Agent's Runner. A ship's agent's messenger.

Marine Surveyors. A generic term for those involved with surveys in a very broad range of activities within the shipping and marine insurance industries. Surveyors in this genre came from a wide variety of primary disciplines, principally those of seafarers experienced in ship operation and engineering, but also of naval architecture and other industrial fields. The recent serious reduction in the number of competent seagoing personnel has seen this area of surveyor recruitment diminishing rapidly.

The three most important types of surveyors supporting shipowners and charterers operations are:

Classification Societies' surveyors. Engaged largely to support the upholding of standards for owners and insurers, they are concerned with the design, building, maintenance and repair of ships to the extent of carrying out surveys to ensure that the standards are maintained. They also carry out statutory surveys where the classification society employing them is approved to act on behalf of Governments. Usually referred to as **Class surveyors.**

Underwriters' surveyors. Largely concerned with determining the nature, extent and cause of damage or the prevention of damage to ships, marine structures, cargoes and the environment. They may be employees of a survey firm or simply sole operators.

Government surveyors. Government employees concerned with the maintenance of standards laid down by statute and associated regulations, many arising from International Conventions. In this role they may act as **Flag State Control** (FSC) or **Port State Control** (PSC) surveyors and may be required to investigate casualties involving ships flying their Government's flag or those of other nations occurring within their own territorial waters.

Lloyd's Agents. The agents appointed by the Corporation of Lloyds in most of the world's main ports. Their role is:

• To report to Lloyd's on the movements of shipping and on other matters of importance to underwriters and the shipping community which occur in their region.

• To appoint cargo surveyors on behalf of Lloyd's underwriters and often to adjust insurance claims under Lloyd's insurance policies.

• To provide an advisory service to the world's shipping and insurance industries within their region. (Many insurance policies instruct an assured to contact the local Lloyd's agent promptly in the event of a claim.)

In recent years the role of the Lloyd's agent has considerably declined due to improved worldwide communications and the increase in cargo insurance written for importers in their own country.

Dockers or dock labourers. Those who work physically to load and discharge ships in the United Kingdom ports. **Longshoremen** (US) and **Wharfies or Watersiders** (Aust. & NZ.)

Seagulls. Not specifically a seaman's term, this was the name used for non-union labour working on the wharf with the approval of the Watersiders' Union in New Zealand when there was a shortage of union labour available; typically university students during the long summer vacation and ships' crews after completion of their day's work.

Trinity House pilots. Pilotage around the coasts of the Great Britain and Northern Ireland came principally under the auspices of *Trinity House which lisenced the pilots. With the passing of the 1987 Pilotage Act this responsibility was transferred to local port authorities.

Deep Sea pilots. In congested areas like the English Channel and southern North Sea, many ships chose to carry a pilot even though they were not in compulsory pilotage areas. This gave considerable professional support to the master who, possibly due to recent dense traffic, fog or heavy weather, may have become seriously fatigued with long hours on the bridge. When bound for a port with compulsory pilotage the deep sea pilot, if lisenced for that port, would usually continue to con the vessel in the port's approaches, thereby saving time, particularly if bad weather might delay a local pilot from boarding. There was usually less need outward bound when the master was more likely to be rested after his leave or at least time off duty. In their respective areas of employment they were also referred to as **Channel pilots** and **North Sea pilots.**

Sea pilot. In some port approaches, particularly those with difficult navigation, one pilot was often compulsory for the approaches and another within the confined of the port. The former was the sea pilot.

River pilot. Even when a *sea pilot was not compulsory a local pilot was nearly always required for the latter stages of entry (often in a river) and for berthing. If a *sea pilot was already on board, the river pilot took over at this stage and either berthed the ship at a riverside berth or took her into the locks where, in some ports, a *dock Pilot might take over for the final berthing. The river pilot was often known as the *mud pilot.

Mud pilot. Another name for the *river pilot in some ports, but in addition to this use the helmsman in Australian and New Zealand ships, when under pilotage in a port area, was also known by this name.

Dock pilot. In the UK, particularly in London, the dock pilot took over from the *river pilot at the lock and conned the vessel from there to her berth, putting her alongside; and vice versa. He was lisenced by the **Company of Watermen and Lightermen,** one of the old London Guilds, (not by *Trinity House) and usually brought his own experienced helmsman on board with him.

This sequence of employing three pilots, sea, river and dock pilot, typically occurred in *liner companies bound for the Port of London. The sea pilot usually boarded off Dungeness (sometimes at Plymouth or Brixham when a passenger ship called to disembark passengers wishing to save time by taking the train to London) and handed over to the *river pilot at Gravesend. The latter then turned the ship over to the dock pilot in the locks at the Royal Docks entrance. Outward bound this was reversed but usually without a *sea pilot being embarked.

Choice pilot. Most *liner companies operating regularly from a UK port chose to have a nominated pilot (their choice pilot) to handle their ships whenever possible. This resulted in a loyalty to the company, a knowledge of its procedures, a familiarity with the handling characteristics of its ships and a rapport with its masters and officers, all resulting in smoother arrangements for arrivals and departures.

Pilotage exemption. In many ports with compulsory pilotage an exemption from employing a local pilot was often granted to a shipmaster who has extensive local experience and was approved, usually by examination, to pilot his own ship within the compulsory pilotage area.

Linesman played an important part in the berthing of ships by taking their mooring wires and ropes and slipping their eyes over the bollards on the quay, later letting them go on departure.

In some ports a boat was required with **boatmen** to take the ship's lines ashore for the linesmen as she berthed but in others the ship was able to get close enough for an attached heaving line to be thrown to linesmen on the quayside.

Two highly respected groups of mariners:

Elder Brethren of Trinity House. The 'directors' of *Trinity House, responsible for carrying out its functions, both professional and charitable. All the Elder Brethren are master mariners or naval officers with several years command experience, and are experts in their profession. They are called upon from time to time to serve as assessors to advise judges in the Admiralty Court in collision and other shipping cases.

Younger Brethren of Trinity House are respected master mariners and naval officers still actively serving at sea, and others prominent in the shipping industry, who are privileged to be invited to become Younger Brethren. Although not employed by *Trinity House, their association assists the Elder Brethren with constantly updated information and experience of day to day matters concerning seafarers, particularly those relating to navigation and ship operations.

Ministry of Transport involvement with trooping:

During the years when troopships and other vessels were required for military operations, in both peacetime and wartime, the following Ministry of Transport organisations or employees were involved:

Sea Transport Service. The department of the Ministry of Transport responsible for the arrangements necessary for the operation of *troopships transporting military personnel overseas, hospital ships in wartime, and freight transports. From time to time, until the late 1950s when almost all trooping by sea came to an end in favour of the use of aircraft, the Government either chartered troopships from their owners or owned them, appointing shipping companies to manage them on its behalf.

Sea Transport Officers. Government employees in the *Sea

Transport Service, the STOs provided the shore-side logistics necessary for the operation of troopships and other vessels under their supervision. They liaised with the ship's owners or managers, and with the military movements personnel. The STO responsible for a district was the **District Sea Transport Officer** (DSTO).

Military personnel involved with trooping services:

The following were involved with troopships operations as part of the military:

O.C. Troops. In the smaller troopships, when the majority of military personnel embarked comprised a complete battalion of a regiment, as was often the case, the battalion's Commanding Officer (CO) was referred to as the O.C.Troops and had overall responsibility for all matters of a military nature concerning the military personnel embarked.

Ship's Commandant. In the larger troopers, a senior military officer, usually a Lieutenant-Colonel, was carried as the senior member of a permanent military staff onboard. He was in overall charge of all military personnel carried except for purely regimental matters which remained the responsibility of the CO of any regiment embarked. (Occasionally an RAF Wing Commander was appointed to this position in lieu of an Army officer.)

Other ship's military staff. In addition to the Ship's Commandant, other permanent military staff were carried. In a larger trooper they might include:

The Senior Medical Officer (SMO)

Nursing staff from the Queen's Royal Army Nursing Service

A Regimental Sergeant Major

Two other Warrant Officers

(Where the *Ship's Commandant was from the Royal Air Force his support staff were from the same Service.)

In addition, a ship's Executive Officer (usually a major) and an Adjutant (usually a captain) were appointed from among the travelling military officers to assist the *O.C. Troops/*Ship's Commandant.

Ship's personnel involved with trooping:

Apart from the troopship's master, with overall responsibility for maintaining a working relationship with the military personnel, the ship's personnel most involved were:

Troop Officer. Apart from a slightly reduced purser's staff, troopships carried the normal complement of officers for passenger ships of their size, but with the notable addition of a troop officer. He was a deck officer, usually of second or first officer's rank, with the specific role of acting as the close liaison between the ship's and military personnel in all matters of mutual concern. The troop officer worked closely with the *Ship's Commandant (or *OC Troops) and his staff, and was responsible to the master for the maintenance of the troop decks and troop deck stores. Nickname: **Troops** or **Troopie.**

Troop deck assistant. Assisting the *troop officer with the satisfactory overall maintenance of the troop deck areas, and particularly with the logistics and distribution of troop deck cleaning materials, was a junior petty officer, often a bosun's mate or a quartermaster.

Others involved during wartime:

Convoy commodore. A retired officer of the Royal Navy or Royal Naval Reserve, of captain's or more senior rank, with overall responsibility for a convoy of merchant ships. Embarked with his signals team in a merchantman, usually in a ship at the head of one of the columns of the convoy, he was concerned with the convoy's formation, course and progress, including any decision for the convoy to scatter if attacked. Large convoys, which could amount to as many as forty ships or more, usually also had a vice and sometimes a rear commodore in case the commodore's ship was sunk.

Senior Officer Escorts. Although the convoy commodore was in command of the convoy as a whole, he was not responsible for the operation of the escorting warships. This naval command was the role of the Senior Officer Escorts, sometimes referred to as the Escort Commander, with whom the commodore worked very closely.

DEMS gunners (Defensively Equipped Merchant Ships). Although many merchant seamen undertook a *Merchant Navy **Defence Course** (below) they were ill-equipped to handle anything more than small machine-guns against low-flying aircraft. Naval gunners, often Hostilities Only ratings, were

---

M.N.D. 4.

A. Merchant Navy Defence Course (Officers), Part II

Name in full ___THOMPSON___   ___CECIL BARRINGTON___
(in Block letters)
Usual Signature ___CBThompson___

Date of Birth ___4/7/1928___

Dis A. No. ___R 337943___

B.S.I.C. No. ___BS 173486___

National Registration No. ___

.de and No. of M of T Certificate ___2nd Mate (FG) 60915___

Session	Subject	Port	Date	Initials of Instructor Officer
11	Gunnery—General			
12	Gunnery—Surface		*7th*	
12A	Gunnery—Surface		*April 1952*	
13	A.B.C. Defence			
14	A.A. Control			
14A	A.A. Control	*London*	*16*	
15	Gun Instruction			
15A	Gun Instruction		*10th*	
15B	Gun Instruction		*April 1952*	
16	Recognition		*Inclusive*	

initially placed aboard merchant ships to man the guns as DEMS gunners but later the majority were from the *Royal Military Artillery. They lived in the crew quarters but usually apart from the crew.

Royal Maritime Artillery (RMA). Army gunners from this regiment served initially in British coasters, but later in ocean-going merchantmen, to man their guns in lieu of naval gunners. Nickname: **Soldiers of the Sea** and **Churchill's sharpshooters.**

Others concerned with ships:

Receiver of Wreck. An important Government employee responsible for administering all aspects of the Merchant Shipping Acts concerning shipwreck and ships' gear or equipment washed up on the shores of the United Kingdom.

Sky pilot. Christian clergyman. Also **Holy Joe.**

Shipmate. The term refers to anyone with whom a seaman has actually sailed. It is used more often than not with a sense of warmth and loyalty but it may be used simply to covey association with another person in a ship. Occasionally it is used when referring to an item of equipment with which a seaman has some familiarity due to being carried in a ship in which he had served, e.g. 'I was once shipmates with an old Kelvin sounding machine'.

BOT acquaintance. A shipmate, although the term is reserved for those who are little more than working companions, and does not implying any sense of warmth towards them.

A sea lawyer. An officer or seaman prone to constantly questioning authority and too eager to assert his rights, placing his own opinion above those in authority. Although seamen were often justified in standing up for their rights, there was never a place for a sea lawyer in any ship and he was rarely popular. The equivalent of 'barrack room lawyer' in the Army and sometimes also **Mess room lawyer.**

Memsahib. Hindustani for a European woman. An officer's wife – his memsahib – was usually very well looked after by her husband's Indian servants when on board his ship.

Friday night sailors. A derogatory term sometimes used in the Merchant Service for those in the Royal Naval Volunteer Reserve who often left their offices on a Friday evening to go to sea in a naval vessel for the weekends, returning to their offices on Monday morning. Similar scornful remarks by merchant seamen, such as **part-time sailors**, were sometimes directed at Royal Naval personnel who, frequently in peace-time, took their ships to sea on a Monday morning and returned to harbour on Friday afternoon for the weekend.

First tripper. The meaning is clearly indicated by the words but they do not suggest the self-consciousness and ineptitude felt by a lad making his first voyage to sea. Once the first voyage was over, no matter whether of only a few weeks or many months, a lad acquired a greater sense of pride and confidence. He was no longer a first tripper.

Greenhorn. An inexperienced member of the crew, usually a *first tripper.

Pleasurer. A pre-sea cadet taking a trip during the long summer holiday on a distant water trawler. These trips took between three and four weeks to Iceland & the Denmark Strait, Bear Island, Spitzbergen, and the White Sea, providing good experience. (The term may have been restricted to the training establishments on the River Humber.)

Shagnasty. A term sometimes used when addressing boys or junior ratings, as in 'Hey you, shagnasty ...'

A Jonah. When a ship encounters an act or acts of misfortune this is attributed to her having someone on board who is 'a Jonah'. (This refers to the biblical figure of Jonah who was swallowed by a whale.)

Hobo. An incompetent shipmate. Also **Sojer** (soldier.)

Black Gang. Heavy-duty customs officers.

Rummagers. Customs officers who searched ships for contraband.

Passenger. Including this term is not intended to suggest that, in this age of air travel, those who pay a fare to travel in a ship belong only to the past. But the old concept of a passenger as a traveller who embarked in a liner at one port and took passage to disembark in another, has almost disappeared except in ferries. Even here there has been some change where travellers are often encouraged to 'take a mini-cruise', remaining on board for the round trip. Nevertheless, according to the Oxford Concise Dictionary the word passenger is still applicable but some shipping companies, captivated by the market-driven language of today, prefer to refer to their cruising public as clients, a word which does not fit with the definition in the same dictionary. Seafarers, though mindful of changes, might be excused for asking, 'What is wrong with the time-honoured term that has served so well for centuries'?

Gully-Gully man. A magician based in Port Said who boarded passenger ships to provide entertainment while berthed there or making a transit of the Suez Canal. Among his many tricks, he was principally remembered for the prolific number of live chicks he could produce from his sleeve!

China Mitchell and George Robey. Two 'famous' names of a couple of Egyptians who supplied labour and materials to ships while in Port Said and the Suez Canal. The story goes that George Robey's profits enabled him to send his sons to Eton!

Sew-Sew Woman. A woman in the Far East who repaired clothes for seafarers, usually going aboard to solicit work as soon as the vessel berthed. The term was also used for women engaged to work in the holds repairing damaged bags of cargo.

Maggie May. A well-known Liverpool harlot of the nineteenth century, and the subject of at least one ballad. She was a real person and not a character from fiction.

Ship swindlers. Seamen's name for ship chandlers.

Crimp. A shoresider who, by deception, violence or drugging, procured seamen for a fee when a master urgently needed a crew to sail his ship. Liverpool, New York, San Francisco and many ports in South America were amongst the most notorious for this evil practice known as **shanghaiing.** By late 19th century crimps had largely disappeared due to legislation which improved the lot of the seaman, but the associated term continued to be used by seamen who complained of being **shanghaied** when they found that the ship they had recently joined did not live up to their hopes and expectations for one reason or another.

Pimp. This term has a similarly unsavoury meaning to crimp but referred more specifically to brothel owners who preyed on seamen and provided them with prostitutes.

Crimps, pimps and banjo players. A sometimes well warranted term for the many corrupt, inefficient customs and other port officials who came aboard in some foreign ports.

CHAPTER TEN

Types & Appearances
of Ships

For a start, let's consider the question, 'When is a vessel a ship or a boat?'

Unfortunately the answer is not simple and starting with sailing ships only adds to the confusion. They are categorised by their rig and a ship is defined as a vessel having three or more masts carrying square sails on each. This distinguishes a ship from a barque, a brig or other differently rigged sailing ship and is one specific use of the word ship, but it is not the principal one in use today.

Apart from also including a definition similar to that above, *The Concise Oxford Dictionary* simply refers to a ship as 'a large seagoing vessel' but to the professional mariner this is an over-simplification and the definition is too imprecise.

The word 'boat' is commonly used to refer to small ships (the uncertain feature of the dictionary definition is reference to size; large is a relative term) but the difficult question is, 'When is it more appropriate to refer to a ship as a boat'?

A small sea-going vessel, such as a 300-ton coaster, is a ship and not a boat in the eyes of most professional mariners, but they would agree that her lifeboats are boats. One commonly held view is that a boat is a small craft which can be carried by a ship. However, even this definition is confused today because some specialised heavy-lift ships can readily carry, albeit as cargo, substantial smaller seagoing ships which could not be called boats by any stretch of the professional seafarer's imagination.

Those unfamiliar with the sea commonly make the mistake

of referring loosely to all ships as boats** and no precise indication can be given of a cut-off point below which boat is a more suitable than ship. It is almost impossible to give a precise definition of ship, but less constrained by space than the dictionary's contributors, a mariner might be expected to widen it. Although still accepting its limitations, particularly in continuing to use a relative term, he might be more comfortable with the following:

'A **ship** is a large, self-propelled, sea-going vessel, usually capable of carrying cargo or passengers, or serving as a warship (except asubmarine which are correctly referred to as a boat.) Small craft usually carried by ships are boats but the term boat does not confine them to this limited purpose. The term ship is rarely applied to craft used for fishing or pleasure although it is appropriate for today's large fishing/factory vessels and many super yachts.'

Craft without a continuous weather-tight deck are properly described as open boats, but it is usual and quite acceptable to describe many more substantial craft which may technically fall within the dictionary's ship description, as boats. This includes packet boat, mail boat and boat train, all of which are, or were, in wide use. As a generalisation though, larger vessels are more properly called ships.

When landsmen refer to large ships as boats, seafarers are apt to cringe, pointing out very firmly that most sea-going vessels should be referred to as ships and scorning the use of boat. Some mariners can be quite pedantic on this point so it may really surprise landsmen when seafarer have no hesitation whatever in applying the term 'boat' to certain types of large sea-going ships. There is often no logic in their use of the term but the practice was very common amongst seamen.

** In Britain, the Minister of Shipping recently committed the unpardonable sin of referring to tonnage tax boats when referring to some of the world's largest ships, including the new giant passenger liner *Queen Mary 2*.

Examples are:

Port boat, Clan boat or **Ropner boat** referring to ships of the Port Line, the Clan Line or the Ropner Shipping Company.

Home boat, a term sometimes used in Australia and New Zealand when referring to a ship on the UK registry running regularly between those countries and the UK which for many years was regarded in these far-flung outposts of the Empire, as 'home'.

Banana boats were small refrigerated vessels built for the banana trade from the Caribbean and Central America.

An Iron boat referred not to the material used in her construction but generally to the ships of the Australian company, Broken Hill Pty. Ltd. Most were named with the prefix Iron e.g. Iron King, Iron Baron, and extensively employed in the iron ore trade from North West Australia.

Lake boat. A vessel built for trading on the Great Lakes of North America. They were long and narrow to fit into the locks and had their bridge right forward with engines aft.

The Tre boats. The ships of the Hain Shipping Company all had Cornish names starting with 'Tre', e.g. Trewidden.

Bay boats were ships of the Moreton Bay class operated by the Aberdeen & Commonwealth Line to Australia before, and shortly after, WW2. They were a good example of a class of relatively large passenger ships being singled out as 'boats'.

Empress boats. Another example included the ships of Canadian Pacific Steamships Ltd. which were named, 'Empress of …'.

The use of the term 'boat' in these cases sounds quite wrong but it was in common use among professional seamen and has, as a consequence, received general approval – even an aura of respectability. Some other examples of the use of boat when referring to ships appear from time to time in the text.

Confused? Landsmen will generally not go far wrong if they refer to all large vessels as ships and not boats.

Ships are of many types, often classified by the nature of the trade in which they ply, but on this basis a ship may fall into more than one category. During the 1875 – 1975 period there were many general categories of ships which have now almost completely disappeared, to be replaced by new types since developed; many of these would have been almost unimaginable in the early part of the period.

OLDER TYPES OF SHIPS

The following incomplete list covers the majority of those once in service but only some of them remain today:

Mail & Passenger Liners
Cargo-Passenger Liners
Cargo Liners
General Traders & Tramps
Tankers
Colliers
Heavy Lift ships
Troopships
Hospital Ships
Cable ships
Cross-Channel Packets
Cross-Channel Train Ferries, Paddle and other
Excursion Steamers
Tugs
Icebreakers
Dredgers
Fishing vessels and smaller craft

In terms of tonnage, but not numbers, passenger and cargo ships of one type or another predominated.

The term passenger ships, which technically meant ships carrying more than 12 passengers, today relates almost exclusively to **Cruise Liners** (some argue that it is not strictly correct to refer to them as *liners), and to some ferries – many of today's enormous ones often now referred to as **Cruise Ferries.** Ships which only occasionally carry mail are no longer termed **Mail ships** as the old Post Office contracts disappeared with the growth of airmail.

Many of the cargo ships of the review period carried up to 12 passengers and were designed for specialised trades, e.g. the carriage of frozen and chilled meat and fruit under refrigeration. Others, usually without passengers, carried general cargoes, while tankers transported oil and, by the latter part of the twentieth century, some had been built to carry a huge range of industrial chemicals, liquid natural gas and propane gas.

In this chapter there are references to many terms and expressions which help to identify ships. Many have disappeared completely with the dramatic change in the appearance of so many ships, cruise liners, ferries and cargo ships in particular. Although some remain today it has been considered prudent to include them all there to give a clearer picture of the features which help to identify a ship or type of ship.

THE TWO PRINCIPAL TYPES OF SHIPS' TRADING PATTERNS

There were, and remain, two important and fundamental aspects of a ship's trading pattern which clearly differentiates one type from another. This has nothing to do with whether they carry passengers or cargo.

Liners. Liners run on a regular route between named ports and adhere, as nearly as possible, to a published schedule carrying cargo or people from A to B. An important shipping term, it does not necessarily refer only to passenger ships, as cargo ships, even those not carrying any passengers, may be liners. The essential point is that they adhere as closely as practical to a pre-determined schedule. If carrying passengers they transport them from one place to another just as would arise when carrying cargo. (This latter point allows those who question the use of the term 'liner' for ships devoted to cruising to argue that these ships take most of their passengers from one place and return them to the same one, the object being not transport but enjoyment of the time on board. Even the few passengers who disembark at a port other than their embarkation port almost always join the ship for the cruise aspect and not the transport from one place to another.)

Tramp ships. Cargo ships with no predetermined sailing schedule called at almost any port in the world to load any suitable cargo on offer for discharge in almost any other port. They picked up and dropped off cargo wherever there was a need, and the routes on which they traded were generally those not covered by any regular liner service. Although many of today's bulk carriers could strictly be referred to as tramp ships or tramps the term has lost favour but it retains some significance as a trading concept.

SHIPS CLASSIFICATION BASED ON THE METHOD OF PROPULSION

Another approach to classifying ships is based upon their type of propulsion as:

Steamer. A vessel whose main engine(s) was steam powered. The steam could be derived from burning either coal or oil in a boiler. This distinguished it from a diesel-powered ship which is referred to as a *motor ship driven by an internal combustion engine. However, the term steamer was sometimes loosely used in the past to differentiate any power-driven vessel from a sailing ship although it is rarely used in this manner today when a necessity rarely arises commercially.

Coal-burner. A steam ship which derived her motive power from steam produced by burning coal in her boilers. The term was used to differentiate these ships from those burning oil fuel either as oil-fired steamers or as motor ships fitted with diesel engines. By the mid-20th century almost no coal-burning ships were still being built; those that were, featured a number of sophisticated innovations which did away with manual stoking of the boilers.

Oil-burner. The term was rarely used in isolation in the way that coal-burner was used. It is assumed today that a steamer will be an oil-burner. But even this is a dying breed as most ships built today are more economically operated as motor ships. **Motor ship/vessel.** Often (but not always) identifiable by having a smaller, squatter funnel and by the appearance of the emission from it. A steamer's smoke would often be blacker and more persistent than the usually paler exhaust from a diesel motor-ship.

Up & Downer. A steam ship with reciprocating engines. In these engines the steam pressure causes an 'up and down' movement of the pistons in the cylinders which, in turn, was made to impart a rotary motion to the propeller shaft. This is quite different from a turbine propelled steam ship where the steam impinges on turbine blades to impart a rotary motion to the shaft. Although many diesel engines also operate with a vertical movement of pistons in cylinders, diesel powered ships are not referred to as up-and-downers. The steam reciprocating engine was sometimes known as a **sewing machine engine** as it ran so quietly and smoothly.

OTHER DISTINGUISHING FEATURES

Liners or tramp ships could look alike except in the case of liners carrying large numbers of passengers when they could usually be identified by the extent of their passenger accommodation. However, the ships in both categories often had quite distinctive features that assisted in identifying or describing individual vessels or classes of ships. Some ships had very clear identifying features. Two of the most clearly evident concerned whether they were flush decked with deckhouses situated on the deck or had their superstructure combined into the hull, as in the first two examples below. Many modern ships tend to lack these individual features, some having a very look-alike appearance. There were several variations on these two common designs in older ships, with a variety of combinations of the basic features of each.

(Readers unfamiliar with the name of parts of a ship used in

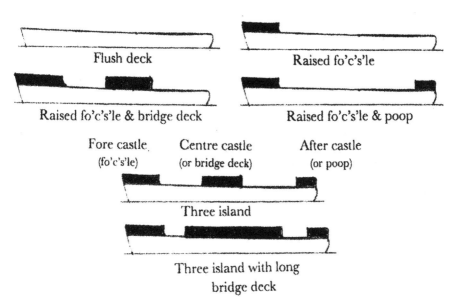

The various 'Island' configurations.

the following few paragraphs may find help in the first two pages of Chapter 11. The illustration on the nest page will also assist with the first few terms.)

Flush Decker. A ship whose deck was flush from forward to aft apart from the slightly concave curve of the deck line as viewed from the side and known as 'sheer'. Although there would usually be a deckhouse with accommodation amidships, and sometimes another right aft, they did not break the continuity of the deck line as they did not extend out to the ship's side.

Three Islander. A vessel having a raised forecastle (fo'c's'le) a raised midship section (centre-castle/centre-island) and a poop, all integral with the hull. These formed the superstructure and were unlike the flush decker's deckhouses as they all extended out to the ship's side, breaking the deck's continuity.

Flush decker with raised fo'c's'le. A variation on the first of the above types, it was quite common for a raised fo'c's'le on an otherwise flush decker as it added useful buoyancy when pitching into a head sea, provided some protection from head seas sweeping aboard and added accommodation for the crew.

Flush decker with raised fo'c's'le and poop. Another variation in which the poop provided benefits aft similar to those of the fo'c's'le. Such a vessel looked a little like a three islander but she differed in having only a deckhouse amidships.

Raised quarter decker. In this design the after deck was raised above the level of the foredeck, often extending from the centre-castle right aft to the stern. A flush foredeck was sometimes combined with a raised fo'c's'le. This type of vessel was common in British Coasters.

Well decker. Some ships had a fo'c's'le and then a short break before a lengthy centre-castle joined a long poop. In profile the deck line would appear continuous for most of its length and the break was known as a well deck and the ship a well decker. In some ships a short break also separated the centre-castle from a long poop, in which case the breaks were sometimes referred to as the forward (for'd) well deck and the after well-deck.)

Liverpool house. Most large, steel square-rigged sailing ships built during the nineteenth century, had a raised fo'c's'le and poop but were flush-decked amidships, with a deckhouse. A small number were also built with a bridge-deck near amidships, similar to the steamer's centre-castle. Known as a Liverpool House it allowed the helmsman and OOW to be better positioned, apart from providing more substantial accommodation than a deckhouse. The post-WW2 survivors, *Pamir* and *Passat*, built at the beginning of the twentieth century, were good examples of vessels with a Liverpool House.

A predominant ship design feature:

'Tween deck. For many years the cargo space in sailing ships comprised a large open space into which cargo was loaded from the bottom of the hold upwards to the weather deck level. As ships became bigger this space became inconveniently large without some horizontal subdivision and a deck was then introduced – a between deck (usually abbreviated to 'tween deck.) It was fitted at about two-thirds of the hold height, thereby providing two levels on which cargo could be stowed. This assisted the separation of cargo intended for different ports and also aided in maintaining a suitable level of ship stability. In the late 19th and early 20th centuries many variations were introduced but they were generally short-lived with one important exception explained in a later paragraph.

'Tween decker. A ship fitted with a deck or decks in her holds. Many cargo ships built during the period were so fitted and they had one, two or occasionally three, 'tween decks. (This contrasts with modern container ships and bulk carriers which have reverted to having deep holds and no 'tween decks. Ro-Ro ships often have permanent, sometimes also temporary, intermediate decks but are not referred to as 'tween deckers.)

This characteristic is really only apparent on close inspection and so has little or no effect on a vessel's external appearance. It is therefore not a useful identifying feature from a distance.

Spar decker. This design was a variation with the space above the 'tween deck of light construction with side openings. Another similar design was that of **Awning decker** which had a lightly constructed 'tween deck space although lacking the side openings. Also similar were **Shade deckers** with a slightly heavier structure. Some of these ships were used for the carriage of cheap-fare passengers, native labour and low deadweight cargoes, sometimes including cattle. They became obsolete early in the 20th century with changes in the Tonnage Regulations. Another variation of the ship, with a lightly constructed deck usually found on small coastal or lake passenger vessels to provide shade, or a promenade, was the **Hurricane Decker**, also now obsolete.

Shelter decker. This was almost the final development of the *'tween decker, built into large numbers of ships until almost the end of the review period. It was a strange concept and a rule dodger. Shelter deckers could be either 'open shelter deckers' or 'closed shelter deckers'. When in the open condition they could reduce their tonnage, the basis upon which many dues were levied. To make this possible the shelter deck had to be technically open to the sea and not watertight. This was achieved by having an additional small hatchway (known as a *Tonnage Hatch) in the deck, with only temporary covering from the weather. There was also a requirement that there was no permanent closure of the bulkheads forming the separation between adjacent cargo spaces immediately beneath the shelter deck. The hatchway down to the hold below this space was required to have covers and the deck was fitted with scuppers which could provide egress for any water and were fittede with non-return valves operated from the shelter deck above. This lower deck then became the *freeboard deck and was thus below the normal weather deck in many ships, i.e. the upper deck exposed to the elements. All this was required to achieve the strange rule-cheating but legal provision for open shelter-deckers. When in the closed condition with these provisions altered they could reduce their freeboard and load to a deeper draft – but this increased their tonnage. The shelter deck rules were an anachronism and were abolished when the 1969 Tonnage Convention came into force.

OTHER SHIPS AND DESIGN PECULIARITIES

Turret ships. Cargo ships designed with very low freeboard at the side decks which were little more than mooring platforms. The bulk of their hulls was raised well above these side decks and accommodated their hatchways. They were built as rule cheaters to reduce Suez Canal dues. A number were built, but they never gained wide popularity although Clan Line ran ten during the last decade of the 19th century.

Trunk deckers. Somewhat similar to turret ships they were more like three islanders but with a 'trunk' for the hatchways, raised above the decks between fo'c's'le and bridge island and between the bridge island and poop. These ships, and turret ships, lacked wide support and were phased out early in the 20th century.

Isherwood system. Ships built to this design ships were constructed with frames and beams laid fore and aft rather than athwartships. The system was more suited to tankers than general cargo ships, only a few of which were built during the early part of the review period.

Hog Islander. A class of vessel built in the USA in a hurry towards the end of WW1 to replace U-boat sinkings. Constructed largely of timber and named after an island in Chesapeake Bay, 122 Hog Islanders were built but they were not a success.

Doxford Economy ship. William Doxford & Sons, ship and engines builders of Sunderland, first produced their 'economy' design of cargo ships in 1934. A number of these motor ships were built, the first type being ships of approximately 9,000 tonnes deadweight with a daily fuel consumption of only 6.5 tons at 10 knots. A later type of approximately 9,500 tonnes consumed 9.5 tons at 12 knots.

Four-master. Most ships had two masts, usually fitted with topmasts. This feature was not therefore worthy of comment unless the topmasts were absent in which case this would assist in identification, even if not with classifying the ship. Three- or four-masted steam or motor vessels were unusual (even more rare were five-masters) so the number of masts was therefore an identifying feature. From about the time of WW2 hardly any ships were built with more than two masts, one mast becoming quite common, and since then conventional masts have seen a steady decline. (Amongst some of the best known four-masters were many ships of the Bibby Line and the Danish East Asiatic Company.)

A Goal-poster. Usually flush deckers whose athwartships pairs of *samson posts were linked together at the top making them look like large soccer goal posts, giving them a distinctive appearance.

Woodbine funnel. The early steamships had very tall, narrow, upright funnels to gain the maximum natural draught for their relatively inefficient boilers. The origin of the term lies in the likeness of these funnels to a cigarette, a very popular brand for many years being the Wild Woodbine. (Funnels began to get shorter with the advent of forced draught made possible by the use of electric fans.)

A straight stem. Ships built in the first part of the period usually had a visible and almost vertical stem post (a steel bar) to which the shell plating was attached.

Raked stem. From about the 1930s ships were being built with a stem-bar that was raked aft as it led from deck to the forefoot below the waterline, giving a slightly more streamlined appearance. This also had the added advantage that collision damage might be confined to a less vulnerable part of the hull above the waterline. Combined with increased flare forward it helped to reduce a vessel's pitching motion as the greater area of hull buoyancy became submerged when the bow plunged into the sea.

A soft stem. A further refinement of the raked stem. Soft stems were often raked aft even more than in the raked stem-bar construction and their principal feature was that the stem, as viewed in plan, had a wrap-around of curved plating outside the stem bar, further enhancing its appearance. Once known as a **Belfast Bow** or **Moulded bow.**

Fiddle-bowed. Once said of a vessel with an old fashioned curved bow.

Maierform bow. A spoon-shaped bow fitted to a small number of cargo ships of European design.

Counter stern. Viewed in plan this is a rounded stern but when seen in profile it sloped forward from just below the deck level to a position well above the waterline. Here it met the exposed sternpost to which the rudder was attached. Also **Eliptical stern. A cruiser stern.** Another rounded stern comprising a plated extension abaft the concealed sternpost and carried vertically down, well below the waterline. The cruiser stern was popular in ships built towards the middle of the period but since the 1970s sterns have often become more chunky and flatter as better suits the carriage of containers and unit loads.

Tumblehome. Rarely seen today. In a cross-sectional view as seen from the stem or stern, this was the inward curve of a ship's hull between the waterline and weather deck so that the beam on deck was narrower than at the waterline. It was a prominent feature in the old wooden-walls of Nelson's day but one of the last vessels to display this feature quite noticeably was the Dutch passenger liner *Oranje,* later *Angelina Lauro,* built in 1939.

Temporary alterations of appearance:

The appearance of cargo ships could be deceptive on first impression depending upon whether they were full of cargo or almost empty, or the manner in which their cargo *derricks were stowed. The following terms would be applied to their temporary appearance:

Down to her marks when fully loaded with her deepest loadline at water level and only a relatively small height of the hull visible.

Light ship or Flying light. Empty of cargo when a substantial height of her hull would be visible above the water.

Derricks flying. On long ocean passages the derricks were invariable lowered horizontally and stowed in their crutches. This gave a ship its customary appearance but for short passages the derricks were often **topped-up** and secured at an angle of about 50 degrees to the horizontal. This could significantly alter a ship's appearance.

LATER TYPES OF SHIPS

This group may seem out of place here as it rightly belongs largely to the current age. Its ships were conceived and born, albeit in small numbers, towards the end of the review period. Container ships. Although many general cargo ships were carrying cargo in freight containers by 1975 it became necessary to build container vessels specifically for this purpose, particularly as more and more specialised containers were made to satisfy more complex cargo needs, e.g. refrigerated produce, chemicals and small parcels of liquids and gasses.

Bulk carriers. These ships came into regular use in the latter half of the 20th century as the smaller 'tween deck cargo ships carrying homogeneous dry cargo were phased out. Larger in size and with unobstructed holds bulk carriers are better suited to the carriage of the larger quantities of the dry, bulk cargo becoming demanded by industry and agriculture. Also **Bulkers.**

Roll-on Roll-off ships. Usually referred to as **Ro-Ros**, these vessels are fitted with retractable ramps up and down which motor vehicles, and cargoes on trailers, can be loaded and discharged. They carry containers, palletised cargo and often large, awkward uncased items of machinery.

Lo-Lo. Meaning Lift on-Lift off. The term, although relatively new, applied to most ships of the earlier period. It refers to conventional methods of cargo handling. The term was introduced to differentiate from *Ro-Ro. There are other variations indicating a mixture of the methods, as in **Lo-Ro.**

OBO. An engines-aft cargo vessel which could carry either liquid cargo (oil, as in a tanker) or dry cargo (as in dry bulk carriers.) OBO stood for Oil/Bulk/Oil to indicate the vessel's dexterity.

VLCC. Very Large Crude Carrier. Large tankers, now often referred to as 'capsize' tankers, able to carry in the vicinity of 200,000 or more deadweight tonnes of oil.

ULCC. Ultra Large Crude Carrier. An even larger version of the VLCC, with a capacity in the vicinity of half a million tonnes. They are a rapidly dying breed.

Parcel tanker. A small tanker which carries a variety of small 'parcels' of chemicals and other industrial liquids in numerous separate and relatively small tanks.

LNG carrier. The carriage of the first liquefied natural gas cargo took place in the late 1950s but has since developed enormously as highly specialised carriers have developed. These ships share with most workhorse vessels of recent years the engines aft configuration but are clearly identifiable either by the several large domes on deck (Moss type) or a lengthy trunking on deck extending almost out to the ship's side (Membrane type). There are invariably also large white letters LNG painted on the ship's side.

Car Carriers. Bulky, wall-sided ships with retractable ramps build specially for the carriage of cars as cargo in huge numbers. Sometimes referred to as **floating car parks** or **floating garages.**

LASH ships. Lighter **A**board **SH**ip. Ships of a different and radical design were built in the 1960s & 1970s to carry barges in lieu of, or as well as, containers, hence the name. The barges (lighters) were loaded with cargo in a similar manner to containers and were then towed to the ship where they were floated on and off at the loading and discharging ports through a large door in the ship's stern.

SPECIAL TYPES OR GROUPS OF SHIPS, MOSTLY ASSOCIATED WITH THE TWO WORLD WARS

Armed Merchant Cruisers. To increase the amount of warships available, a number of passenger ships were requisitioned by the Admiralty in both World Wars and used for patrolling sea areas to enforce blockades. Fitted with medium-sized guns and partly manned by naval officers and ratings in addition to some of their original Merchant Service officers and ratings, they were commissioned as naval vessels.

Nickname: **Admiralty Made Coffins** after the initial letters of their type. Being almost entirely without any armour plate they were very vulnerable to enemy gunfire. (Two famous AMC's sunk while fighting German surface warships during WW2 were HMS *Jervis Bay* and HMS *Rawalpindi*.)

10ᵗʰ Cruiser Squadron. Some very well known passenger ships, requisitioned as armed merchant cruisers during WW1, formed a major part of this important naval unit which spent many months patrolling the Denmark Strait between Iceland and the North of Scotland to prevent German ships escaping the blockade. WW2 saw a limited revival.

Hospital Ships. Many passenger liners were similarly requisitioned by the Government, albeit unarmed and retaining their merchant ship status, to provide mobile, floating hospitals in wartime. Painted white, with a green band right around the hull, a Red Cross painted on each side of their funnels and topsides, and illuminated at night, they were protected by the Geneva Convention, although not all German aircraft pilots honoured this code during WW2.

Q-Ships. During the First World War, at the height of the U-Boat campaign, several cargo ships were fitted with concealed guns and carried a naval crew disguised to look like merchant seamen. The guns were hidden until brought into action when a U-Boat surfaced to call for the ship to be abandoned prior to being torpedoed. Later, U-Boats, wary of being surprised, remained submerged and sank their prey without warning. Consequently the use of the Q-Ship soon declined. Lieut. Commander W.E.Saunders RNR won the only New Zealand naval Victoria Cross (then with a blue ribbon) after an action against U-93 in 1917 while commanding HMS *Prize* (Q21).

Troopships. During the Boer War and in both World Wars many passenger ships were requisitioned by the Government to carry troops overseas. They were temporarily refitted to increase their carrying capacity but were rarely modified with any special feature to fit them for their task. After the war they almost all returned to their owners and, after refits, resumed normal passenger services. (Such was the contribution of the *Queen Mary* and the *Queen Elizabeth* it was considered that their vast troop-carrying capacity had probably shortened WW2 by as much as a year.)

Before WW1, and between the two World Wars, peacetime trooping took place, principally to and from India, and almost entirely by permanent troopships. After WW2 and following the partition of India they were engaged in servicing and relieving British troops on a much wider scale. This largely arose with Japan and Korea, but elsewhere within the Commonwealth they carried relief battalions for the garrisons stationed in outposts like Hong Kong, Singapore, and Gibraltar.

Today, in peacetime, British troops are moved around the world by air. But until the late 1950s the Government either owned or long-term chartered passenger ships built, or converted, as permanent **troopers** distinctively painted white, with a blue band right around the hull. They had a yellow funnel and flew either their owner's or manager's house flag. Their ensign was the Red Ensign, or the Ministry of Transport blue ensign if owned by the Government. The principal shipping companies owning and/or managing these vessels were Bibby Line, British India and P & O.

Woolworth carriers. The name given to a type of convoy escort aircraft carrier, most of which were built hurriedly and cheaply, principally in the USA, and generically named after the then very familiar low-cost retail stores. Some were completed on merchant ship hulls, two well-known ones being HMS *Nairana* and HMS *Vindex*, both taken over while still on the stocks. (These two ships were rebuilt after the war as *Port Victor* and *Port Vindex*.) Woolworth carriers were small, light aircraft carriers classed as warships, operated by the Royal Navy but their function was essentially that of escorting merchantmen in convoy.

CAM ships (**C**atapult **A**ircraft **M**erchantmen). From about 1941,

in the absence of sufficient escort aircraft carriers, some convoys
had to rely for their air protection largely upon a cargo ship in
the convoy fitted with a catapult on the fore deck. About 35
were modified for this role. This catapult was directed straight
ahead of the ship and, when required, a fighter aircraft (usually
a Hawker Hurricane) was catapulted into the air. Unable to
land back on board, the aircraft was ditched and lost with the
intention of recovering the pilot from the water after ditching
but a number were lost.

MAC ships (**M**erchant **A**ircraft **C**arriers). A significant
improvement on CAM ships these were also merchant ships
flying the Red Ensign, fitted with a flight deck like an aircraft
carrier and able to fly off and on a small number, usually four,
fighter aircraft. Cargo working gear on most ships would have
prevented aircraft operations so MAC ships were restricted to
the carriage of oil or grain. 19 were converted for this role – 6
were grain carriers and 13 oil carriers. In some cases they were
later rebuilt and converted back to ordinary merchant ships.

Convoy rescue ships. Converted for the role of picking up
survivors from ships sunk in convoy, these ships included many
small passenger vessels. They rescued over 4,000 British and
Allied seamen in WW2.

War ships. During the two World Wars a number of merchant
ships were built for the British Government and their names
prefixed with War, e.g. War Brahmin; their names reflected
this temporary ownership. During WW1 these vessels, many
built in the USA, came under the direction of the Shipping
Controller but were managed on a day-to-day basis by British
shipping companies.

Empire ships. During WW2 there were principally two types
of vessel that acquired this prefix:

(i) The majority were war-built vessels, temporarily owned
by the Ministry of Shipping – later renamed the Ministry of
War Transport – but managed by shipping companies. They
were mostly built in the United Kingdom (a number were of

one class of 7,000 ton ships), and in the USA. Some were either lent to, chartered or purchased by the British Government, and a number comprised old tonnage completed in the USA as part of their WW1 building programme but completed too late for hostilities. Of those built in Britain, both cargo ships and tankers, some were single ships of one particular design but others comprised classes of similar ships. Most acquired the prefix, Empire (e.g. *Empire Chieftain)* and totalled well over a thousand.

(ii) Also given Empire names were ships captured from the enemy during hostilities or taken by Britain as reparations after the War ended. They generally took the same prefix and included many passenger ships, e.g. *Empire Fowey*' ex-German *Potsdam.*

Oceans, Forts and Parks. These were also war-built standard cargo ships completed in large numbers in North America but designed in Britain. 60 Oceans, all coal-burners, were built on the West Coast of the USA (e.g. *Ocean Strength*) and the numerous Forts were similar but Canadian built and named after that country's forts (e.g.*Fort Stickine).* The Parks, built in Canada and named after Canadian parks, were similar in appearance but were oil-fired. They were owned by the Canadian Government and largely manned by Canadian crews (e.g.*Algonquin Park*).

Liberty ships. Built in the USA, the first in late September 1941, the Liberty ships were prefabricated, mass-produced and all welded, 11-knot, oil-burning ships, most of which closely followed a British tramp ship design. (Apart from the huge number of general cargo ships of around 10,850 dwt tonnes, there were also 32 built as tankers, deliberately very similar in appearance to dry cargo ships and with most of their tanker features hidden to deceive the enemy. There were also 24 colliers.)

The Liberty ships' speed of construction and their vital role in overcoming the very serious loss of merchant ships from the unrelenting U-Boat attacks in the North Atlantic became one of the great WW2 legends. Produced in their hundreds, some were built and launched in as little as a week (the record was 4 days 15 hours from laying the keel.) Said to have been 'built by the mile and cut off by the yard', more than two and a half thousand were launched during the war years.

Those that came under Ministry of War Transport bareboat charter (200) were named with Sam as the first part of their names (e.g. *Samesk*) and became known as **Samboats.** Although doubtless the choice of name was influenced by the notion that 'Uncle Sam' had lent them to Britain, it is said that the real reason for the name was that the British Government classified them as ships having their **S**uperstructure **A**ft of **M**idships. Many survived the war and were either returned to the USA or sold to British shipowners as temporary tonnage until new ships, built to their company's design, could replace them.

Victory Ships. Faster than Liberty ships, and also built in the USA but to an American design, they were mass-produced cargo ships of a higher standard. They appeared much later in WW2 and were appropriately named with 'Victory' as their last name, e.g. *Ripon Victory.* After the war many came, like the liberty ships, into the hands of British owners as temporary replacements for their war depleted fleets.

US Emergency ships. Many other ships were built during the war to American designs under the US Maritime Commission's emergency shipbuilding programme, the majority being known as C-1, C-2, C-3, T-1, T-2, T-3 designs. The cargo ships, denoted by the 'C', were fast ships for their time and, together with the tankers, designated by 'T', were mostly American owned although a number came under the Red Ensign. Of the tankers, the best known in the British Merchant Service were the T-2s; all-welded, turbo-electric tankers of which more than 500 built. One, the ***Ohio,*** earned immortal fame when, as part of Operation Pedestal, the most heavily mauled of all the Malta Convoys, she remained afloat just long enough to deliver her cargo of oil fuel to the beleaguered island.

Chants (An abbreviation of Channel Tankers). Small war-built tankers built in Britain in large numbers. Some operated after the war as dry cargo ships. They were nicknamed, **'Churchill's Holy Answer to the Nazi Terror'.**

Post-War replacement tonnage. During the war the war-built and captured ships were largely allocated to various British shipping companies to operate on behalf of the Government. When the War was over many were sold to British shipping companies – often their wartime managers – as temporary tonnage until replacements for their war-devastated fleets could be built. These war-built ships later again changed hands, often to foreign buyers.

SD-14s. This was a class of standard ships developed after WW2 by the British shipbuilder Austin & Pickergill. Built in large numbers they proved to be very successful general cargo ships but this type of vessel lost favour as containerisation took over.

Fortunes. Originating from Japan, this was another class of standard ships which fond favour with many ship operators, but it too suffered the same fate, and for the same reason, as the SD-14s.

The Little Ships of Dunkirk. Almost too well known to mention, these small merchant ships, tugs, fishing vessels and yachts, earned their place in history for the part they played in the Evacuation of Dunkirk in 1940 when several well known coastal passenger vessels, and a number of other craft, were lost.

MISCELLANEOUS SPECIAL SHIPS

Loggers. Ships built for, or employed carrying logs both underdeck and on deck. Two features of purpose-built log carriers were the large stanchions (posts) fitted outboard on deck to restrain the logs, and the swinging derrick at each hatch. While these vessels could be described as **timber ships** the term was more often used to describe vessels carrying sawn timber which was also stowed below and above deck, and to which special regulations applied.

Flatiron colliers. Built to carry coal from the North East Coast to the River Thames, they were built with very low superstructure and could lower their masts and funnels to go under the bridges above Tower Bridge. This gave them a very flat profile and, as their nickname suggests, a likeness to a domestic iron. They discharged their cargo at Battersea, Wandsworth and Fulham power stations but with the decline in the riverside coal-fired power stations, they have now largely disappeared.

Light-ships/vessels. Rarely moored far from land these little ships, which were usually manned and fitted with a small lighthouse, were employed in relatively busy coastal waters to supplement shore-based lighthouses in places where an ordinary navigation buoy was inadequate to provide sufficient visibility. They have largely been replaced with very large buoys (LANBYs) of a type not considered practical some years ago before the advent of reliable, solar powered electronics. Although a few light-ships remain in service around the world, they largely belong to a past age and are more likely to be found today in Maritime Museums.

Pilot cutters and pilot boats. Pilots boarding a ship entering a port usually embarked from a small boat, the pilot boat, or disembarked into it after piloting the ship out of the port. The pilot boat was usually a tender belonging to a larger, parent vessel, the pilot cutter. The pilot cutter cruised or anchored on station in the vicinity of the approaches to their pilotage district and some famous ones were of a distinctive and colourful character. In more recent times there has been a strong trend towards using fast pilot launches based ashore in the vicinity of the pilotage grounds. Some ports have used helicopters.

Cable ships. Although there are still cable ships their equipment is now so much more sophisticated that they hardly resemble the early cable layers concerned with laying and servicing the first sub-ocean telephone and power cables. However, many are still distinctive in appearance with huge sheaves at bow and stern for the cables to run through the ship while being laid or repaired.

Coasters. Small vessels, once employed in large numbers, principally in the coastal and short sea trades of Northern Europe, although other parts of the world had their own, often distinctive, coastal vessels. They once served as carriers of all kinds of commodities, agricultural produce, foodstuffs and manufactured goods carried to and from numerous small ports. Today, their role almost everywhere has largely been taken-over by huge road juggernauts and other vehicles carrying containers form one country to another, particularly throughout Europe. Coasters were often nicknamed **Rock Dodgers** or *P***ond Hoppers** by deep-sea men.

Weekly boat. UK coasters were often known by this name, as their crew were paid on a weekly basis. In many cases the crew also provided their own food and paid the cook.

Dumb barges. Barge without their own propulsion and requiring to be towed.

Reefer ships. The abbreviated name for vessels which were specially fitted for the carriage of refrigerated cargoes.

Meat boats. *Reefer ships which carried principally frozen and chilled meat, but usually had some non -refrigerated spaces for general cargo.

Emigrant Ships. Emigrants from Europe to North America provided employment for a number of passenger ships before and after WW1. Again, for a few years after WW2, a number of the older ships were employed carrying emigrants to parts of the Commonwealth, principally Australia and New Zealand, under assisted passage schemes financed by their governments.

Miscellaneous:

Rust buckets. A term given prominence in recent years for badly maintained and often dangerously operated ships that put their crew and the environment at risk. They are usually sailing under Flags of Convenience.

Flag of convenience. In order to minimise costs many shipowners registered their ships in countries that require minimal fees. In most cases these countries have consequently much lower standards of safety and ship maintenance than the traditional seafaring nations.

Jumboised. This refers to a vessel that had been lengthened by adding a new section somewhere within her overall length, usually around amidships. This increased her earning capacity.

A Bone in her teeth. A ship's bow wave, but the term is usually only used when conveying that a ship is steaming particularly fast – at a rate of knots – as was the case with some of the large transatlantic liners.

The Queens. This term was affectionately used as a collective term for the liners, *Queen Elizabeth* and *Queen Mary* which, in post-WW2 years, jointly ran the express Southampton-New York service of Cunard.

Ocean Greyhound. Often used more by landsmen than seafarers this refers to a fast ship such as many of Cunard's North Atlantic liners.

Windbag. A term used for a commercial sailing ship by seamen in steam ships.

Daddy's yacht. Used in a slightly derogatory sense by fellow crew when one of them expected to receive better treatment, more congenial work, improved feeding and comfort than he was receiving on board his present ship. His shipmates might then enquire of him, 'What do you think this is – your Daddy's yacht?' It was also occasionally used in a more favourable context where one ship in a company enjoyed a particularly good reputation and was a favourite in which to sail.

Floating Fifth Avenue. A luxury passenger liner and particularly appropriate for a North Atlantic liner on the New York run.

Bum Boat. A small local boat which came alongside ships at anchor, typically at Port Said and other Middle-Eastern ports. It was used by hawkers peddling their wares or soliciting passengers wishing to be transported them between the ship and the shore, or vice versa. When used for passengers as a 'water taxi', it was known as a **Wallah-wallah** in Hong Kong and as a **Dhysa** in Malta.

Coffin ships. During the 19th century when Samuel Plimsol was campaigning to reduce the serious loss of seamen by introducing load lines, this term was frequently applied to the many ships lost by serious overloading. It was offten contended that unscrupulous shipowners deliberately sent their ships to sea in this unseaworthy condition to collect inflated values from their insurers.

The mail steamer. Not strictly a term used by seamen, it was used more by shoresiders in far-off parts of the Empire who anxiously awaited the arrival of the ship with the mail from home (the UK). The arrival of the mail steamer at Bombay, as elsewhere, was a keenly anticipated event in their lives.

The Children's Ship. The name by which the Ellerman passenger liner, *City of Benares*, was known after being sunk by a U-boat on 17 September 1940 in the North Atlantic while carrying evacuee children to North America. Her sinking caused considerable anguish in Britain, raising a hue and cry over the inhumane conduct of the U-boat war.

The Officers' ship. Port Line's *Port Gisborne* was so named for a time during the depression when she was manned almost entirely by officers who were grateful to have employment even at reduced rates of pay. In 1931 she carried 18 ex-apprentices – there were no deck boys or ordinary seamen as all the ABs had Second Mates certificates – and the bosun was said to have held a Masters' certificate. She was known in Port Line as, 'The Officers' ship'.

MN Defence Courses. In some United Kingdom ports, in preparation for the probable hostilities, the Government instituted special defence courses, with the co-operation of the Royal Navy, for merchant seamen (1937 for officers & 1939 for ratings.) Much of the equipment involved was very basic, some having about as much sophistication as in the TV programme Dad's Army. When the country was plunged into war the courses doubtless gave some confidence to the crews of merchant ships who were assisted to make the best use of their very limited defensive armament. The courses continued for some years after the war.(See illustration on page 155.)

Convoys. Sailing a number of merchant ships together in a convoy for their protection goes back hundreds of years, but in the WW1 the convoy system was not introduced until 1917 to combat losses from German submarines. In WW2 it was started almost as soon as the war began but the lack of escort ships severely restricted their effectiveness. Eventually the convoy system proved to be very effective, and as U-boat losses increased so did the successful arrival of convoys. Ships in convoy would often be in three or more columns and include forty or more merchant ships, the largest comprising 167 ships. The principal convoy assembly points were the River Clyde, Halifax (Canada) and Freetown (West Africa) but smaller convoys were later formed elsewhere from such ports as New York and Gibraltar.

Russian convoys. All convoys were given an identifying number and as with some other reminders of the war years, it has been felt appropriate here to include the number of the most devastated and famous of the convoys to Russia in 1942. In **Convoy PQ 17,** comprising thirty-five ships, twenty-four were sunk; in **Convoy PQ 18,** thirteen of its thirty-nine ships were lost. (While the losses from the Russian convoys were exceptional, it should not be overlooked that many Atlantic convoys to and from Britain suffered horrific losses too, and Operation Pedestal, the famous, heavily escorted life-and-death convoy to Malta, also suffered a terrible mauling.)

Operation code names. Several of the most important naval operations of the Second World War that involved merchant ships were:

Operation Dynamo – The evacuation of Dunkirk.

Operation Pedestal – The vital Malta convoy in which the tanker *Ohio* earned her master the George Cross.

Operation Torch – The invasion of North Africa.

Operation Husky – The invasion of Sicily.

Operation Shingle – The Anzio landings.

Operation Neptune – The naval part of operation Overlord, the invasion of Normandy.

De-Gaussing. In order to combat the magnetic mine, developed by the Germans early in WW2, it was necessary to neutralise the inherent magnetism of steel ships. This was achieved by securing copper cables horizontally around the topsides of the hull and passing an electrical current through them all the time they are in a magnetic mine danger zone. This was known as De-Gaussing. Merchant ships had to be able to de-magnetise themselves with permanently fitted De-Guasssing gear, as the magnetic field surrounding them varied with the cargo they were carrying. (Warships are often **De-Permed**, an occasional process whereby their residual magnetism is more permanently removed by temporarily passing electric cables vertically around the hull and topsides to form a coil through which current is passed only while in harbour at a de-perming berth.)

Deceptive appearances. In order to confuse enemy warships, particularly U-boats, considerable use was made in WW1 of dazzle camouflage. It was less used in WW2, but some deception was achieved with the building of a number of new ships with upright **stump masts** and **upright funnels** with no rake in them. This was extended in some cases to having **fashion plates** (the cut-away plates at the corners of the well decks) of different lengths on different sides, thereby changing the apparent aspect of the ship and causing some confusion regarding her course when viewed through a periscope.

Pakeha, Waimanu & Marami. Early in WW2, these three Shaw Savill Line cargo ships were converted into decoys for the Royal Navy. The first two were effectively disguised as *Royal Sovereign* class battleships and the third as the aircraft carrier *Hermes*.

A prefix before a name:

Although there were exceptions, merchant ships generally did not use a prefix in the manner of naval ships which use HMS (Her Majesty's Ship) although ownership of merchant ships was, in a few cases, conveyed thus:

RFA. Royal Fleet Auxiliary as in RFA *Resource.*

HMT. Her Majesty's Transport. The prefix for a ship owned by, or operated for, the Government for the carriage of military personnel, stores or cargo, generally in peacetime. The prefix was particularly used for troopships, e.g. HMT *Empire Fowey*, and was not generally applied to cargo ships chartered during times of conflict. Hospital ships often used the prefix HS. (Other than vessels of the *RFA which have a more direct naval connection. no Government Transports are in service today.)

P & O. Peninsular and Oriental Steam Navigation Company's ownership, e.g. P & O *Himalaya*. (The use of this prefix has been discontinued.)

A special role prefix:

For many years, but largely now discontinued, a prefix was used to denote the role in which a ship was involved:

RMS. Royal Mail Ship, as in RMS *Queen Elizabeth*. As all First Class mail goes by air today and there are few special Post Office mail contracts with shipping companies, the term has fallen into disuse. (Ships carrying Royal Mail under contract flew a Royal Mail pennant from their foremast and often received priority handling in ports and shipping canals.)

A propulsion prefix:

The type of a ship's propulsion was conveyed thus:

SS. Steam ship. The term has fallen into disuse, as most ships are now motor ships.

TSS. Twin Screw Steamship was sometimes used.

MV. Motor Vessel (Occasionally **MS**, for Motor Ship.)

QSMV. Quadruple Screw Motor Vessel. Shaw Savill's *Dominion Monarch* used this prefix.

QSTS. Quadruple Screw Turbine Steamer. The *Queen Mary* sometimes used this prefix.

RMMV. Royal Mail Motor Vessel. *Capetown Castle* was an example.

TEV. Turbo-electric vessel. P&O's *Viceroy of India* used this prefix. Strangely, similar initials for diesel-electric powered vessels were rarely used.

A post-WW2 'Victory' ship.

CHAPTER ELEVEN

Parts of the Ship

Some parts were peculiar to vessels of the years between 1875 and 1975 and have almost completely disappeared from modern ships – for example those relating to coal-burning vessels. Others belonging predominately to this era may still be found in some modern ships and have been included because they largely originated during this earlier time.

A few of the terms included in this chapter border on the professional but have been included because some appreciation of them is essential to those who wish to understand the description of many types of ships.

THE PRINCIPAL PART S OF THE HULL

Superstructure:

In mediaeval fighting ships, whose principal role was to carry soldiers into battle against the enemy fleet, the troops fought from 'castles'; one in the bow, one amidships and one at the stern where the ship's officers were also stationed. Later, merchant ships retained structures in these locations, but not for the same purpose. They are now referred to in the overall description of some ships as 'islands' although the actual names of two of the original 'castles' have been retained.

The forecastle. (Pronounced 'Folksul' as in 'Folk' and 'sul' with a long 'u'. It is usually abbreviated to Fo'c's'le – the phonetic spelling and as used throughout this book – sometimes to F'x'le and occasionally to Fo'castle.) It is the forepart of the ship and used to provide accommodation for many of the crew, usually the deck hands and the firemen and trimmers. It also contained the cable locker and frequently the Bosun's Store and

Carpenter's Shop. Some steamships in the late 19th and early 20th century had only a small anchor deck known as a **monkey fo'c's'le** but when it became an important part of the superstructure it was referred to as the **top-gallant fo'c's'le.** Later, the first part of the name was dropped and it gradually became common to speak of the deck, the area over the fo'c's'le and on which the windlass was situated, as the **Fo'c's'le head.**

Centre castle. The central area above the weather deck, when extended out to the ship's side with which it was integral, was part of the superstructure. It usually contained crew accommodation and was known as the centre castle, particularly in oil tankers before the bridge and the deck officers' accommodation was transferred to the stern, as is usual today.

The Poop. Important in the sailing ship era, this third 'island' on some ships provided protection against being overwhelmed by a following sea breaking aboard which often swept the helmsman away from the wheel. It also served to provide crew accommodation and additional buoyancy aft, and as protection to the steering engine or motors below. In many ships a deckhouse is fitted on deck aft and although not extending out to the ship's side and integral with the hull, it was sometimes referred to, but not strictly correctly, as the poop.)

Decks:

A deck is a horizontal platform corresponding to the floor in a house and usually named to correspond with the purpose it serves, e.g. Boat Deck – the deck on which the boats are stowed. But this is not always the case. The names of decks can present some difficulties to those unacquainted with ships and naval architecture. There certainly was some lack of consistency in their use at sea.

Main deck. This is a particularly important deck, continuous through the length of the ship, contributing substantially to her structural strength.

Tonnage deck. The term for a deck used in the computation of a vessel's tonnage. It was often the *weather deck but in the case of some *shelter or similarly decked vessels it was the watertight deck below.

Freeboard deck. This was the deck from which the freeboard was measured.

Shelter deck. Properly used, this was the term for the deck above the tonnage deck in a *shelter deck ship and the one which fits the first description below for the *weather deck. However, the term came to be used frequently in the later 20th century shelter-deckers, not so much to describe the actual deck itself as to refer to the cargo space sandwiched between it and the tonnage deck beneath it.

Weather Deck. Adding further confusion for the layman (and often the seaman too!) the term was sometimes applied to the uppermost continuous deck which, as its name implies, kept out the worst of the weather from the hull –the deck which, seen from a distance, certainly appeared to warrant the name. However, on account of some strange features of the Tonnage Regulations at that time, in *shelter deckers and the variety of other *'tween deckers common at the turn of the 19th century, the uppermost watertight deck in the hull was often the deck below and referred to as the weather deck.

While seafarers used the above three terms to describe decks performing an important function, passengers were required to familiarise themselves with other descriptions for the several decks where cabins, public rooms and ship's utilities were situated – **A-Deck, B-Deck. Promenade Deck, Boat Deck** etc. This was not entirely straightforward as some passenger ships began the lettering from the bottom deck upwards and others from the top deck downwards.

MISCELLANEOUS PARTS OF A SHIP

Tonnage hatch. A requirement of the strangely contrived shelter deck rules was that a vessel had to have a small deck opening, the width of the ship's hatchways, which was not to be used to carry cargo and was not properly secured against the weather. Often used as a storage for ships' cargo gear and stores which could stand a possible wetting, it was often erroneously referred to as the **dunnage hatch**, partly because of the similarity of the name and also because it was often temporarily used to store dunnage. Also **Tonnage well.**

Thornycroft funnel. Thornycroft was the name of the shipbuilding and repair company which initiated the design of a particular type of attachment fitted to the top of a funnel intended to assist in carrying the smoke and smuts clear of the decks. When fitted to the P & O ships *Himalaya* and *Chusan* after they had experienced problems, their funnels' appearance was significantly altered and became quite distinctive.

Admiralty topped funnels. The term given to funnels fitted with a 'hat' on top for the same reason as in the case above case. They were common in some earlier warships and gave them a distinctive appearance. Many of the older Orient Line ships built between the two World Wars featured this device too. Also, **Cowl-topped funnels.**

Welsh bonnet. The name given to the funnel cap of the later, post-war Orient liners, sometimes referred to rather incorrectly as a Dutch cap.

Flying bridge. The catwalk above the main deck on the smaller, older tankers which linked the fo'c's'le and poop to the midships accommodation.

Half deck. Traditionally the deckhouse on the weather deck in which the apprentices were berthed in sailing ships. In later ships the apprentices were often berthed in a cabin adjacent to the officers' accommodation but the term was retained for the apprentices' accommodation no matter where it was situated.

Room. In many ships seamen used this term in preference to **'cabin'**. The term was not used for dormitory type accommodation but for a smaller living/sleeping space usually containing from one to four, or possibly six berths. In some companies the term cabin was used for officers' sleeping accommodation and **stateroom** was usually applied to passenger accommodation. See also *Peak and *Glory hole.

Dining Saloon. Often simply **Saloon,** the name given in a cargo ship to the place where the master, passengers (if carried) and usually the officers, had their meals with steward service. For many years the name was used in passenger ships, but towards the end of the review period, it changed to **The Restaurant** as a wave of post-war sophistication swept aboard. As marketing jargon reached new heights and choice became a byword, passenger ships tended to have several passenger restaurants, each with its own special name and often with ethnic food choice.

Dance space. For many years almost all but the larger transatlantic liners used part of their passenger decks as a dance floor. These areas, frequently provided with a bar, cane chairs and tables were generally protected from some of the weather by a deck above, and could be closed off in more inclement weather by temporary side shutters. As part of the marketing drives for US passengers after about the middle of the 20th century some ships later enclosed these spaces permanently, upgrading them with soft furnishings and renaming them, **The Ballroom.**

Jalousie. A slatted closure allowing ventilation. Doors to accommodation and wardrobes were often jalousie doors.

Escape panel. In wartime, interior doors to accommodation usually had a panel in their lower half that could be readily pushed out by a blow, as from a boot. This was to allow escape in an emergency as doors would often jam as the result of a mine or torpedo exploding.

Compactum. This item of furniture consisted of a tall, wooden cabinet with a mirror near the top with a small built-in water tank concealed behind it. Beneath the tank was a small, round washbasin that hinged open when in use and emptied into a tank underneath when returned to the closed position. It belonged to the days before running water was available in passengers' cabins, the water tank being frequently filled and emptied by a steward.

Fresh water tap. Also belonging to the time when the convenience of running water was not readily available in ships, a single tap with lock and key, under the control of the Chief Steward, was often the sole source of fresh water for the crew. It succeeded the fresh water pump in sailing ships and lasted in a few ships for several years after WW 2.

Chains. A folding platform, usually on the side of the weather deck just forward of the bridge, which when lowered to the horizontal was stood on by a seaman heaving a lead-line to take soundings. The results were called out to the bridge. The act of taking soundings this way was referred to as **heaving the lead** and should not be confused with *swinging the lead. The lead could be **armed,** a good practice in which a plug of tallow was inserted into the hole at the bottom of the lead. This was intended to pick-up a sample of the seabed for comparison with the charted information.

Triatic stay. The wire stay fitted in many ships and spread between the foremast head and the funnel to provide a point high above the bridge from which to suspend flag halyards. Rarely found in ships today where flag halyards are usually made fast to a small signal mast usually found above the bridge. Also **Jumper stay.**

Rod and chain steering gear. For many years the steam steering engine coupled to the rudder at the stern was connected to the ship's wheel, usually amidships, by means of rods and chains. The gear required good maintenance and frequent lubrication, unlike modern electric or hydraulic connections to the electric steering motors.

Scotchman. A length of steel pipe surrounding the forestay and main stay in ships with traditional masts to prevent these stays becoming damaged by chafe from the cargo runners working the cargo hatches below them. In sailing ships they were wooden battens or pieces of hide lashed to backstays and shrouds to prevent sail chafe on these wires.

Lifeboat covers. After commercial sailing ships had given way to steamships, lifeboat covers became a prime canvas item for the crews' attention. Although the canvas tarpaulins used as hatch covers also required repairs from time to time they needed much less work than boat covers which were often made on board. They were constantly in the weather and subjected to soot, sometimes hot, from the funnel. Many a young apprentice learnt to sew canvas by working on boat covers alongside the lamp trimmer or an experienced AB. Modern, enclosed lifeboats have done away with the need for them.

Crucifix. A type of cleat, in the form of a cross, principally associated with the securing of rope falls on old-type lifeboat davits, and rarely seen today.

Bright work. Unpainted metal such as brass, and varnished wood. Because of the labour required for its upkeep, it is rarely seen today except in smart passenger ships.

Bridge cabs. Long before the advent of enclosed bridges it became fashionable for a while to build ships with a small area of the bridge wings partially enclosed. These cabs, often constructed partly of varnished teak and glass above the steel lower part, provided some shelter for those on the bridge. Cabs were particularly welcome in foul weather when the lookout could be kept behind glass but away from the central wheelhouse. The *Queen Mary* of 1936 was a classic example of a ship fitted with cabs.

Dodger. Intended to enable persons to 'dodge' the full effects of strong winds and driving rain, dodgers were originally made of canvas. They simply provided a barrier to protect anyone behind from the full strength of the elements, forcing the wind and rain upwards and over the top. They were particularly necessary on a ship's open bridge, and when used around the fore part enabled the OOW, with his eyes just above the dodger, to keep a better lookout. Steel dodgers, particularly those curved outwards at the top and with a baffle in front, were effective successors to canvas dodgers.

Scuttle. The term in general use for an opening porthole, particularly in the ship's side. When open, its main purpose was to allow fresh air and more light into the compartment which it served.

Deadlight. A round steel plate with rubber inlay close to its perimeter, which could be screwed hard down upon a closed *scuttle. It was usually hinged immediately above the scuttle for the purpose of backing-up the scuttle glass and preventing its being smashed in heavy weather.

Eyebrows. Riveted or welded outside and just above a *scuttle, there was often a small, curved, steel channel looking a little like an eyebrow. Its purpose was to deflect water from above so that it went around, rather than through the scuttle when open.

Dogs. A term used for the securing mechanism for scuttles, doors and small hatch lids which were required to be watertight, typically in the ship's side or on the weather deck. This type of closure usually had a rubber gasket surrounding it and the dogs were required to apply pressure when securing so that the rubber was compressed, thereby providing a watertight seal.

Gunport door. A heavy, watertight steel door on hinges fitting into an opening in the hull plating, usually of passenger ships. It was well secured by *dogs when at sea, and when opened in the vicinity of a port it was often the place where passengers, pilots and port officials embarked and disembarked. (It had nothing to do with guns except that the smaller hull openings for the guns in the old wooden walls – 19th century and earlier warships – bore this name.)

Pilgrim ports. For a time some Blue Funnel Line ships carried Moslem pilgrims between the East and Jeddah. They were accommodated in the *'tween decks with embarkation and disembarkation access through shipside doors, a form of gunport door, known as pilgrim ports.

Frahm's anti-rolling tanks. A moderately successful design of anti-rolling device once fitted to several large passenger ships. Many attempts have been made over the years to reduce rolling and one of the more successful methods, before the advent of the now common gyro-controlled stabiliser fins, was by means of water tanks at the side of a vessel in which the transfer of water was induced to be out of phase with the roll of the ship. In some types of ships they have staged a comeback.

Bibby alleyway. In passenger ships many inboard cabins in the accommodation were provided with a narrow alleyway, about four feet wide, to the ship's side with a porthole (scuttle) at the end. Its purpose was to give access to natural light and fresh air. The idea probably originated in Bibby Line passenger ships but later became common in other ships until air-conditioning overcame the cool air problem.

Burma Road. A long, sometimes poorly lit, main working alleyway. In passenger ships this alleyway was usually a little above the waterline, running much of the length of the ship and adjacent to many of the essential work areas, e.g. butcher's shop, baker's shop, storerooms etc. which led off it.

Cross-alleyway. An athwartships, working alleyway, sometimes found in the engine room or pursers stores area in a passenger ship and usually provided with a gunport door at each end.

Chastity belt. Several Royal Mail Line passenger ships were built with an open deck space separating the officers' accommodation, situated beneath the bridge, from passenger accommodation just abaft it on the same deck. The name was acquired for obvious reasons although the design may not have been deliberately incorporated to protect the honour of lady passengers. Another suggested reason, albeit perhaps unlikely, was that it provided some protection for the officers from passengers joining in South American ports with the intention, as pirates, of overwhelming the bridge and taking control of the ship.

Mast house. A steel structure creating a shelter around a mast at weather or upper deck level. It sometimes served as a small storeroom, a housing for winches and often as an access to a cargo hold below.

Booby hatch/trap hatch. A small entrance from the deck into a cargo hold, with a lid that closed onto a coaming and could be secured weather-tight. This small, separate hatch could be locked and provided a safe and convenient hold entry. Many ships were built without them and consequently entry to the hold could then only be made with a main hatch cover off, and entrance was then gained over the hatch coaming. This exposed the person to a relatively high degree of risk of falling into a sometimes empty hold.

Butterworth locker. The locker in a tanker in which the tank cleaning gear was stowed.

Monkey Island. The area, above the wheelhouse in most merchant ships where the standard compass, and later, the gyro bearing-compass, was situated, together with the Radio Direction Finder aerial.

Pulpit. The monkey island was usually surrounded by varnished, teak bulwarks. The standard compass on the *monkey island, was mounted on a raised platform to assist clear, almost all-round visibility. The monkey island with this platform bore some resemblance to a pulpit.

Telescopic topmasts. Until WW2 most ship's masts had either integral topmasts or fitted topmasts and only some of the latter could be lowered in the event of navigating under a low bridge, as was essential on the Manchester Ship Canal. Originally, topmasts in steamships followed the pattern of those in sailing ships where they were fitted above and forward of the lower mast and secured by a fid in the mast-band. Later, those intended to be lowered were designed to fit into the lower, steel mast, telescope fashion, to simplify lowering. This gave a significantly altered appearance.

Christmas Tree. A lightweight mast on top of the bridge used for displaying flag or light signals. It carried flag halyards, radio aerials and often a variety of coloured lights. Originally found on some ships with two conventional masts without topmasts, it is now commonly the only mast.

Boot topping. A wide band of a ship's hull between the top of the anti-fouling paint on her bottom and the main hull colour, usually painted in a distinctive colour to enhance the appearance. It usually had anti-fouling and anti-corrosive properties. The area was also referred to as **the wind and water strakes** being between these two elements, particularly in a cargo ship which varied her draft considerably depending upon her state of loading. The term is also used to describe the actual paint applied to this area.

Dado. A bulkhead on the weather deck of a coal-burning ship was sometimes painted in a dark colour up to half-height. This made it less inclined than an all-white bulkhead to show the dirt after coaling.

Glory hole. The dormitory style stewards' accommodation in passenger ships.

Peak. Similar to the above but generally applicable to any dormitory type accommodation for the crew, regardless of their department.

Berth. This word has at least three meanings.
• A bunk or bed in a cabin
• Employment in a ship – in the sense, he obtained a berth in her, meaning that he joined her to serve in her in some capacity or other
• The space alongside a dock wall, wharf or jetty to which the ship is made fast.

Punkah Louvre. The punkah was originally a fabric flap suspended from the ceiling of a building in hot climates pulled back and forth to produce a cooling draft of air. In the Indian sub-continent, the worker pulling the operating cord was the **punkah wallah.** As ships became more mechanised, electric fans were used and then later incorporated into metal trunking to blow fresh air along it to cool the interior. Openings were made in the trunking wherever the air was required and these were fitted with nozzles to allow the air to be concentrated and directed wherever desired, or shut off. This mechanical system became known as punkah louvre ventilation and its effectiveness was enhanced by the introduction of air conditioning, which either warmed or cooled the air as required.

Panama lead. The special type of fairlead necessary when transiting the locks of the Panama Canal whose **mules,** (lockside towing locomotives) were usually high above the level of the ship's mooring deck. Panama leads were completely oval in shape, unlike normal fairleads which are open at the top, and have rounded, soft edges to minimise chafe.

The following terms were often used by seafarers, the first two a little flippantly but the third with some justification as Chinese junks, and some Mediterranean craft, had a pair of eyes painted on each bow to enable the vessel to see where she was going.

The sharp end. The bows.

The blunt end. The stern.

The eyes of the ship. The fore part of the fo'c's'le.

A North Atlantic passanger ship of the 1950s.

CHAPTER TWELVE

Ship's Gear & Equipment

Many items our parents and grandparents used in the home have no place in our lives today and it was inevitable that the same would occur at sea. Most of the items mentioned in this chapter are not to be found in modern ships but belong to the period with which this book is concerned. They cover a wide range.

Scupper boards. For many years ships' scuppers (drain pipes) often discharged overboard at whatever level in the ship's side was convenient. When in port, to prevent dirty water, and more unpleasant liquids and residues from falling onto the quayside, into lighters and boats alongside, or onto the crew painting the ship's side, wide wooden boards were suspended over the outlets on a rope from the main deck. This ensured the water dribbled down the ship's side rather than squirting out from it. Scupper covers were usually of timber construction but were sometimes made of canvas with the bottom side weighted down with broken *fire-bars. Scupper boards which were hung over the sewage discharges were **chocolate boxes.**

Some ships had a vertical steel channel riveted or welded to the hull as baffle plates for the same purpose. However, standing out from the hull, they could cause problems, particularly when berthing or in ports where a ship might range back and forth along the quay. To overcome this problem with overboard discharges some ships continued the scupper pipe down inside the hull to the waterline. Also **baffle boards.**

Thunderbox. When occasionally, for some special purpose, ships carried extra native crew for a short while, they were generally not permitted to use the ships toilets, so a WC-like wooden contraption was lashed to the stern rail for their use.

Gash chute. A chute down which all the galley and other refuse could be dumped into the sea. It was usually attached to the stern rails on the lowest open deck aft but in passenger ships with a galley below decks a chute was fitted through the ship's side above water level.

Gash buckets. These were waste food receptacles. The use of the word gash, on its own, could be applied to anything spare, e.g. 'Have you got a gash knife please?'

Rosie. The name usually applied to the galley gash bucket but also often given to any waste-paper basket.

Scuttle chute/scoop. To assist the entry of fresh air into accommodation ventilated by opening scuttles, a round, metal chute was temporarily poked through it to scoop as much air as possible into the ship which, when steaming ahead, made its own wind. Sometimes old beer cartons with their lids removed were poked through scuttles in the crew accommodation but they looked very untidy. Before air-conditioning it was not unknown for captains of passenger ships encountering a following breeze of the same speed as the ship in the Red Sea, to make a 360° turn to get some air flowing through the ship for a short while.

Scuttle state board. This was a wooden board on the bridge of passenger ships, inscribed with the names of each deck with opening scuttles, and a manually operated indicator to show clearly which scuttles were open or closed. Before air-conditioning, scuttles were frequently opened for ventilation, particularly in hot weather, but this could only be permitted in fine weather and when there was little sea or swell. With the onset of less favourable weather it became necessary to close the lower deck scuttles and if the sea and swell increased then those on the higher decks were progressively closed too. It was usually the responsibility of the OOW to 'keep a weather eye open' and order the opening and closing of scuttles as necessary.

The scuttle state board, kept up to date with each change, acted as a reminder to him of the present state of the scuttle openings.

Fiddles. Wooden bars around the perimeter of a table. They were capable of being hinged up or down, or simply secured onto tabletops, to prevent plates and dishes falling off when the ship was rolling. (A further precaution was to dampen the tablecloth to which china and cutlery tended to stick.) Metal bars were used on galley stoves for the same purpose.

Fort Knox. Sometimes said of the storage locker for new tools or equipment kept carefully locked against pilferage by the crew.

Lord Kelvin's balls. Properly known as spheres this disrespectful name was given to the soft iron spheres mounted, one on each side, of the binnacle containing a magnetic compass. They were fitted to correct for the magnetic influence on the compass caused by a ship's steelwork and took their name from William Thompson, ther first Baron Kelvin (1824-1907), a physicist who made a major contribution to compass design.

Straining bar. In most ships the side separation bulkheads of compartments containing WC's (**the heads**) were fitted with a wooden bar at sitting height which could be grabbed for steadiness when the ship was rolling heavily. However, it was more often seen as assisting in the fulfilment of nature's demand and was referred to as a straining bar.

Doxford house Flag. A name used sarcastically in ships fitted with Doxford diesel engines, to refer to the 'Not Under Command' signal – the display of two black spheres in a vertical line on a flag halyard, as required by the Collision Regulations to convey an inability to manoeuvre as required by the Rules. Although Doxford engines offered certain advantages they did appear to require shutting-down at sea for urgent repairs rather too often which left single-screw ships unmaneuverable. This impression may not have been wholly justified but came about because, at one time, Doxford's horizontally opposed economy diesels were fitted in greater numbers in British-built cargo ships than any other diesel engines.

Fleming gear. For many years most ships' lifeboats were propelled by oars or sails. Motors were fitted to some but were often unreliable and in due course a manual method of driving a relatively large diameter propeller was devised. Known as Fleming gear it consisted of a number of vertical levers located at the boat's thwarts (bench seats). On being worked backwards and forwards by the crew, the Fleming gear drove the propeller whose shaft was geared to the levers. This was a less skilled and tiring operation than rowing a lifeboat with heavy oars. (Reliable diesel engines and covered lifeboats, inflatable life rafts and electronic position indicators have largely overcome the problem of rescue from an abandoned ship once an evacuation has been successfully achieved.) Fleming gear was sometimes unofficially referred to as *Armstrong's patent.

Limousines. Partially enclosed, launch-like boats, slightly more comfortable than the customary ships' lifeboat but useable for the purpose in an emergency. They were carried in some passenger ships and were used when anchoring off ports with no suitable shore-based launches to covey passengers to and from the shore.

Insurance wire. A moderately flexible, very heavy steel wire, often of 6 inch (150 mm) circumference, wound onto a drum for ease of handling. (Ropes and wires were referred to by their circumference rather than diameter during most of the review period). Although its name, once in very general use, suggests that it was an insurance requirement no evidence has been found to link it with such an origin. Classification society rules referred to it as a towing wire. It was carried in most ships, occasionally used as a mooring wire, but primarily for use in the event of the vessel requiring to be towed or undertaking a tow.

Fire wire. When berthed alongside in port tankers and ships carrying dangerous goods were usually required to have a short length of mooring wire made fast on deck and hanging over the offside bow and quarter. In the event of fire breaking out, either on board, or close-by ashore, the wires could be quickly picked-up by tugs to pull the ship away.

Ralston stability indicator. The trade name of an instrument, comprising a balanced 'table' on which a scaled, outline plan of a ship was engraved and upon which weights could be added or removed. Its purpose was to observe the effect of making similar changes to the weight distribution in the ship herself. With this instrument the operator could determine the ship's stability in any state of loading. Stability was usually the mate's responsibility and a mathematical calculation was a time-consuming, complex matter when undertaken from basic principles. It could be more quickly and easily determined by the Ralston stability indicator. Today this is done even more simply and quickly with a suitable computer programme. (The stability of a ship at any time was dependent upon a number of variable factors with the principal influences being the density and location of the cargo in her holds, together with the quantity of fresh water, ballast water, and fuel oil in her tanks.)

Lodicator. An instrument not unlike a stability indicator in principle but used in tankers and bulk carriers to assist in planning which tanks to fill and holds to use for cargo. It calculated the stresses imposed on the hull depending upon their choice and provided an indication of the sheer forces and bending moments in any state of loading.

Breeches buoy. An item of life-saving equipment with which the seafarer was once required to become familiar. It was not carried by ships but was held ashore for rescue purposes in the event of a ship stranding. It comprised a lifebuoy with a pair of canvas breeches attached beneath it, suspended from a block (pulley) that travelled horizontally on a rope span. A lighter rope, sometimes in conjunction with a block and tackle (a pulley & rope system) with its heaving end ashore, was attached to the buoy and used to drag rescued seamen to safety. Ideally this was intended to be achieved above the water but was often more in than out of it. Another light rope was the recovery line required to return the buoy to the ship for further rescue attempts. The system was used with pyrotechnic signals which were also used when RNLI lifeboats or ship's boats were involved in a rescue attempt. Helicopters and inflatable rescue boats have made the breeches buoy obsolete.

Norwegian Patent Fog Horn. As a back up in case of failure of the ship's principal foghorn, her whistle or siren, ships carried this cumbersome mechanical device emitting a loud grunt when its handle was turned.

Malim Sahib's Hindustani. The name of a small, paperback book written by Captain C.T. Wilson of the Bombay pilot service, which was to be found in the kit of almost every officer serving in ships with an Indian crew. Although some of the crew spoke passable English the failure of an officer to address the crew in Hindustani was seen as infra-dig and this useful book gave a valuable introduction and working knowledge of the language used by these seamen.

Green River knife. A sheath knife of very good quality and well suited to use aboard ship, often carried by seamen. Another type of knife favoured by seamen was a simple, cheap cobbler's knife for which a canvas (occasionally leather) sheaf was made by its owner. It was always said that every good seaman carried a knife for his daily work and shipboard emergencies, particularly in sailing ships. (The ship's *articles contained a clause allowing the master to impose a fine on any member of the crew possessing a dangerous weapon, which might include a heavy-bladed hunting type of knife. The fine was on the basis of every day on which the weapon was retained but a proper seaman's sheaf knife, of the type described above, was exempt from any such penalty.)

Handspike. Together with a fixed bladed knife, a small marlinspike by this name was also carried in a sheaf by seamen.

A Manchester spike. A good seaman carried a sheath knife and a handspike when working on deck. Those regarded as poor seamen, particularly draft dodgers joining the Merchant Service to avoid post-war compulsory military training, were sometimes said to carry a 'Manchester spike'. This, derogatory, and largely Liverpool expression, implied they were probably carrying a comb or a nail file in their pockets in lieu of a seamanlike sheath knife and spike.

Handy billy. A very useful small tackle (rope and pulley combination) jocularly referred to as a **Convenient William.**

Steam purriwallah. The Lascar seaman's term for the radar — literally steam lookout man.

Chinese dynamo. An oil lamp, usually fixed to a bulkhead. Also **Paraffin dynamo** or **Bulkhead dynamo.**

Bogey (Bogie). The coal stove fitted in the accommodation of old style ships.

Fearnaught. A coarse, grey cloth possessing thermal insulating properties. Before more efficient materials were developed it was used in ships' refrigerated chambers as a sealant for the doors and sometimes for coats worn by those who worked in them. Occasionally used as cold weather gear in the sailing era.

IN WARTIME

During the two World Wars merchant ships carried special additional equipment to assist them in eluding the enemy and defending themselves against attack.

Bridge name boards. Introduced in wartime as a means of displaying or hiding a ship's name when required, they each consisted of two horizontal wooden boards, one above the other with hinges between them. They were usually mounted on the outside of the monkey island, one set on each side, with the ships name painted on them in large letters. The lower one was fixed and the upper one hinged above it so that by folding the upper over the lower the ship's name could be concealed, or alternatively displayed by the reverse process. The ship's name was only unmasked when assembling a convoy or in a friendly port. The usual peacetime display of the name on either bow or across the stern was painted out in wartime. After WW2, even though the ship's name was then clearly painted on both bows and the stern, this practice of displaying the name above the bridge continued but without the facility for concealment. In some ships the name was displayed even more elaborately with night–time illumination. Cut-out lettering on a horizontal 'box' containing light bulbs became popular and in some ships even neon lights spelling out the ships name, sometimes on the side of the funnel were also used, i.e. P & O's *Himalaya*..

Zigzag clock. A type of alarm clock fitted in the wheelhouse, it differed from a conventional alarm clock by being capable of having several alarm times set on it if desired. Basically similar to a typical bridge clock, it had a brass ring around its face with movable, but lockable, contacts attached. These could be set to sound a battery-operated alarm at any required time to alert the OOW to alter course and begin the next leg of a zigzag. The zigzag, with variable direction and random lengths for each leg, made it difficult for a submarine to aim a torpedo at the ship and was an important anti-U-boat defence.

Signal code books. During hostilities ships were required to carry code books to enable secret communications when necessary. They were kept in the master's safe and were either weighted or carried in weighted bags for throwing overboard to prevent capture by the enemy in the event of abandoning ship. Later, the Cold War with Russia during the second half of the 20th century brought with it tensions between NATO and Warsaw Pact countries. In preparation for possible hostilities, British merchant ships were provided with signal code books and other secret or confidential manuals which were required to be kept in the master's safe. From time to time, for exercise purposes, signals were sent by the Admiralty requiring masters to refer to their code books and send appropriate replies. (Although radio silence was observed as fully as possible there was no need for a code book, and never any hesitation in breaking silence, to send QQQQ, meaning that a ship was under attack from a surface raider.)

Mersigs (Merchant signals). The name by which the merchant ships' code book was known.

Naval Control of Shipping (NCS). During the two World Wars the routeing and many other aspects of the operation of merchant ships came under the control of the Admiralty. Some merchant ships, usually fast ones, sailed independently of convoys or naval escort but the majority were formed into convoys under the direct protection of the Navy and, when possible, of the Royal Air Force Coastal Command. Although naval control ceased very shortly after the end of hostilities a dormant system for NCS existed throughout the 20th century Cold War when provision was made for the reintroduction of full naval control in the event of hostilities. Naval officers, many of them reserve officers, were NCS Officers and carried out exercises from time to time. With the cooperation of the ships' owners, officers holding these normally dormant posts boarded British ships in home and Commonwealth ports to test the system.

Fog buoy. Many merchant ships in convoy during wartime had difficulty keeping station on one another even in fine weather. When fog came down the difficulty reached nightmare proportions. To give assistance, ships were provided with a fog buoy, a floating device which was towed astern and scooped up water to form a plume likely to be visible to the ship astern even in moderate fog, helping to avoid a collision.

Paravane. An item of equipment regularly used by minesweepers and provided to some merchant ships. It was designed to cut floating mines loose from their moorings. Paravanes were streamed from the fore part of a ship, one on each bow, and attached by a wire designed to sever a mine's mooring wire. The paravane acted like a fishing vessel's otter board carrying the wire well away from the ship towards its beam. One lucky merchant ship, the *Port Chalmers,* was saved from possible sinking by its paravane which picked up, not a mine, but a torpedo probably fired at it.

Hurry-up bag. During the war tankers and ships carrying dangerous goods kept a bag filled with essential survival gear readily available in case of having to abandon ship in a hurry. Also **Grab bag.**

Chase-me-Charlies. During WW2 German aircraft flying from air fields in captured Brittany, around Brest, would attack ships within range in the Eastern Atlantic using guided bombs by this name.

Winston Specials. *Convoys were given letters and numbers to indicate their type and operational areas. Those comprising passenger ships routed via the Cape of Good Hope, calling at South African ports and carrying troops for the Middle and Far East theatres of war, bore the prefix WS and became nicknamed 'Winston Specials'. One very special and unusual convoy in 1941, WS-12X, particularly warranted this nickname. It sailed from the UK to Halifax NS with British troops where, especially requested by Winston Churchill to Roosevelt, the troops then embarked on US transports escorted by American warships for Cape Town and Bombay. (The US was still neutral at this time.)

Defensibly Equipped Merchant Ships (DEMS). During WW2 most merchant ships were fitted with some armament for self-defence. This armament, usually 25 to 50 years old, was woefully inadequate against most threats the enemy could impose. It was frequently a 4-inch (sometimes 6-inch) surface target weapon accompanied by a small number of anti-aircraft guns. Its presence probably gave a boost to morale. (See also Chapter 9 – DEMS gunners.)

The odd variety of weapons usually comprised some of the following:

4-inch naval gun. Many merchant ships mounted a 4-inch gun of a type that was often carried by warships before WW1. It was mounted on the poop, principally for defence against surface submarines and commerce raiders. This weapon had been in service for many years in the Royal Navy and most of those fitted in merchant ships were quite old versions.

Oerlikon cannon. A 20mm quick-firing gun principally for anti-aircraft use and fitted to many merchant ships. (Neither **Pom-Poms**, nor their replacement, the **Bofors,** were fitted in any numbers in merchant ships.)

Hodgkiss machine gun. Principally carried in the early years of WW2 by merchant ships, it was not a particularly reliable or effective weapon.

Lewis machine gun. A light machine gun widely used in the early stages of WW2.

Holman projector. Simple in design & operation, this crude form of air defence comprised a steel tube about 3-foot long (1 metre) attached to a steam or compressed air source of propulsion, and projected a rocket with a hand grenade.

Parachute And Cable (PAC). Anti-aircraft parachute and cable device projected into the air but offering only very limited protection to the ship from attacking aircraft. A larger version of something similar was known as the **Fast Aerial Mine.**

Pillar-box. A defensive weapon, it was a crude and elementary forerunner of subsequently more successful rocket-launchers. It comprised a sort of rotating box-shaped turret with small, unsophisticated rockets on either side. Two other items of anti-aircraft rocket launchers fitted in some ships were the **Pig Trough** and the **Harvey Projector.**

Blimps. Barrage balloons. Tethered to moored ships, particularly in the Thames Estuary, they offered some protection from low flying aircraft forcing them to fly higher. They were not carried by ships during the ordinary course of their voyaging.

Admiralty Defence Net (ADN). A merchant ship adaptation of the anti-torpedo nets carried in naval ships. It was used with only limited success.

CHAPTER THIRTEEN

Working Ship

At sea, the deck officers, engineer officers and ratings were engaged in either watch keeping on the bridge or in the engine room, or on day-work. The latter involved general maintenance for most of the time, including a good deal of cleaning and painting.

In port, the deck officers usually had a more relaxed watch-keeping role, being responsible for the overall safety of the ship and for the efficient stowage and handling of the cargo. The deck ratings were then either required for gangway watch-keeping duties or were engaged in general maintenance (ship-side painting could now be carried out) or rigging the cargo gear for the stevedores. The engineers and engine room ratings also had a more relaxed watch-keeping routine for the auxiliary machinery, the majority of them being fully involved with day-time maintenance while the main engine(s) was idle.

It was at sea that the Purser's Department was most able to work to a routine as it wined and dined the passengers and attended to their every need. Once a passenger ship arrived in port and the passengers either disembarked or went ashore sightseeing, the pursers, stewards and galley staff, still with responsibilities for passenger comfort, were also busy attending to officials from the local customs and immigration departments, replenishing stores, particularly fresh produce, and preparing to embark new passengers.

CREW WORK, EQUIPMENT AND MATERIALS

Many of the terms associated with the Engine Room and Pursers /Catering Departments were discussed in earlier chapters. The colloquial terms and expressions that follow refer largely to the daily work of the deck crew and the equipment they used although some terms are equally applicable to the work of all the crew. A good deal of the work aboard ship was concerned with cleaning and painting. It produced a number of terms relating to this work and the material used for it.

Smoke-oh! A break from work for a short period of relaxation with a cup of tea or coffee and a cigarette, usually mid-morning and mid-afternoon.

Job and finish. A job of work that had to be completed before the hands could knock-off. It was sometimes a goodwill gesture which might allow them to finish their work early as a reward after such dirty jobs as blacking down the rigging or painting a funnel or mast. It could also be a ploy to get the work completed as quickly as possible. Occasionally a task had to be completed before the hands knocked-off even though it might require them to work long after normal knock-off time and the order 'job and finish' was then viewed much less favourably. Also **Job & Knock.**

Field Day. A day during which extra work was carried out involving hours beyond a normal day's work, often with watch-keepers working during their watch below. It was an infrequent requirement but on occasions some crew might be called upon to make extra efforts, usually to complete an important job which would otherwise adversely affect the ship's safety or operation. (Once payment for overtime for ratings was introduced this practice mysteriously diminished, but not for the *apprentices to who overtime was not paid.)

To turn to. To start work, as first thing in the morning, or after a break such as smoke-oh.

Put me on a shake. To call someone for his watch or other work when he was asleep – as in, 'Put me on a shake for 0500'.

Homeward bounders. Worn and patched working clothes worn for the last leg of a voyage and dumped on arrival at the final port. The term was also used for unduly large, widely spaced and usually hurried stitches made when sewing canvas. Anything less than about four stitches to a needle's length was generally considered untidy and, particularly if carelessly made, justified this disparaging term. Very neat work required about five to six stitches to the inch but four was common for ordinary work. Also **Dogs' teeth.**

Windyhammer. A pneumatically driven machine capable of chipping the paint and rust off a steel deck many times faster than any unfortunate rating or apprentice with an ordinary chipping hammer. Some machines were electric driven.

Bilge diving. The often filthy job of cleaning out the bilges after cargo had found its way into them frequently arose after carrying grain when the job became all the more unpleasant due to grain rotting in the bilge.

Tank diving. Similar to *bilge diving when the residue in a cargo oil tank had to be removed by hand before reloading. Depending upon the nature of the previous cargo it could be a most unpleasant task.

Bilge & Tank soundings. A part of the routine of any well-run ship with the carpenter regularly sounding the ballast and fresh water tanks, and the bilges. Usually occurring at about 0700 and 1800 each day, in some ships the second set of soundings was completed earlier in the afternoon to avoid having to pay overtime. The carpenter recorded the soundings in a book kept for that purpose on the bridge. They were later transferred to the deck log after inspection by the mate. A similar routine took place in the engine room where the fuel tank soundings were recorded in the engine room log.

Oiling round. Another routine job which was the responsibility of the carpenter, sometimes delegated to an apprentice or deck hand. It was frequently reserved for Saturday mornings and usually involved oiling every weather deck door dog, lock and hinge, the windlass, roller fairleads and other deck equipment except winches which were usually the responsibility of the engineers. In ships with **rod-and-chain steering gear** oiling round was such an important task that it was usually carried out twice a day.

Docking Stations. Usually simply **Stations.** This term was applied to the places where the officers and deck hands attended for a vessel's arrival or departure from port. It was customary for the master and third mate to be stationed on the bridge, the mate on the fo'c's'le and the second mate aft. A fourth mate, when carried, would often be stationed at the gangway. (In P & O, and some other liner companies, this was varied with the mate on the bridge with the master and fourth mate, and the third mate on the f'oc's'le). The term 'Stations' was also used for Fire and Boat Stations and Emergency Stations, the places where the crew mustered for drills and emergencies.

Organised confusion. Often the crew name for Fire & Boat drill.

Rat's nest. A tangled heap of rope or cordage that took time to sort out before use. Also **Bunch of buggers. Bunch of bastards.**

Liverpool splice. There is more than one method of splicing an eye in a wire rope and a commonly used one is the relatively simple Liverpool splice in which all the tucks are made with the lay. It is suitable for standing rigging but not running rigging where heavy strain could cause it to unlay. Wires are rarely spliced aboard ship today. Most are supplied from the factory already 'spliced' by a machine that clamps an alloy ferrule around the parts of the wire to be joined. This alternative is usually referred to as a **Tallurit splice.**

Dog's cock. A back splice in a fibre rope.

Cunt splice. Properly referred to as a **cut splice,** the vulgar name arises from the shape of the finished splice which forms an oval opening between the two pieces of rope spliced together.

Post Office splice. A type of splice used by radio officers in making up wire radio aerials.

Panama Splice. A method of joining two wires by clamping their overlapping ends together with bulldog grips, or making an eye by clamping two parts of a wire together with them.

Slippery hitch. A bend or hitch that comes undone because it was improperly made.

Wammy. A short length of rope, rope yarn or twine used as a temporary stopping or fastening, e.g. to bind together the several turns of a mooring wire or topping lift around the bitts (a type of cleat) to prevent them springing off.

Irish pennants. Rope yarns, light line or other untidy ends left hanging loose and liable to flap in the wind.

Clew up. Often used in the sense of concluding or squaring up a job, or closing down an operation, e.g. an order to, clew up the hold means to close it by putting the hatch covers on. The term originated in sailing ships and referred to hoisting the clew of a square sail to its yard so as to spill the wind, usually preparatory to furling it.

Loss of Doss. Additional overtime work reflecting loss of sleep.

Eight hours day of arrival. Work for the company prior to cargo working at extra pay.

Armstrong's Patent. An operation performed solely by manual effort was said to be done by using Armstrong's patent or **Norwegian steam,** and sometimes **handraulic.**

A work up. Heavy labour, often under pressure

To drop (or pick up) the pick. To anchor (or weigh anchor). The anchor was also sometimes referred to as the hook.

Mediterranean moor. In some small Mediterranean ports, particularly those used by yachts and ferries, a vessel moors stern-on at right angles to the quay with bows to either a buoy or her anchors. Access to the shore may be by either boat, or a gangway over the stern. The system is also used in other ports where swell conditions might cause damage if lying alongside, e.g. Madras. It also enables maximum use to be made of available quay space.

Penang moor. At one time ships in this Malaysian port anchored off when working cargo to and from lighters. Local regulations required ships to use two anchors to limit their swing but when the anchorage was not crowded it was common to use one anchor only and to lower the other below the surface of the water to look as though she was anchored by both.

A Shackle (of cable – 15 *fathoms). Although still in use in the Merchant Service for an anchor cable's length measurement it is mentioned here because the Royal Navy made a change in the mid-20th century from 12 fathoms to follow the Merchant Service's practice. An anchor cable is made up of several lengths (shackles) each of which is joined to its neighbour by a device also known as a shackle.

The Old Man's rounds. The Captain's inspection of living quarters, the galley, storerooms and other important parts of the ship. There was a statutory requirement for the master to ensure reasonable standards were maintained on board by carrying out regular inspections. The number of people accompanying him usually depended upon the size of the vessel and in a large passenger ship his entourage might include, the chief officer, chief engineer, purser and chief steward. The steward or rating responsible for the inspected area was also required to be present at inspection).

Gone ashore for a loaf. A sarcastic answer to an enquiry about a seaman's whereabouts if he could not be found when the ship was at sea, particularly when required for work. Also **Gone up the road for soap and matches.**

Working the head. Used in a somewhat similar context to the above, particularly where a little cunning was involved or a 'sickie' invented as an excuse to avoid work.

Swinging the lead. Dodging responsibility, usually feigning illness or idling on the job. (Not to be confused with *heaving the lead.)

Tot. A tot of rum, usually authorised by the master as a special appreciation to members of the crew who, in difficult circumstances, had completed a particularly tough and unpleasant job, e.g. cleaning oil residues from a tanker's empty cargo tanks or securing deck cargo at sea in heavy weather in a cold climate.

If a person dies at sea the bosun, by tradition, would sew the body into its canvas shroud and receive a tot for his efforts. (In the Royal Navy a tot may be issued to celebrate a special occasion, e.g. a Royal wedding, and is known as, Splicing the Mainbrace. The term owes its origin to the considerable difficulty experienced when the occasional need arose in a sailing man-o-war to splice the large diameter rope of which this item of rigging was made.)

Bosun's Manual. Although the title refers only to a bosun, this book, published by Brown Son & Ferguson in 1944, was an excellent guide for all deck ratings and junior officers seeking guidance in many aspects of their work and duties.

Sugi-Mugi. The words, of Indian origin, refer to a solution of caustic soda and water, sometimes with the addition of *soft soap, used for washing paintwork. Although there was a commercial brand of soap powder of this name it was rarely used because most *lamp trimmers (deck storekeepers) had their own formula for the best cleaner. The act of washing paintwork was known as **sugi-mugiing**, more often abbreviated to **sugiing** (sometimes spelt **soogying**). A more miserable job than sugiing deckheads (overheads) full of rivets with *dangleberries, on the weather side of an open deck on a cold windy day after coaling ship, is hard to imagine. Apprentices soon learnt not to get offside with the mate.

Soft soap. Made from various types of animal or vegetable oil and potash; a good cleaning agent often used in sugi-mugi.

Bathbrick and colza oil. Badly tarnished brass, particularly with an accumulation of verdigris, was frequently cleaned initially using ground-up bath brick in colza oil (rape-seed oil) often applied with old bunting, a rough material saved from worn-out flags.

Carbolasene. Pink liquid soap in 5-gallon containers.

Fleet (of painting). A horizontal length of hull plating that could be painted by one or two men on a stage without moving it along.

Banjo Fleet. This was a particularly difficult part of the vessel **to** paint or *suji when working from a stage. Painting overside on heavily riveted hull plating or areas difficult to access might be so described.

In for a haircut and shave. Said of a vessel dry docked briefly for the sole purpose of scraping off the marine growth from her underwater areas. After cleaning these areas were usually recoated with anti-fouling paints but this occurs much less often today with the improvement in the paint's anti-fouling life and the development of underwater cleaning by divers with mechanical equipment while the ship is afloat.

Skyhook. An imaginary work aid on which a bosun's chair could be conveniently hung when an instruction was received to clean, paint or otherwise work on a part of the ship with difficult access high above deck level.

Holystone. A block of soft sandstone used to scour wooden decks. It gained its name because the deck crew usually used it when on their knees, although sometimes large holystones were fitted into a steel frame secured to a long wooden handle. The verb relating to their use was 'to holystone'.

Bible & Prayer Book. These refer to the usual two smaller sizes of hand-held holystones used for getting into awkward corners.

Bear. Heavy, steel framed broom with short stiff bristles used for *barbarising wooden decks, often improvised from a large square block of wood to which was nailed part of a-coir doormat, heavily weighted and fitted with a long handle.

Mutton cloth. While almost any old, clean rags were used for the rougher cleaning jobs on board, this soft, woven cotton cloth was used for finer cleaning work. Often referred to ashore as stockinette, it was also used extensively for the wrapping of lamb and mutton carcasses for refrigerated shipments.

Cotton waste. Ships carried this cheap by-product of the cotton mills by the sackfull for both deck and engine room use in mopping up oil, paint and other spills and excesses.

Causticing. A process in tank cleaning when changing from dirty oil (crude, heavy oils and diesel) to refined products. A drum of caustic soda was suspended in the tank and a steam hose stuck into it. The caustic steam produced helped clean the residue that normal tank washing left behind.

Sand and Canvas. The materials commonly used, with a good deal of 'elbow grease' and water, to clean and freshen woodwork, commonly teak handrails and other untreated wooden surfaces. The canvas was usually a piece of old fire hose and, with the sand, the effect was that of a very coarse, but not particularly aggressive, sandpaper.

Barbarise. The term used when wooden decks, having become particularly dirty and oil-stained after lengthy stays in port, were cleaned with long-handle brooms using caustic soda, sand and water. (Today it might be difficult to imagine that some cargo ships built for the liner companies to carry refrigerated cargoes, had wooden weather decks throughout their entire length.)

Holiday. Small areas missed when applying paint, sometimes difficult to avoid when of the same colour as the previous coat.

Dangleberries. Rivets securing a deck above to beams overhead invariably had small, dried, drips of paint hanging down like small stalactites. The hard drips became progressively larger with each coat of paint and were the source of much pain and misery for the crew whose knuckles suffered considerably when washing paintwork in cold weather on open decks. The pain was exacerbated when the washing water contained, as it usually did, mild caustic soda.

Blacking (or blackening) down. A dirty job which consisted of applying *Stockholm tar to standing rigging for preservation. Other concoctions usually involving fish oil and grease were used. It was usually accomplished by lowering a seaman by means of a gantline (a rope rove through a pulley above) while seated in a bosun's chair attached to the standing rigging by the bow of a shackle surrounding the stay. This method of working was sometimes referred to as **riding the stays.**

Burlap shroud. A hesssian cloth covering sometimes worn by seamen painting aloft or blacking down when in a bosun's chair, to protect themselves from paint splashes.

Chaining the rails. A simple but ingenious method of chipping rust and old paint from rails by wrapping a small chain around, holding both ends and using a sawing motion.

Save-all. The term might also be applied to an old tarpaulin spread on the deck when painting overheads to keep it free of paint splashes. (An alternative use of the term will be found in the Chapter 14 on Cargo and Cargo Handling.)

Stockholm tar. The resin derived from certain conifers produced a good preservative for rope and other materials. Much of it came from Scandinavia.

Blacklead. Also called **graphite** and **plumbago,** a good dry lubricant which, when mixed with tallow, was often used to grease the pins and sheaves of blocks.

Manhelper or manhelp. The name given to a length of bamboo, 6 –12 feet long (1.83 – 3.66 metres) to which a paint brush was lashed, usually at a 45° angle, when required to paint areas which were difficult to reach. Also **Striker** and **Long-arm.**

Gazinta. Small dog's leg paint brush on which the painting head was offset at an angle to the long handle to facilitate painting awkward corners. It 'goes-into' odd small spaces.

Painting with a wad. A mutton cloth or cotton waste wad was used to paint rails or other objects for which a brush was impractical, or at best made for very slow work.

Red lead. Once an everyday preservative coating applied to clean, bare steel before applying the undercoat and finish coats. It was supplied to ships either as red-lead powder for mixing with boiled linseed oil on board or ready-mixed, but now is largely replaced by proprietary producta.

CHAPTER FOURTEEN

Cargo and Cargo Handling

The arrival of the steamship during the 19th century, and its eventual replacement of the sailing ship as a cargo carrier, did little to change the methods by which cargoes were loaded and discharged.

In square-rigged sailing ships the ends of the yards, the horizontal booms across a mast to which sails were attached, provided a convenient place to attach a cargo block (pulley) high above a wharf or lighter. The mast stay was equally suitable for a second block to be suspended immediately over an open hatchway. These blocks provided a lead for the wires, one end of which was attached to the cargo hook and the other to the winch drum to work the cargo in or out of a hold and over the ship's side.

Steamship designers soon cottoned on to the idea and ships were then built with *derricks taking the place of yards, the derricks being attached either beside the masts, or to *Samson posts. This allowed the continued of the traditional method of cargo handling and the basic, well tried and tested method of handling *break bulk cargoes changed very little for many years after the demise of the sailing ship. In time hydraulic and electric winches replaced steam winches and later mechanical fork hoists assisted cargo handling; but even these changes did not alter the basics of cargo handling and stowage for many more years.

Slowly, after the introduction of steamships, the handling of *bulk cargoes, such as coal and grain, became an increasingly sophisticated process, advancing beyond the laborious process of shifting bagged commodities by hand. Conveyor belts and pneumatic devices significantly simplified and sped-up bulk cargo handling.

During the latter part of the 20th century more efficient types of derricks appeared briefly, but it was the introduction of the freight containers and specialist *container ships, beginning in earnest in the 1950s, which really brought about the huge change in cargo handling. By about 1980 this new generation of ships, together with *Ro-Ro ships, revolutionised cargo handling on many of the worlds' major trade routes and began to influence most of the others, bringing with it a whole new language.

Although a few ships still handle cargo by the traditional methods, changes started to occur with the introduction of new devices like shrink-wrapped pallets and pre-slung bundles, both of which brought about the disappearance of some of the traditional equipment. The disappearance of conventional stevedoring gear escalated as container-handling devices were developed and now includes special container cranes, huge fork hoists, straddle carriers and Ro-Ro trailers.

Very few of the old terms are still heard in the docks and on the world's waterfronts. They do not constitute part of today's nautical language but were in constant use by merchant seamen until the 1970s.

PROFESSIONAL AND COLLOQUIAL TERMS ONCE COMMON

(The standard work on cargo stowage in British Merchant ships for many years was, *Stowage– the Properties and Stowage of Cargo* by Captain R.E. Thomas, first published in 1928 and generally referred to as **Thomas's Stowage**.)

Cargo stowage:

Break bulk. This important term used to differentiate methods of cargo stowage has two meanings, as an adjective and as a verb:

(i) (Adj.) A term applied to cargo that is unpackaged or

individually packaged and loaded directly into a ship's hold as in a traditional cargo ship. This distinguishes it from cargo loaded into freight containers and conveyed in them aboard a ship. It is not unusual, even in a specialised container ship, for one hold (usually the forward hold) to carry break bulk cargo as it is usually an awkwardly shaped area for container stowage. (ii) (Verb) To open a cargo hatch and commence discharging bulk cargo at the ship's first port of discharge. This is referred to as 'breaking bulk'.

Overstow. Ideally cargo would be loaded into a hold or 'tween deck so that it was easily accessible at each discharge port in turn. On occasions, due to poor planning or late arrival alongside the ship, cargo for a later port of discharge might have to be stowed over cargo for an earlier one. This would then require extra handling on arrival at the earlier port as the later port cargo was shifted out of the way to gain access. This would be described as an overstow, to be avoided whenever possible.

Ship's gear and fittings:

Today's ships generally rely upon shipboard or shore-side

A single derrick with its topping lift and guys.

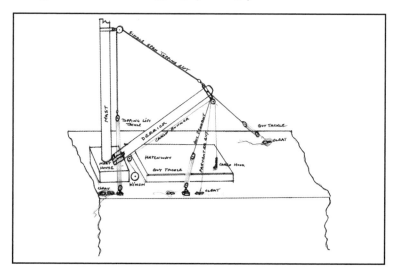

cranes, conveyors, or wheeled vehicles, to load and discharge their cargo. Consequently the terms relating to *derricks and *winches are becoming obsolete.

Derricks. Originally of wooden, but later of steel construction, these were cargo booms (a term used in the USA) attached to the masts or *derrick-posts by a **gooseneck** (a swivel allowing horizontal and vertical movement). They could be used singly as a swinging derrick or with another, as in the *Union Purchase method, and replaced the sailing ship's yards for cargo handling. (Derricks are said to be named after a public hangman named Derrick, who used a similar device.)

Union purchase

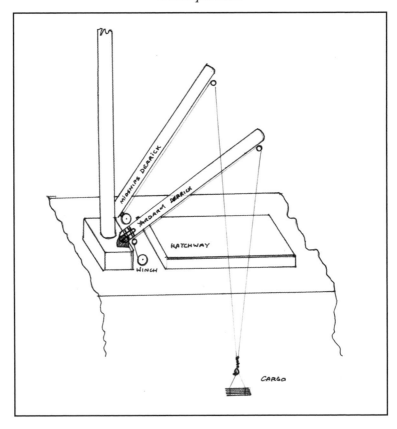

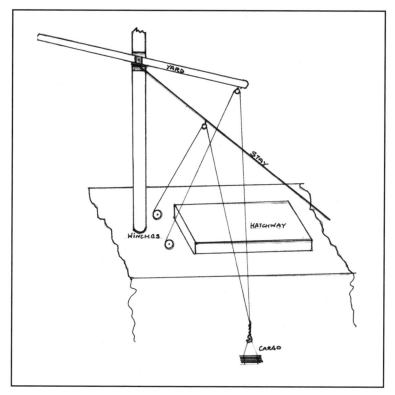

Yard and Stay Method

Samson post. Vertical, tubular steel posts beside a hatchway and to which derricks were attached. Also, **Derrick post** and **King post.**

Mast House. A box-like steel structure on deck around the base of a mast in some ships, with the derricks attached on each side. It also served as a convenient place for storing ship's gear and occasionally small parcels of cargo. With doors opening onto the deck it sheltered electric sockets and switches for cargo working lights and often provided access to the holds below.

Union Purchase. In this time-honoured, method of cargo handling mentioned above, two adjacent derricks had their wire *cargo runners shackled together with swivels to the cargo hook and were worked in tandem to enable cargo to be loaded into or discharged from the hold below. With one derrick over the open hatchway and the other over the ship' s side cargo could be worked into or out of the hold by heaving on one runner while simultaneously slacking the other. This was much the same as with the sailing ship's **yard and stay method,** the only variation being the substitution of one derrick for the yard and another for the stay. (See diagrams on page 226 & 227)

Yardarm derrick. The derrick in the Union Purchase arrangement that was positioned over the ship's side, above the quayside or lighter − the equivalent of the sailing ship's yardarm.(See diagram page 226)

Midship derrick. The derrick positioned over the hold − in the same position as provided by the sailing ship's stay. (See diagram page 226)

Swinging derrick. Instead of loading/discharging cargo with two fixed derricks, as in the Union Purchase method, a single swinging derrick was sometimes used. There were three methods of doing this and in each case the derrick used as the swinging derrick was the one on the side of the ship adjacent to the quay or lighter to/from which the cargo was to be loaded/discharged. (It was rarely used for a lift of more than about 30 cwt. (1.67 metric tonnes.)

(i) Instead of making the guys fast they were taken to separate winches and worked in tandem as *'steam' (i.e. powered) guys, heaving and easing as required to swing the derrick.

(ii) The outboard guy, taken to a winch, swung the derrick to a position over the shipside discharging/loading point. The inboard guy, passing through a block at the head of a derrick fixed on the opposite side of the hatchway, had a weight suspended from it. This weight had to be heavy enough to pull the swinging derrick back over the hatchway and without the weight reaching the deck.

(iii) The ship was listed towards the loading/discharging quay or lighter and the inboard guy rigged as the steam guy. When discharging, the derrick was allowed to swing by gravity towards the ship's side under the control of the steam guy which was eased when the cargo had been lifted above the hatch coming. When loading, the steam guy swung the derrick back over the hatchway against the resistance of gravity acting on the cargo and derrick. (This method lacked some of the control of (ii) above. It was usually confined to use in small vessels with only one derrick at a hatchway.)

Dead man. The weight used on the inboard guy to return a swinging derrick to its position over a hatchway.

Steam Guy. A wire or rope rigged to the guy pennant of a derrick, rove through blocks and led to a winch. It was used to swing the derrick as required. Originally used with steam winches and later with electric winches, it remained a 'steam' guy.

Jumbo derrick. Most derricks had a Safe Working Load (SWL) of 3, 5 or 10 tons (3.05, 5.05 or 10.16 tonnes) but for heavy lifts a more substantial one was required, and 30, 50 (30.48, 50.80 tonne)or occasionally a 100-ton (101.60 tonne) jumbo derrick (usually abbreviated to Jumbo) was fitted in some ships. Specialist heavy lift ships today have cranes capable of lifting 1,000 tonnes and even before their introduction jumbo derricks had increased considerably in capacity.

Stulken derrick. (Sometimes spelt Stulcken). A patented type of swinging derrick fitted to a few ships in the second half of the twentieth century.

Hallen derrick. Another patented derrick of the same period which had a similar function but operated in a different manner. They were fitted to several Federal Line ships built in the late 1960s. A similar, **Velén derrick**, was fitted on standard design ships of the SD14 class.

Cargo runner. A wire of about 2.5 inches (64mm) circumference with an eye at one end, shackled to a swivel and a cargo hook. It passed through a block at the derrick head, then down the length of the derrick to another block at its foot before being wound onto the drum of a winch. The cargo was lifted and lowered on this wire.

Topping lift. The device required to raise and lower the derrick and hold it at the required working height. There were three types: (See diagrams)

(i) A wire tackle (a system of wires and pulleys) whose blocks were made fast at the derrick head and at the top of the samson post, or outer end of a mast table (an athwartships platform larger and stronger than a spreader for the shrouds). One end of the wire was taken a deck winch for lifting/lowering and when the derrick head was at the correct height the topping lift was made fast to a cleat on the deck or mast house.

(ii) A larger, single-span wire between the derrick head and at the top of the samson post or outer end of a mast table was led through a block and down to the deck. A tackle was attached to its working end and led to a winch, being subsequently made fast as in (i).

(iii) As in (ii) above except that the end of the single-span wire leading down to the deck had a small tackle and a heavy chain attached to it. The tackle was led to a winch and the chain, rather than the tackle, was made fast on the deck.

Preventer. This term has a general use and as its name suggests it was a back-up to prevent an accident in the event of the failure of the item which it was backing-up. It was particularly applied in cargo working to a back-up derrick guy when it was known as the **preventer guy.**

Bull wire. Usually a wire of similar dimensions to a cargo runner, it was attached to an item or bundle of cargo in a hold, through a snatch block attached to the ship's structure also within the hold. (A **snatch block's** side could be opened so that the wire could to be inserted without having to pass an end through the block.) The other end of the bull wire was taken to a winch via a lead block and used to assist in dragging cargo horizontally from the 'wings' into the 'square' of the hatch from which it could be hoisted out.

Register of Cargo Gear. Ships were required by law to

maintain a register of their cargo gear, recording its details, testing, inspections, surveys and other matters related to it safe use. Failure to maintain the cargo gear in good condition and accurately record the relevant information often resulted in substantial delays in port before a Government inspector was satisfied that the safety of the local dock labour was not prejudiced.

Winches. Situated on deck, occasionally on or in mast houses, close to the heel of the derricks, they provided the mechanical power for raising and lowering the cargo. Until about the early 1920s when electric winches first appeared, winches were almost always steam driven after the era of those operates solely by manpower. They were invariably very noisy in operation and the steam pipes feeding them emitted an occasional, loud bang, a **steam hammer.** These winches frequently disturbed the sleep of all on board when working cargo at night. The noise from the several winches running together, and also intermittently, was such that the resulting cacophony was often known as **The Clarke Chapman Symphony,** taking its name from the best known manufacturer of these winches.

Very cold weather caused many problems and when temporarily not in use the winches were kept running out of gear to prevent damage by freezing. In these conditions the leaking steam condensed into water and frequently formed rivulets running across the deck. They then froze and became dangerously slippery. Until about the 1930s no seats, or shelter from the sun, were built-in and the winch drivers, who often spent long hours at their post, commonly made temporary seats and erected crude but effective canopies. These comprised a simple wooden framework tied with rope yarns, and a rough-woven mat above. The timber and mats were from taken from the *dunnage used for cargo stowage.

Cranes. Only a small number of ships were fitted with their own cranes until about the 1970s when they gained in popularity, being much more common today although many *bulkers have no cargo gear at all, relying on shore equipment. The development of electric shipboard cranes was delayed for many years by technical difficulties but the earlier ships fitted with cranes used hydraulic power. The 1930's P & O passenger ships of the 'R' class were good examples of ships with hydraulic cranes.

Hatch covering. Many passenger ships, whose hatches were usually small, had hinged steel, one-piece hatch covers but the covering on the open deck of cargo ships was very basic as explained below. *Shelter deck ships also had a similar arrangement at a lower level where, in theory at least, the hatchways were required to be watertight.

Until the advent of the steel *MacGregor patent hatch covers, traditional cargo ship hatch covering for many years comprised several component parts:

(i) **Hatch beams**. Of similar profile and dimensions to the underdeck beams adjacent to the hatch opening, they were slotted into place inside the hatch coaming (the sides of the hatch), acting as athwartships bearers for the *hatch boards. When in position they restored transverse strength at deck level where the underdeck beans had been cut to allow for the open hatchway. Roller beams were a later improvement; they could be pulled out of the way to one end of the hatchway rather than be lifted out to allow access.

(ii) **Hatch boards** made of wood, usually about six feet (1.83m) long, two feet (0.61m) wide and at least three inches (76.2m) thick, they were strengthened with a metal band and fitted with a handhold at each end. Lifted in place by two men and paced fore and aft, they usually spanned two or three beams and provided the structural covers for the hatch opening.

(iii) **Slab hatches.** A later improvement, quicker and less dangerous or demanding, they consisted of three or four hatch boards secured together, side by side, and lifted on and off by derrick or crane.

(iv) **Tarpaulins.** Large sheets of heavy canvas spread over the hatch boards, covering the entire hatchway, they provided a waterproof covering. Normally there were three such tarpaulins covering each open deck hatchway, the top one always in very good condition whereas others might be older and slightly worn. In port the good tarpaulins were often removed to keep them from possible damage by stevedores.

(v) **Coaming bars and wedges.** The tarpaulins were kept in place by long, flat steel bars slotted into brackets spaced at intervals around the outside of the coaming and tightly secured by hardwood wedges.

(vi) **Locking bars.** Flat steel bars laid across the covering tarpaulins at intervals and secured with padlocks. Their purpose was twofold: they provided some security for the tarpaulins against heavy seas on deck and also against possible entry by thieves (often the crew) intent upon pilfering attractive items of cargo. (Alternatively, rope would be stretched across the tarpaulins in a close lattice pattern and securely lashed down.)

Beam legs. Comprising two lengths of wire, each with a beam hook spliced into one end and a common ring into the other, they were used to lift hatch beams by a derrick or crane.

The lids. The commonly used term for steel hatch covers of the *MacGregor, or similar type. **Drop the lids** was often the mate's instruction for closing this type of hatches.

MacGregor steel hatch covers. The MacGregor Company developed considerably improved hatch covers towards the middle of the twentieth century. They consisted of large, electrically or hydraulically operated steel lids that folded and stowed out of the way of cargo working. Operating them required little more than the movement of a single lever. Their inherent strength did away with the need for hatch beams which would otherwise have had to be removed and shipped each time a cargo hatch was worked.

Rain tents/hatch tents. Because of the time and effort required to close a conventional hatchway when it rained during a period of working cargo, a simplified type of temporary cover was devised. It consisted of a canvas cover like a large camping tent, suspended over the hatchway beneath one or more derricks. It could be either bell-shaped, and supported over the hatchway with a single derrick, or rectangular with a fore and aft ridge and suspended from a derrick at each end of the hatch. Tents had tie-downs all around their base and gave good, temporary weather protection in port in all but the wildest weather.

Dunnage. Material used in a ship's hold to facilitate and improve the stowage of cargo. It consisted principally of timber, usually 2"x2", 3"x3" & 6"x1", (50 x 50 mm, 75 x 75 mm & 150 x 25 mm) together with roughly woven rush or palm leaf **mats**, heavy brown waterproofed paper with sisal reinforcement, and old tarpaulins. Dunnage was used to prevent cargo coming into direct contact with the ship's steelwork and some cargoes which sweated under certain climatic conditions causing wetting to adjacent cargo. Well-placed dunnage also aided good ventilation as a preventative measure against sweat damage and, particularly if nets were used, made a good separation between blocks of cargo destined for different ports. The preparation of a hold for refrigerated cargo often entailed extensive dunnaging with large quantities of timber nailed in place in a regular pattern before reducing the hold to the required loading temperature. Some dunnage was carried in ships but most of it was brought from the shore just before loading.

Butter and egg battens (or laths). Smaller wooden dunnage used to assist air circulation around crates of these refrigerated commodities.

Tomming off. The securing of break bulk general cargo by means of wooden shores and some lighter timber nailed and wedged in place against the ship's structure to prevent cargo shifting in heavy weather when not supported by adjacent cargo. Wire was also used when better suited to the cargo to be secured –this method of securing was then referred to as **lashing.**

Hog lashing. A lashing applied in a criss-cross fashion to a deck cargo of timber when the load has attained roughly half-height during loading. The term is not obsolete but is almost entirely restricted to the timber trade.

Hatch plugs. In insulated holds of refrigerated ships it was necessary to ensure that the hatchways were thermally sealed, as with all the other boundaries comprising the hold structure. Thick, wooden, insulated hatch plugs about 3 foot square (900 mm) and about 10 inches deep (250 mm) were wedged between the beams in the hatch square after loading, their edges sealed above with brown paper and glue. The space between the top of the plugs and the underside of the hatch boards laid over the beams, was filled with sawdust to improve the insulation.

Brine pipes. In the older refrigerated ships, before the system of blowing cold air through the refrigerated spaces was introduced, cold brine was circulated through pipes attached to the deck-heads and sides of the holds.

Heating coils. Many valuable vegetable oils (e.g. palm oil & coconut oil) were carried in the deep tanks of cargo ships, particularly from the Far East to Europe. They usually solidified when cold and had to be heated to allow them to be sufficiently liquid for pumping out at destination. Heating coils through which steam was circulated, and usually capable of being removed so that the deep tanks could be used for dry cargo, were fitted for this purpose.

Ventilation. Appropriate ventilation is a prerequisite for the successful carriage of many cargoes but it was well into the 20th century before effective mechanical ventilation was introduced into new ships. For many years all ventilation was by natural means usually achieved by large, open-mouth ventilators on the weather deck, *mast houses, and *samson posts. They were known as **cowl ventilators** and were trimmed into the wind to obtain maximum introduction of fresh air. Another type, **mushroom ventilators**, later became more common being less vulnerable to collecting rain and spray in bad weather.

Windsail. A long, cylindrical ventilator made of canvas, having a forward facing open hood at the top to catch the wind. It was usually temporarily suspended from a derrick over an engine room skylight, a tanker's cargo tanks or a cargo hatch to catch the wind and improve ventilation.

Specials lockers. Valuable or attractive goods such as liquors, cigarettes and personal effects, known as **special cargo**, but not requiring the extra-special treatment mentioned in the paragraph below were stowed in specials lockers in a hold. Their key was the personal responsibility of a designated officer. A cadet or quartermaster and/or a specially employed shore-side watchman, temporarily responsible for the key, had to be present during loading and discharging.

Specie room. Lockable space within a hold used for particularly high value cargo such as currency, works of art, precious gems or metals. Its key was usually entrusted only to an officer who was required to be present when its contents was loaded or discharged. After loading and securing, the master was usually required to keep the key in his safe until it was drawn again by the officer responsible for specie. In order to conceal the presence of specie, no detail indicating its nature was shown on the cargo plan and the information was available to as few people as possible. Also **Bullion room.**

Shifting boards. Owing to the tendency of grain to slide from side to side very readily when a ship rolls, its carriage has long been governed by strict regulations. For many years, ships normally used for general cargo were required to have their holds divided longitudinally by wooded boards fitted prior to loading grain in bulk.

Hatch feeders. Since grain settles due to movement and vibration, the Grain Regulations required ships to fit a wooden hopper in the hatchway to top-up the space below as the grain settled, and so maintain a full capacity within the shifting boards.

Save-all. A large square of canvas reinforced with rope edging and with lengths of rope at its corners joining at a common ring, used to gather up the rubbish for removal when a cargo hold was swept out after completion of discharge.

Clusters. For many years ships did not have suitably positioned, fixed lighting to assist cargo-work at night, so portable lights were positioned on deck, in the holds and overside. Called clusters, they were so named because they had a number of light bulbs arranged in a circle beneath a reflector/guard. Some so-called clusters had a single light bulb. In *white crew ships it was often an apprentice's job to collect them from the lamp trimmer's store, and test them each night before dark. They were easily damaged and frequently failed.

The Stevedoring Company's gear:

Some of the larger items of lifting equipment were rarely carried in ships but were provided by the contracted stevedoring company in the port of loading or discharge.

Meat net. A square rope net attached by its corners to ropes joining at a common lifting ring which was slipped over the cargo hook on the *cargo runner. It was used to load and discharge chilled or frozen meat or other refrigerated cargo. (Wire and rope nets were also used to handle many items of general cargo.)

Tray. Rectangular wooden platform with a wire at each corner joined in pairs onto a ring for lifting small items of cargo, typically cheese crates and butter boxes.

Skip. Not unlike the wooden tray but of steel, it had three shallow sides and the fourth open to allow easy transfer of small items such as heavy boxes or metal ingots. It was fitted with lifting lugs for attaching to a four-legged hooked or shackled wire bridle.

Sling. A fibre rope about 20 feet (6.10m) long with its ends spliced together to form an endless loop. Placed under and around an item of general cargo, with one bight of rope passing through the other, the grip tightened as the weight came upon it when lifted.

Wool snotter. Usually of fibre rope about 12 feet (3.66m) long, with a small eye-splice in each end. Used in a similar manner to the sling when handling bales of wool, but with one eye passed through the eye in the other.

Chain sling. Similar to a wool snotter, it has a metal ring at each end and was used in a similar manner for lifting steel sections.

Drum hooks. Attached as a pair to a length of chain, they gripped the drum's lip at each end as the weight was taken up. Also **Can-hooks.**

Plate hooks. Used for lifting steel plate. Like the drum hook, used as a pair on a length of chain, they gripped the edge of the plate as the weight was taken up.

Timber dogs. Similar to plate hooks but with their own special type of grips more suited for lifting timber.

Car spreaders. Two lengths of metal or wood a little longer than the width of a motorcar, each had a wire lifting-bridle attached. The bridles comprised wire rope and a small mesh net that was passed under the car's wheels before lifting. The spreader was intended to kept the wires clear of the car's bodywork but lack of care often caused damage to the car's wings.

The stevedores' personal gear:

*Dockers in the countries with a good standard of living usually had their own tools and personal gear which assisted in performing their role of stowing the cargo efficiently, or in removing it from a tight stowage position. This included:

Bale hook. A steel hook attached to a wooded handle and held in the palm of the hand with the hook projecting between the fingers, resembling the substitute for Captain Hook's lost hand. It gave a docker a sound grip on heavy or bulky items of cargo such as bales of wool or other cargo not likely to damage by tearing. Also **Wool hook.**

Bag hook. Similar to a bale hook but with two very much smaller hooks, side by side. It was used when handling hessian-bagged cargo susceptible to tearing.

Boot wraps. When loading or discharging frozen meat the *dockers in a hold could not avoid walking on the mutton cloth covering the carcasses. To prevent dirt contamination they wrapped clean hessian, provided by the stevedoring company, around their boots.

Personnel:

The following comprised the principal persons from ashore concerned with cargo stowage. They worked in cooperation with the ship's officers.

Stevedore. Although 'a stevedore' was the generic term for all who loaded and discharged cargo it was customary to refer specifically to the person in charge of the whole operation on any particular ship, as **The Stevedore.** He was sometimes known also as **The Supervisor** and was frequently a qualified master mariner.

Stevedore foreman. As the name implies, the person in close charge of the dock labour and responsible to his boss, *The Stevedore.

Docker. The term commonly used in the United Kingdom for stevedores generally, i.e. the cargo labourers. Also, **Longshoreman** (USA) **Wharfie** or **Watersider** (Australia and New Zealand).

Seagull. A term used in Australia and New Zealand for non-union labour which worked part-time on the wharf, e.g. university students during vacations.

Tally clerk. Shipping companies usually contracted with firms employing reliable individuals known as tally clerks to record (tally) every item of caro loaded or discharged from their ships. These firms were often separate from the stevedoring companies.

Wharfinger. In the United Kingdom, a shipping or stevedoring company employee who received cargo at the quay or wharf transit shed before shipment, or after discharge from the ship and before delivery to a carrier. In Australia and New Zealand it usually referred to the employee of the port authority responsible for the care of its wharf and cargo sheds.

Hatchman. A *docker whose role was to station himself adjacent to an open hatchway during cargo operations for safety purposes and to direct the crane or winch driver using hand signals. Also **Hatchie**

Winch (or crane) driver. A docker or port authority employee who was instructed by the hatchman when to operate his winch (crane) to raise or lower cargo. Also, Winchman or winchie (Craneman or cranie).

Gang. The collective name for a group of *dockers when working as a team.

Spell. A short break from working with the gang when a *docker would relax for a few minutes, usually out of the hold or away from the ship's side or warehouse.

Dirt money. Extra money was often paid to dockers when handling dirty, dusty or obnoxious cargo such as bagged cement, carbon lamp black or fishmeal.

Stoop money was sometimes paid when working in confined spaces. (New lavatory pans, frequently shipped loose and separated in stow by straw, were said to have been the subject of a claim for 'degradation/embarrassment money' by Australian and New Zealand wharfies when at the height of their disruptive powers in the 1950s. One correspondent even mentioned 'Bee money' when a bee troubled them and would not leave a hold.)

Miscellaneous:

Cargo plan. Cargo was loaded to a carefully predetermined plan to ensure adequate stability and trim of the ship, minimum over-stowage and maximum access at discharge ports, i.e. avoidance of any need to shift cargo due to over-stow as a consequence of a subsequent port's cargo covering it. On completion of loading a large, pre-printed outline plan and profile of the ship's cargo spaces was prepared in considerable detail using a colour code for each discharge port. The completed plan indicated the position of as many items of the cargo as possible. Some cargo plans became a work of art.

Cargo list. The list provided at each loading port, accompanying the *cargo plan and stating the stowage position of all cargo loaded. It was more detailed than the cargo plan but lacked its visual impact.

Manifest. A document required by Customs authorities at each port of departure and arrival listing all the cargo on board. It was compiled from details on the *bills of lading.

Bill of Lading. A very important document in world trade (now adapted in many cases for use by electronic means) was issued by the master to the shipper, based upon information in the *Mate's receipt. It acknowledged receipt of the cargo, showed the shipping marks (identification), stated the quantity of cargo shipped, provided evidence of the contract of carriage and acted as a document of title. If the carriage was not subject to the terms and conditions of a *Charter Party, this information would be stated on the bill of lading.

As a receipt it usually contained a statement such as, 'X' in number packages, said tocontain (description) received on board in apparent good order and condition. This number of packages would then be expected to out-turn at the discharge port in similar condition. Occasionally, a tally into the ship might suggest a lesser number of packages loaded than indicated in the pre-prepared documents, in which case a bill of lading for say 120 packages, might be claused, 'Received on board 117 packages, three more in dispute; if on board to be delivered'. Sometimes, even with an undisputed quantity loaded, a full out-turn did not take place as the odd small item could be overlooked in a large hold with cargo remaining on board for a later port. The ship would then be responsible for the short-delivery. An amusing but rather tall story is told of a ship which loaded a number of elephants at an Eastern port (live animals often formed part of a ship's cargo) and some uncertainty arose

over the number when the bill of lading was completed and
issued by the ship's agent after the ship had sailed. As a safeguard
it was claused in the customary manner, 'X' in number elephants
received in apparent good order and condition, one in dispute:
if on board to be delivered'. Presumably there was not too much
difficulty at the discharge port after the bill of lading quantity
of 'X' elephants has been disembarked, in finding a missing
elephant if it was still on board.

   Another story is told of a mate, given to a sense of humour
but often where least appropriate, who incurred the master's
displeasure with an entry in the *Deck Log Book. A contingent
of the Royal Irish Constabulary was embarked for a passage to
another port. He recorded the event as, 'Received on board 36
fathoms of Bobbies in one fathom (6 foot) pieces'.

Mate's receipt. The cargo officer's receipt stating the shipping
marks, quantity and condition of the goods received from a
carrier delivering the cargo to the ship on behalf of a shipper
who later exchanged it for the *Bill of Lading.

Charter-party. The document detailing the terms and
conditions of the charter arrangements when a ship, or space
in her, is hired by a major shipper contracting with the
shipowner for the hire. Frequently abbreviated to CP.

Deck cargo. For a variety of reasons (lack of hold space,
awkward machinery, dangerous goods etc.) small quantities of
cargo were sometimes carried on an exposed deck often
atshippers' risk. Ships which carried substantial quantities were
required to comply with special Deck Cargo Regulations. Apart
from being the obvious name for cargo so carried, the term
'deck cargo' was also a sarcastic term for the result of an oil
spill on the deck of a tanker.

Full & Down. A vessel is said to be Full & Down when all her
cargo space is filled and she is at her appropriate loadline mark.
This situation was not common because relatively light cargoes
might fill the ships to capacity without being heavy enough to
put her down to her marks. The reverse was sometimes the

case with heavy cargoes such as iron ore.

Below her marks. A ship which submerged her loadline was said to be below her marks and therefore overloaded; a statutory offence. When loading in fresh or partly fresh water (as in a river) a load-line could be submerged by no more than would be naturally corrected when she entered the higher density sea water, and by any weight reduction which would occur from consuming fuel on passage to the sea. Also **Over her marks.**

The Slam. The sound at the start and end of the working day in port when all the ships' steel hatch lids were opened and closed at about the same time. This term may have been confined to the Port of London.

Drop the sticks! An order sometimes given to lower the derricks to their sea stowage position.

Gate tally. Tally clerks and others required to keep a count (tally) of cargo loaded and discharged usually did so by counting in groups of five, recording the first four items on a tally sheet with successive vertical strokes (each representing the numeral one) and the fifth with a diagonal slash across the other four (卌) giving the appearance of a country gate.

Bamboo tally. In the Far East it was not unusual for cargo to be tallied in and out by using bamboo sticks which could be transferred from one place to another, usually a pair of boxes, provided for the purpose,

Cargo Brand. The term was applied to items of cargo pilfered from the holds by the crew for personal use, typically clothing and other 'attractive' items. When this occurred it was usually said that the cargo had been **broached.**

Freezing works. Abattoirs. In the countries from which large quantities of frozen or chilled meat were shipped, principally Argentina, Australia and New Zealand, the freezing works played an important part in their export trade. The animals were usually slaughtered and processed here before being loaded into insulated railway trucks and road vehicles for conveyance to the ports. Many freezing works were situated at the ports and had their own berthing arrangements for ships immediately adjacent to their meat store where a conveyor belt might be used instead of trucks.

Red label. Registered mail. Mail was shipped in bags and usually consisted of two types, registered mail and ordinary mail. The former received special treatment on account of its value and vulnerability to theft. Its loading and stowage in a *specials locker was supervised personally by a deck officer, (the mail officer) who signed for its receipt. Woe betides a mail officer whose out-turn of **reds** at the discharge port was one short.

Diplomatic mail. Occasionally low priority mail from a British embassy or consulate would be carried by a British ship and entrusted to the mail officer's personal care. It was usually shipped in very small quantities and was commonly held in the mail officer's cabin or locked cupboard in the officers' accommodation.

Shipowners' rain. Rain that fell at night in port when there was no planned cargo working and so did not delay the vessel's turn-round, to the shipowner's delight.

Godown. The name by which a warehouse, usually a wharf transit warehouse, was known in the East.

Railway box/car. A van that could be detached from its bogeys and carried on deck, customarily aboard ships owned by the railway companies in the North and Irish Sea trades. A similar arrangement in the USA with road vehicles was the forerunners of today's freight containers.

Sea freighter. A type of small freight container, supplied to shippers by the Union S.S. Co. of New Zealand for its trans-Tasman cargo services in the 1970s. It could be collapsed and, occupying a minimum of space, was returned empty to any ports where there was an imbalance in export and import trade. It was later withdrawn.

Six-foot case. An oblique reference to a coffin which was sometimes carried as cargo.

Dumping. Wool was normally shipped covered in hessian as 'single bales' but to save shipping space the equivalent of two bales were sometimes compressed together under great pressure to produce a single bale only a little larger than an ordinary single one. Known as a **dump,** it was very heavy for the stevedores to handle but saved shipping space.

Telescoping. The term for lamb and mutton carcasses cut into two halves to save shipping space with the thinner rear end being stuffed inside the wider front end.

Bung up and bilge free. The stowage of wooden casks containing liquids required special care. To prevent the largest part of their circumference (the bilge) from bearing their full weight when stowed horizontally they were lifted slightly above the surface on which they were stowed by placing wooden wedges (quoins) either side of the bilge. Then, to prevent leakage they had to be turned with their bung (the plug for the filling-hole in the bilge) uppermost. They were then bung up and bilge free.

Butterworth system. Widely used method of tank washing in oil tankers using hot seawater sprayed through rotating nozzles inserted into special openings in the deck.

Sludge. Unpumpable residues remaining in a tanker's cargo tanks after discharge.

CHAPTER FIFTEEN

Watchkeeping and Timekeeping

Commercial shipping operates almost entirely non-stop, day in day out, except on the rare occasions when a ship may be laid-up, out of commission.

Normal operation at sea requires some members of a ship's crew to keep her steaming towards her next port of call, 24 hours a day, but even in port it is rarely possible to dispense with all crew involvement. Even lying idle in a dock or alongside a wharf, electrical generating machinery will usually have to continue running to maintain essential services, and if working cargo there will be a need for its loading or discharge to be supervised. Precautions also have to be taken against the risk of fire and unauthorised entry on board.

This type of continuous crew input requires some form of shift work and the seafarers' term for this is, watchkeeping.

WATCHKEEPING AND ASSOCIATED DUTIES

The word 'Watch' had two meanings; one refers to a period of time, the other to a group of persons.

(i) Watch – A period of time

The 24-hour day is divided into periods. Crew not on day-work keep a watch, day and night, usually of four hours' duration. Watches are named as follows:

Midnight to 0400	Middle watch
0400 to 0800	Morning watch
0800 to Noon	Forenoon watch
Noon to 1600	Afternoon watch
1600 to 2000	Dog-watches
2000 to midnight	First watch

Although some vast changes have taken place to British shipping in recent years the principles of watchkeeping have generally not altered but occasionally some variations may be found.

Early steamships tended to follow the pattern of the sailing ships in the majority of which the crew allocated to watchkeeping were divided into two groups that simply alternated their periods of duty. But, as steamships became larger and carried more crew some shipping companies changed to a system involving three groups which gives a shorter period on duty and more time off.

The two systems provide for either:

4-on, 4-off. Four hours on duty followed by four off. (**The two-watch system**). (Known also as **Watch & Watch** and sometimes as **Watch-about**).

4-on, 8-off. This comprises four hours on duty followed by eight off. It is also known as the **three-watch system**).

In 1936 the two-watch system was abolished as a routine practice in British ships of 2,500 tons and over. It had been demanding on all the watch-keepers but particularly on the officers. The two deck officer watchkeepers in many ships were the mate and second mate who both had other duties in addition to watchkeeping. (The master did not usually keep a watch but in some ships today with minimum manning, the master is obliged to do so to comply with the now mandatory three-watch system.)

The system used depended on the number of people available. Variations included **6-on, 6-off**, or anything mutually agreed between the officers and approved by the master. In some trades, typically coastal and short-sea, and for some special purposes, 6-hour watches are usually kept and there are other variations.

Dog-watches. In the 4-on, 4-off system many ships used the dog-watches as two 2-hour watches within the 4-hour period – 1600 to 1800 (**First Dog**) and 1800 to 2000 (**Last Dog**). The purpose was to break the cycle so that the same men would not have the same watch day after day. (Last was always used in the

Royal Navy for the second of the two dog- watches but 'Second' appears in books of a respected Merchant Service publisher.)

Scandanavian watches. This variation consisted of five watches in 24 hours:

1300 – 1900, 1900 – midnight, midnight to 0400, 0400–0800, 0800–1300. It was worked in some ships, particularly Scandanavian as its name suggests. Also **Norwegian watches** & **Swedish watches.** There were other variations for the crew employed in some ships operating special services such as pilot cutters.

Standing watches. In a 4-on, 8-off system, particularly in a ship with a large crew, it was usual for the watch-keepers to remain in the same watch for lengthy periods, often for an entire voyage, except in port. Thus there were three groups of watch-keepers in the 12-hour rotation: 12-4, 4-8, 8-12 and each kept to his same period during each cycle.

Ratings sometimes changed watches after a period in port but this seldom applied to the officers. Most ships, other than coasters, carried three mates but many well-found ships carried four or more.

In ships with a master and three mates it was the almost universal custom for the mates to keep the watches shown in the left hand column on the next page. Where four mates were carried the same watches were sometimes kept but with the fourth mate keeping watch with the mate.

Where the fourth mate was sufficiently experienced and the captain had confidence in him he would usually have a watch of his own without the mate as shown in the right hand column. In merchant ships the watches were usually known by their times rather than their proper names (as in the Royal Navy) and were the same AM and PM.

The allocation of officers' watches:

Although practices could vary, the general pattern of watchkeeping in British ships was usually:

Three-mate ship	Four-mate ship
12 - 4 watch – **2nd Mate**	**2nd Mate** (until the change noted below when it was kept by **3rd Mate.**)
4 - 8 watch – **Mate**	**Mate** with the 4th Mate (until the latter gained the Master's confidence as a sole watchkeeper when it was kept by the **2nd Mate.**)
8 - 12 watch – **3rd Mate**	**3rd Mate** (until taken over by **4th Mate** if approved by the Master).

Terms relating to watches:

The old man's watch. The 8-12 watch was the Master's watch in ships with an uncertificated or inexperienced third or 4th Mate on the bridge. This was because, at night, the Master was usually not asleep for much, if any of this time, and was therefore ready for an urgent call to the bridge if required. It was often said that he probably spent much of the watch looking through his for'd facing windows.

Graveyard watch. The Middle Watch (midnight–0400) and the least popular watch with most seamen on account of the broken sleep and the possible boredom because most shipboard activities were suspended for the night.

Star watch. Sometimes the 4-8 watch was so referred by deck ratings. It was a popular watch because in some ships it gave them ample opportunity for earning overtime by working part of their watch below.

The watch below. Apart from being the interval between spells of watchkeeping duty on the bridge (or engine room), those in the next duty watch were collectively referred to as the watch below. While theoretically officers were off duty during their watch below it was frequently necessary for them to work during these periods, or at least part of them, to attend to other duties.

(There was an expression of disapproval, even of disgust, for a seaman who was perceived by his shipmates to be 'crawling' or 'sucking-up' to the mate. It was chanted disparagingly in his presence – **'May I come back next trip, Sir, if I work my watch below?'**)

Watch on, stop on. This is almost the opposite of *job and finish which applied to day-workers. A period on watch normally has clearly defined start and finish times but on rare occasions it was necessary to remain on watch without any certain time of finishing. For example, when a ship is making port in foggy conditions and extra lookouts or other functions were required without any certainty of a relief available before the danger was over. Also **Go on, stop on** and **Chinese watches.**

Keeping the deck. The OOW was said to be keeping the deck. The term originated in sailing ships where there was very rarely a bridge, and the OOW was usually stationed aft on the poop deck. The term persisted into the steamship era when most ships acquired bridges and was still used well into the 20th century. Also said of an officer keeping a cargo watch or anchor watch.

Reliefs. A watchkeeper was relieved by another officer or crew member who would take over his watch-keeping duties on completion of a watch, or because of a need for the watch-keeper to go below for a meal or other reason. Meal reliefs were not usually required for the forenoon (third mate) and afternoon (second mate) watch-keepers, who usually ate breakfast and lunch respectively, before going on watch. This was not practicable for the evening watch-keeper (the mate) and, particularly in tramp ships it was customary for the third mate to relieve the mate for his evening meal from 1700 to 1730.

Marking the passage of time:

Time on board ship was notified by striking a bell, and a small bell was usually fitted just outside the wheelhouse with its lanyard extended to reach the helmsman who could use it without leaving the wheel. When it was necessary for a person to be instructed to strike the bell to indicate the time, the correct term was **'make it'**, e.g. 'Make six bells', but it was usually left to the helmsman to keep an eye on the clock and make the bells at the appropriate time. Some bridge and engine room clocks struck the time in this fashion automatically but it was still helpful to use the wheelhouse bell as it could usually be heard further away and alerted others around the ship. During the night hours it was usual to suspend its use.

The textbook model for timekeeping was:

One bell at half an hour after the start of the four-hour cycle, i.e. 0030, 0430, 0830, 1230, 1630 & 2030.

Two bells half an hour later at 0100, 0500, 0900, 1300, 1700 & 2100.

Three bells half an hour later again.

The strikes then increased by one bell for each half-hour until the end of the watch except as explained below.

Seven bells was sometimes made at 0720 and 1120 instead of 0730 & 1130. This allowed the *watch below forty minutes (an extra ten minutes) to prepare as they were required to have their breakfast or dinner before going on watch. **Seven-bell meals** were served at these times.

Eight bells indicated the end of the watch, 0400, 0800, Noon, 1600, 2000 and Midnight.

Flogging the clock. The common but unofficial term for adjusting the ship's time necessary to account for any change of longitude, upon which time is based. It resulted in the day varying in length by anything from a few minutes to as much as half an hour or more, depending on the ship's course and speed. To accommodate this change the clock was put forward (sailing east) or back (sailing west), to keep in step with local, or zone, time.

Method of making the bells:
The second bell of each two bell group followed immediately after its predecessor, but the odd bell which indicated the half-hour, or the next two bell group later, was made after a short interval, e.g. three bells would be struck as strike-strike-interval-strike. There were often other variations than those for seven-bell meals and included one bell a quarter of an hour before the beginning of a watch as a notification to the *watch-below that they were on duty in fifteen minutes. For the night watches this shorter warning was usually considered adequate for them to awaken and dress, and for the day watches they were already up and dressed so it served as a final reminder. Even though the bell might be silent at the designated times they were always referred to as so many bells and an officer called at say 2345 for his watch at midnight would be told, 'One bell, Sir.' (It was expected that advice on the weather also be given so that he could dress appropriately.)

Make eight bells. The one exception to the helmsman making the bells without instructions was at Noon when it was customary for the OOW to order it, and if the captain was on the bridge his approval would first be sought to, 'Make eight bells, Sir?'

Bell to Bell. Literally meaning on and off watch exactly on time, the expression was sometimes used for a seaman who gave no more time to his work than was strictly required. It might be said in a derogatory sense of anyone unwilling to give a little extra of himself, as in, 'He's a bell to bell man'; the landsman's equivalent of 'clock watcher'.

Sixteen bells. It was the tradition that the youngest member of the crew struck sixteen bells at midnight on New Years Eve – eight bells for the old year and eight for the new.

(ii) **Watch – A group of persons**
A watch consisted of a team with a specific, common overall duty. It could be concerned with the ship's safe navigation or propulsion and was usually for a specific period of time. The number of persons in a watch was determined by the complexity

of the duties required by it and the number often increased with the size of the vessel. Some ships operate today with a one-man navigation watch, two being required at night, but during the review period ships invariably had several people in a watch; bridge watches in most ocean-going ships usually comprised four or five men. Automation has now made it possible for engine rooms to be unmanned for lengthy periods whereas it was once common to have at least four, and several more in large steam ships particularly if coal-fired when a large number of firemen and trimmers would also be necessary.

A watch could also be for other specific purposes in port, such as ensuring the proper stowage of cargo (**cargo watch**) and safety of the ship (**fire watch** or **gangway watch.**)

Officer of the Watch. Usually abbreviated to OOW, he was the officer responsible to the master for the safe navigation and handling of the ship during his period on watch.

Engineer of the Watch (EOW). The engineer officer responsible to the chief engineer for the engine room during his watch.

Not all ships operated exactly the same systems but a **typical 4-hour navigation watch** might have included:

The Officer of the Watch (many passenger ships had two).

An apprentice or cadet (if carried and not employed on day-work).

Three seamen who alternated duties as helmsman, lookout and stand-by man. (In passenger ships and many Indian crewed cargo ships at least one of the seamen would be a quartermaster, an experienced helmsmen for whom steering was a specialist role.)

The officers usually remained in the same watch pattern day after day but the three ratings, often two able seamen (ABs) and an ordinary seaman (OS), generally moved on one place after each watch so their pattern changed daily. The usual rotation of duties for the ratings, varied slightly in some ships but where the wheel trick was of two hours duration, it usually

Another Beuttler cartoon, from early in the 20th century entitled
'An officer at last – Impressions of his first watch.'

conformed to the following pattern:

	Hour one	**Hour two**	**Hour three**	**Hour four**
Seaman 1	Wheel	Stand-by	Wheel	Lookout
Seaman 2	Lookout	Wheel	Stand-by	Wheel
Seaman 3	Stand-by	Lookout	Lookout	Stand-by

During the day-watches the stand-by man was usually allowed a smoke after coming off the wheel and before reporting to the bosun to work on deck with the rest of the deck hands. During the night watches he could usually stay below in his accommodation but, both day and night, he was on call to the bridge if required. In the period shortly before the change of the watch he was required to call the *watch below at the appropriate time in readiness for their taking over for the next watch.

If the OOW required either the stand-by man or a cadet on the bridge, often with reasonable haste, or an unscheduled relief for the lookout or helmsman, he blew a code on his pea-whistle:

One blast for the standby man

Two blasts for the cadet or apprentice

Three blasts for the relief lookout

Farmer. The seaman who had two stand-by hours and two lookout hours with no *wheel trick. One suggested origin for the name was that, in the days of sail when the livestock had to be fed and watered, this was the duty of the seaman who had the first and last hour's stand-by. Another, less charitable, was simply that any farmer could perform the stand-by and lookout functions but not that of a helmsman.

Wheel trick. A period of duty at the wheel, usually not more than two hours.

The navigation lookout. Apart from the requirement for a lookout from the bridge by the OOW and often a seaman too, there was a need for a seaman to maintain a lookout for shipping from the fo'c's'le head. Paradoxically, as ships became larger their masts often became shorter and less suitable for crow's nests, the traditional lookout position, while bridges and fo'c's'le heads grew higher than many smaller ships' crow's nests. In any event it became desirable for a lookout to be kept from a lower level than the bridge as small craft are more likely to be silhouetted against the horizon instead of being 'buried' against the sea.

Lookout signals. The fo'c's'le bell, rather than a telephone, was used to signal sightings of ships or other objects to the bridge, one bell for a sighting to starboard, two for port and three for dead ahead. Four drew the OOW's attention to the fact that the lookout had not been, or wished to be, relieved.

In P & O and the Blue Funnel Line, the port and starboard signals were reversed. The

rationale for this was that in a strong wind, or if the OOW was busy, two bells were more likely to be heard than one and the OOW thereby more likely to be alerted to something being in sight somewhere. For compliance with the Collision Regulations the starboard side is usually seen as the danger side due to a need to give way to a vessel crossing from starboard to port; there is therefore an argument that it is preferable to keep the most efficient lookout on the starboard side.

A typical engine room watch might have included:

> The Engineer of the Watch
> A Junior EOW
> 2 Wipers and greasers
> 8 Firemen and trimmers (only in a coal-fired ship)

Keeping ship. In port it was usual, except in passenger ships, for both the deck and engineer officers to break watches, i.e. stop the routine watch-keeping pattern, and for one of each to be **the duty officer** in their respective departments. They might remain on duty for 12 or even 24 hours and were permitted to sleep during some of this time provided a responsible rating was on duty and alerted to call them in an emergency. However, cargo operations required a constant vigil and the duty deck officer would have a restricted period of duty and was expected to be constantly aware of the cargo operations taking place.

When on duty in port he was said to be keeping ship and was often referred to as the **shipkeeper.**

Bells had other than simply watchkeeping uses:

The fo'c's'le bell. The principal bell, larger than the bridge bell and usually cast with the ship's name, was fitted on the fo'c's'le head. Its minimum dimensions were subject to BOT regulations as the bell was an essential item of navigation equipment.

Ringing the fo'c's'le bell. A fog signal for ships at anchor when rung rapidly for about five seconds at intervals not exceeding one minute, and in ships over 100 meters in length it was immediately followed by the striking of a gong at the stern. This bell rung rapidly for about thirty seconds was also a fire alarm.

The bell as an anchoring signal. When letting go or weighing anchor the fo'c's'le bell was used to indicate to the bridge the number of shackles of cable that had run out, one stroke for each shackle. When the anchor broke out of the seabed it was said to be aweigh which was indicated by its rapid ringing for a few moments. The bell was preferable to the telephone as it did not distract those receiving the message on the bridge and might be more audible over the rattle of the cable passing noisily over the windlass.

Church bell. In passenger ships the fo'c'l'le bell was often tolled as a church bell to summon those wishing to attend.

Visitors' bell. As sailing time approached in passenger ships the fo'c's'le bell was sometimes rung rapidly for about 10 seconds at intervals of ten minutes to warn visitors to depart. It was usually accompanied by an announcement over the public address system.

The bell as a font. If a child was to be christened on board by a clergyman (often the *Mission to Seamen chaplain) while a ship was in port, the fo'c's'le bell would be unshipped, turned over and fitted into a wooden framework made by the ship's carpenter to serve as the font.

CHAPTER SIXTEEN

Navigation and the Ship's Position

Because the navigation of the ship was carried out by the officers, usually with little or no assistance from any deck ratings, it is not surprising that there is less slang associated with this aspect of ship operation. This chapter therefore contains many less colloquial expressions or slang terms and most included are of a more professional nature, though this does not alter the importance of preserving them as part of the nautical language. Methods of navigating a ship have drastically altered in the past three or four decades and many terms once associated with navigation have already been replaced by new ones belonging to the electronic age.

The navigator. All deck officers were commonly referred to as navigating officers but in most merchant ships the second officer was usually designated, The navigator. He was directly responsible to the master for the availability and care of the charts, nautical publications and all navigation equipment except sextants which were invariably the personal property of the deck officers – rarely were they supplied by a shipping company to its vessels. (The frequent exchanging of officers abroad by means of flying today, often to provide regular leave, has necessitated the removal of heavy items from their baggage. Consequently sextants now form part of a ship's equipment.)

The watchkeeping officers. As explained in chapter 15, in ships with three deck officers it was customary for the *third officer to keep the 8–12 watch, the *second officer the 12–4 and the *chief officer the 4–8. Many cargo ships in the leading British shipping companies carried a *fourth officer who often kept a watch with, or in lieu of, the chief officer.

If there were two officers on the 4–8 watch, the morning and evening twilight star sights were sometimes taken by the more experienced officer, but that would usually depend upon the experience of the junior officer and upon the importance which the master placed upon the accuracy of the ship's position by the stars. In the open ocean, if the weather was likely to be satisfactory for fixing the ship's position by the sun at noon, star sights were of less importance unless they were being relied upon when making a landfall after a long ocean passage.

Passenger ships usually carried additional officers. The pattern varied considerably between shipping companies but frequently a ship would carry a *first officer as the senior of the watchkeepers (the chief officer being a day-worker) and an additional second and third officer, consequently there were usually two certificated officers on each watch. (Cunard and Orient Lines were notable for employing as watchkeeping officers only those holding Masters' Certificates.)

NAVIGATING AND POSITION FIXING

Essential to the ship's safe navigation and timely arrival at loading and discharging ports was the maintenance of a careful check upon the ship's track. For this, an accurate determination of the ship's position was necessary and the navigators of British merchant ships in the past generally maintained very high standards. Today electronic aids make this relatively simple, and usually highly accurate. GPS has revolutionised bavigation.

In sight of land the OOW took frequent compass bearings to keep track of the ship's position, sometimes under the master's occasional supervision. These bearings were hand plotted onto a paper chart upon which had been drawn the intended track of the vessel as directed by the master. Horizontal angles between two terrestrial objects and vertical angles of objects such as hills and lighthouses, taken by a sextant, were also used to fix a ship's position with the aid of plotting instruments, principally parallel rules and dividers.

Blue Funnel Line, which carried its own hull insurance, had clearly specified tracks recorded in a manual and which were later inserted on their ships' charts in ink by the navigator. Most companies generally gave less direction in this although some had lists of way-points (a term not widely used before the advent of satellite navigation) for recommended tracks, but in most cases masters used their own discretion in deciding on appropriate courses between ports.

Basic plotting equipment:

Admiralty charts. All British merchant ships carried sets of Admiralty charts printed on high quality paper and covering the areas in which they traded. (During at least the first half of the review period many Admiralty charts, known as blue backs, were printed on a very sturdy and long lasting blue, linen-backed paper.) Admiralty charts were regarded by the Courts as providing the necessary standard to which charts should comply and were required to be kept up to date from Notices to Mariners supplied free of charge by the Hydrographic Office of the Royal Navy. (Its name has since been changed when it became an independent commercial operation.) For some radio based navigational systems admiralty charts were over-printed with additional and relevant information, e.g. Decca lattice charts in the earlier days of that system's operation. (The early years of the 21st century are seeing the cautious introduction of electronic chart systems which may lead to their almost universal use before very long).

Parallel rules. Chart plotting was facilitated by the use of a pair of rulers that could be moved parallel to one another. Originally made of wood, they were later made of either brass or plastic and a popular type, still known today as **Captain Field's,** had a protractor engraved on them. A later development, **a roller rule**, comprised a single brass or plastic ruler with a pair of rollers which would maintain its direction when carefully slid across a chart from one part to another.

Other instruments used for this purpose were square protractors (one patented type was a **Douglas protractor**) and a pair of triangular protractors, but neither received much favour in British merchant ships.

Dividers. Similar to the simple item of length measuring equipment familiar to many school children and draftsmen for use on paper, the navigator's 'pair' of dividers retained the simple straight legs but was usually more robust and made of brass (non-magnetic). Another type of dividers was later introduced, largely for yachtsmen, in which the upper part of each leg was made semicircular. Known as **bow dividers**, having regard to their upper-leg shape, they were intended to simplify single-handed use but generally they did not find favour with professional navigators who found little difficulty in using conventional dividers with one hand.

Nautical publications. Apart from the *Nautical Almanac* a number of official nautical publications were required to be carried by British merchant ships including *Admiralty Tide Tables, Ocean Passages of the World, Sailing Directions* and various others.

The slide rule. Although never seriously challenging the importance of nautical tables for the calculation of position lines based upon celestial observations, this fairly basic mathematical instrument was used by some navigators for the more basic navigation calculations. (Hand-held **navigation calculators,** and **computer programmes** have since found a place with navigators for astronomical sights and other calculations.)

Terrestrial position fixing – Instruments:

Standard compass. The name given to the principal, and mandatory, magnetic compass required by the regulations which also provided that, together with the steering compass, it was to be corrected for ship's magnetism by a licensed compass adjuster. It was the principal and only major item of ship's equipment used to determine position when in sight of land until the introduction of radio and radar based equipment.

Gyro compass. Working on an entirely difference principle, devoid of the earth's magnetic influence, this compass was first developed in the early part of the 20th century. It relies upon a spinning rotor (a gyroscope), driven by electricity, and the earth's rotation. This enables it to point to True North rather than Magnetic North. Although subject to some mechanical errors which could be allowed for, it is steadier than a magnetic compass when a ship is rolling, and is without the deflecting influence of a ship's and the earth's magnetic fields. It has largely replaced the magnetic compass for all practical purposes although the magnetic compass still has a value as it is not subject to electric power and mechanical failure.

Terrestrial position fixing – Methods and terms:
Vertical sextant angles. The *sextant had some limited value in terrestrial position fixing. It could be used to determine a position circle upon which a ship lay, by measuring the vertical angle of a lighthouse and other objects of known height and position.

Horizontal sextant angles, obtained in pairs between three or more visible, charted objects could also be used to fix the ship's position.

Other methods of fixing a ship's position by terrestrial means, albeit less certain, included three point bearings and two bearings with a run between. These required no more than a compass observation of a charted object at intervals and a record of the course and speed of the ship.

Raising the light. Navigating coastwise at night, a lighthouse will first be seen as an occasional beam of light when still just below the horizon, particularly if there is some cloud. Before the advent of electronic position fixing instruments it was useful to watch this **loom of the light** until the exact moment it appeared over the horizon as a spot of light. A simple calculation would provide the distance off, i.e. the distance of the sea horizon, and if the time of raising the light was recorded and a compass bearing taken of it, the ship's position could be determined quite simply.

The Day's Work. When terrestial or celestial observations were unavailable and chart plotting was impractical due to the small scale of a chart, it was necessary to make the best estimate of the ship's position by other means. This was achieved from the record of compass courses steered, with allowances made for natural and ship related magnetic influences, (or gyro errors) estimated currents, wind and weather conditions experienced over a period. The day's work was the term used to describe the sometimes rather tedious computation necessary using predetermined, tabulated and published trigonometrical solutions (**Traverse Tables**) to arrive at the best estimated position.

Astronomical position fixing – Instruments and equipment:

Sextant. (See also under terrestrial position fixing). The standard and essential instrument for navigating out of sight of land for many years until the advent of satellite navigation. Its value lay in its ability to measure accurately the elevation of a heavenly body above the horizon and thereby enable the navigator, with the assistance of a nautical ephemeris and trigonometrical tables, to obtain a position line.

Chronometer. A very accurate time-piece, of which two were normally carried, used to check the time to the nearest second of all sextant observations used in determining a position line. Chronometers were checked for accuracy daily whenever possible, usually by a radio time signal, and their **rate** (progressive error) recorded to provide against the possibility of being unable to obtain a daily check on rare occasions. In some places, Greenwich included, before the advent of reliable radio time signals for chronometer rating, a tower was erected within sight of the port area having a time ball above it which was dropped daily exactly at noon.

Star globe. The equivalent of a globe presenting an image of the earth, a star globe provided a similar spherical representation of the heavens showing the principal stars. The positions of the planets, which constantly vary, could also be temporarily marked following reference to the Nautical Almanac. It could be set for any time of the day or night and assisted a navigator in finding the approximate height above the horizon and direction of any heavenly body whose altitude he wished to determine accurately by means of his sextant. This was particularly valuable for evening star sights as the stars would otherwise be difficult to find until the twilight was far enough advanced for them to shine brightly, and in company with others. (While the increased darkness aided star identification it had an adverse effect on the clarity of the horizon so early identification and location was helpful)

Rude Star-Identifier. This was a less bulky alternative to a *star globe and comprised a disc of about 8 inches (204 mm) diameter and served much the same purpose as a star globe.

Inman's Tables. The lengthy spherical trigonometry calculations required to obtain the *position lines mentioned below could be assisted by using certain mathematical tables and over the years many books containing them, together with data from pre-calculated solutions, appeared on the market. One of the earlier sets of these tables once in common use was provided by a clergyman with an interest in mathematics, the Reverend Inman.

Norries Tables. A further compilation of similar and other useful information for the same purpose. They became the vogue some years later and were very popular with Merchant Service navigators in the 1930s and 1940s.

Burtons Tables. Following soon after *Norries Tables*, the simplified Burton's Tables became the standard work for a later generation of navigators. *Martelli's Tables* also caught the fancy of some.

Alt-Az tables. (Abbreviation of Altitude and Azimuth.) Shortly before WW 2 the mathematicians made a further significant contribution for the benefit of air navigators by pre-computing the solutions to innumerable spherical triangles and tabulating them in this set of tables. These were required because the speed of aircraft made it necessary for their navigators to achieve higher speeds of calculation than was then possible or needed by marine navigators. There was a compromise as these Air Navigation Alt-Az tables sacrificed some accuracy.

Sight reduction tables. The Royal Navy also required pre-computed solutions to spherical triangles and called for the publication of similar tables. As mariners preferred to achieve a slightly greater accuracy this resulted in bulkier volumes but neither speed of calculation nor weight of paper was of as much importance as to air navigators.

ABC Tables. A set of mathematical tables extensively used by navigators which enabled the bearing of the sun to be calculated with much greater speed than by the more laborious process of spherical trigonometry. They also served a useful purpose in some other calculations.

Nautical Almanacs. British ships were invariably supplied with *The Nautical Almanac* published by Her Majesty's Stationery Office (HMSO). The ephemeris in it was essential for calculations to fix a ship's position following sextant observations of heavenly bodies, and for determining compass errors after taking bearings of them. Many ships also carried copies of other publishers' almanacs and navigation information.

Electronic calculators. In the 1970s one or two firms introduced battery operated, hand held, navigation calculators that incorporated essential data from the nautical almanac. These calculators simplified and sped-up the calculation of position from observations of heavenly bodies.

Astronomical position fixing – Methods and terms:

Taking sights. Making sextant observations of the sun, stars and other heavenly bodies used to fix a vessel's position when out of sight of land. This was followed by a series of spherical trigonometry calculations to determine the ship's position from which the course to any point en route could be calculated.

Shooting the sun. Making a sextant observation of the sun. Also **Taking a sun sight.** (A similar expression to the latter was used with the appropriate adjective when taking observations of the moon, planets or stars.)

Fixing the ship. The term for ascertaining the ship's position following observations of heavenly bodies or terrestrial objects.

When out of sight of land, and the position to be determined by the celestial objects, the following was the daily routine in most ships:

• Stellar observations were taken at morning twilight by the 4–8 watch-keeper and a position obtained. (Note the reference to 'twilight' as it was necessary to see both the celestial object and the horizon simultaneously.)

• During the forenoon, an observation of the sun was obtained by all the watch-keeping officers, including the master.

• The results of 2 above were combined with another sun sight at noon to determine the ship's position at solar mid-day (i.e. noon by the sun which was then at its maximum altitude, and bearing due north or south. However, this was usually not exactly mid-day by the time the ship was keeping.

• An afternoon sun sight was taken by the 12-4 watch-keeper. (This was little more than a useful check on the sights in the 8-12 watch and some help if later star sights were unobtainable, e.g. due to overcast conditions.)

• Later, evening twilight star sights were taken by the 4-8 watchkeeper and a position obtained.

In most British merchant ships the master would lead the team, usually consisting of at least the second and third officers, in taking a forenoon sun sight, and another at noon. Depending upon his judgment of the 4-8 watchkeeper's competence, the master might also take evening stars and sometimes also morning stars when approaching an imminent landfall. This practice varied very little, although in a few of the larger companies, notably P & O, the master never took sights and relied entirely upon his navigator, aided by the other junior watch-keeping officers.

Sumner lines. In 1837 an American master, Captain Thomas Sumner, made an interesting discovery that demonstrated the value of a single sun sight. For a time the resulting position line was named after him and his discovery led to a better understanding of the use of position lines in celestial navigation.

Long by Chron. (Longitude by Chronometer). There was more than one method of calculating a position line obtained by astronomical observations and almost universal Merchant Service practice, except when the sun was on the meridian at noon (*Mer.Alt.) was by the Long by Chron method.

Marq St Hilaire. Named after a French naval officer in 1875, this method achieved a similar result to that of *Long by Chron and was also known as **The Intercept Method.**

Mer Alt. (Meridian Altitude). A position line could be simply calculated from an observation of the altitude of a heavenly body when it was exactly on (or very close to) the meridian. For the sun this occurred at solar noon when it was at its maximum altitude and bore exactly due north or south of the observer; and at varying times for other bodies.

The Noon Position. This was adjusted for any small time difference between the solar noon and ship's mid-day, and always treated as an important moment in a ship's daily routine. This position was achieved by obtaining the sun's *mer alt and combining it with the previously obtained position line from a forenoon sight with an allowance for direction and distance covered in the interim. Also when available by terrestial means. This position was then used to determine the course and average speed made good for the day from the previous noon.

The day's run. Apart from its navigational value in calculating the average speed from Noon to Noon and subtracting it from the previous Noon's distance still to go, the day's run also had a social importance in passenger ships where a **tote** was run by betting on the day's run. At noon the ship's siren was sounded, the tote closed and shortly afterwards the navigator announced the day's run from the previous Noon. The successful punter was paid out with a proportion of the takings customarily going to seamen's charities.

Other navigation instruments and related terms:

Steering compass. The secondary magnetic compass which was fitted in the wheelhouse in front of the wheel, for the helmsman to steer by and was duplicated at the emergency steering position at the stern. In later ships a steering compass, separate from the *standard compass,was often not fitted and reliance was placed upon a periscope which allowed the helmsman to read the standard compass on the *monkey island above.

Slate board. In sailing ships where frequent alterations of course were common due to wind shifts, and often the need to tack to make progress to windward, it was usual for the OOW to keep a record on a slate board of each course alteration during his watch. Later, in steamships, a slate on the wheelhouse bulkhead was used for a while to remind the OOW and helmsman of the course being steered. In due course even more elaborate course boards were provided employing numerals painted on wood, or engraved on plastic, for display in a suitable holder.

Boxing the compass. An unusual term, it refers to repeating aloud all the thirty-two points of the compass (each of eleven and a quarter degrees) in consecutive order. The earlier compasses contained 4 Cardinal points (e.g. North), 4 Half-Cardinal points (e.g. North-East), 8 Three-letter points (e.g. North-North-East) and 16 By-points (e.g. North-by-East, usually written as NxE). Today the term, and an understanding of it, has almost entirely disappeared as direction is invariably given in degrees rather than in points of the compass.

Quarter-points. The sub-division achieved by dividing each of the 32 points of the compass into quarters produced units known as quarter-points. Although some seafarers today may

The mariners' compass

be familiar with the main 32 points of the compass mentioned above, few would recall the time when a ship was conned by giving helm orders in quarter-points. To test a candidate's knowledge, an examiner for an officer's Certificate of Competence would usually require him to recite all the quarter points between, say South-West and North-West without any mistakes. This ability to 'box the compass in quarter-points' was still an essential requirement to pass the oral examination for a Second Mate's Certificate until at least the latter part of the 1940s. (It was not nearly as easy as it may sound because the quarter-points did not follow a continuous clockwise pattern all round the circle and reversed periodically, becoming anti-clockwise each time a three-letter-point was reached.)

Autopilot. An automatic steering device, in much more general use today than during the third quarter of the 20th century when it was first introduced. The autopilot used at sea was sometimes referred to as **Iron Mike** but generally it did not acquire this name nearly as frequently as a similar instrument fitted to aircraft.

Common log. An early means of ascertaining a ship's speed, it comprised a triangular piece of wood with a short length of cord attached to each corner, one attachment being simply a tight-fitting peg which could be made to release when required to assist recovery. With the three cord legs as a bridle attached to a length of rope knotted at measured intervals and wound onto a hand-held drum, the wooden shape was dropped in the water at the stern. With the drum running free as the rope ran out, the knots on the rope leaving the drum were counted after a fixed time interval determined by using a sand glass. They belonged largely to the days of sail and early in the steamship era before *patent logs were invented. Also **chip log** and **logship.** (An earlier method of checking speed was to drop a piece of wood over the ship's side well forward and record the time taken to reach a position near the stern Sometimes known a **Dutchman's Log.**)

Patent log. The Walker 'Trident' log was a very successful and widely used brand of patent log, a measuring instrument which recorded the distance steamed by a ship over a noted period of time, thereby providing speed through the water. Comprising a *rotator, *log line, *governor and a recorder (*log clock), it was originally fitted to the ship's stern rail (the taffrail) and referred to as a **taffrail log**. Later developments include some logs that fitted small impellors or sensors on the hull, employing Doppler, Pitot tube and electro-magnetic principles.

Rotator. A brass, propeller-like fin which, when towed on the end of the patent-log line induced rotation.

Log line. The length of plaited rope with a wire core which linked the rotator of a patent log to the *governor, a small fly-wheel, which helped to even-out any irregularities in its rotation.

Log Clock. The instrument that recorded the number of rotations of the log line on a patent log. Attached to the taffrail on earlier models it was later improved when fitted on a *log boom beneath the bridge to save the excursion aft to read it. A still later model had a distant-reading electrical log clock in the chart room.

Log boom. Usually fixed by a swivel to the ship's side below the bridge, this boom was capable of being swung out horizontally at right angle to the ship. This kept the *log rotator clear of any undue influence from the propeller wash and ship's wake. The outer end of the boom had a 90° change-of-direction device affixed to it and to one part of which the *log line was attached. A short length of line was then attached to the other part and the boom's position allowed the inboard end of this line to be attached to the clock on a rail at the ship's side, or on wing of the bridge above, rather than at the stern, making it much more convenient to read.

Echo-sounding machine. This electronic sounding device revolutiionised navigation and hydrographic surveying by providing almost instantaneous soundings and removing much of the drudgery of sounding with either a sounding line or wire

Kelvin sounding machine. Invented by Lord Kelvin, this was a mechanical instrument fitted on deck at the stern, or at the ship's side amidships when provided with a boom. It consisted of a thin wire on a drum, a lead weight and a brass sheath lowered by gravity and controlled by a brake. The depth of water was determined after the sheath, containing a replaceable, glass, open-ended tube containing silver nitrate, had been recovered on board after reaching the bottom of the sea. Depending upon the depth of water, the pressure forced seawater up the tube and altered the colour of the silver nitrate. Comparison with a graduated boxwood scale, after the tube's recovery on board, indicated the depth of water. In early versions rewinding the wire onto the drum was by hand – a very lengthy and tedious operation – but later electric motors were fitted. In similar fashion to the *patent log, the Kelvin Sounding Machine later employed a boom closer to the bridge enabling the depth to be reported more easily from there.

Arming the lead. The reliability of later electronic echo sounders has completely the use of the deep-sea lead and even the hand lead line. However, there was a time when they were the only means of obtaining a sounding and they had one advantage over their electronic successors. The lead itself had a hole at the bottom, an open pocket that could be packed with tallow – the act of arming the lead – to pick-up a sample of the seabed. When compared with the information on the chart, the seabed material sticking to the tallow sometimes assisted in determining the vessel's position.

The patent log and the deep-sea sounding machine were fitted in ships for much of the review period, being only slowly displaced by more sophisticated equipment. Until about the time of WW2, they, together with the sextant, the chronometer, the echo sounder, the radio direction finder and the gyro compass, were about the only items of navigation equipment available. A WW2 invention, *radar began to become available commercially shortly after the War and from then on many other electronic navigation aids were introduced in quick succession.

Today the almost universal Global Positioning System (GPS) employing navigation satellites and computers in the receivers, has almost entirely eliminated the need for these old-fashioned navigation methods involving sextants and trigonometrical tables, except as a back-up in rare instances. Rarely do ship's officers now carry their own sextants although ships usually provide one sextant on the bridge in case of emergencies where there is a need to resort to basic principles.

Radar. (**R**adio **A**id **D**irection **A**nd **R**ange). This navigation aid detects the presence of above-water objects (e.g. other ships and natural, geographical obstructions) even when visibility is nil, as in darkness and fog. It has served the dual purpose of providing an 'electronic lookout' for dangers and a navigation aid giving a bearing and distance of objects which, if identifiable on the chart, materially aid position fixing. Its fitting is now mandator but until as late as about 1960 a number of well-found ships, owned by respected shipping companies, chose not to fit it.

Decca Navigator. A British development this was a simple-to-use navigation aid having shore-based transmitters and a ship-borne receiver employing radio frequencies for relatively short-range use. Initially, to determine the ship's position, it had to be accompanied by a navigation chart overlaid with coloured, curved lines depicting the radio waves emanating from its shore-based stations. Later development of this navigation system enabled the receiving instrument to provide a direct read-out of latitude and longitude. It was discontinued by about the end of the 20th century.

Loran. This American development was a relatively longer-range system. Both a Loran A and a Loran C navigation system employing sophisticated receivers were used for many years and also operated on radio frequencies. Loran was very much less common than *Decca in British merchant ships during the period but it was used extensively in the North Atlantic liners.

Consol. This was a radio navigation aid that radiated a signal from a shore-based transmitter but did not require sophisticated equipment to receive them. It could be used with a conventional broadcast radio receiver but its use was confined to Northern European waters.

Radio Direction Finder (R.D.F or more usually D/F). Radio beacons around the UK and many other coasts transmitted a continuous tone, each having a slightly different frequency. This was followed by its call sign in the Morse code. Using the ship's D/F instrument the radio officer could tune to these beacons and take a bearing on two or three in turn. This enabled the navigator to fix the ship's position, not necessarily with great accuracy, but was particularly valuable when poor visibility or overcast weather prevented fixing by visual means. It was also used to obtain a bearing of a ship transmitting a distress message and helped to locate her. (The presence of a D/F in a ship could usually be detected by the single or double steel loop mounted above the bridge but modern electronic navigation systems have made the system obsolete.)

Miscellaneous

Nichol's Concise Guide. The standard navigation textbook for most of the period, found amongst the study books of almost every aspiring second mate, it came in two volumes although only Volume 1 was commonly encountered. The Royal Naval equivalent, **The Admiralty Manual of Navigation** in three volumes also found a place in some Merchant Service officers' reference material, together with the highly respected American equivalent known simply as **Bowditch.**

Lecky's Wrinkles. The abbreviated and common name for **Wrinkles in Practical Navigation** by Captain Squire Thornton Stratford Lecky, at one time a Pacific Steam Navigation Company master. It was an extraordinary and remarkable tome of some 800 pages, recording the worthy captain's very wide experience and providing an enormous amount of practical guidance to navigators on all aspects of navigation. First published in 1881, it was a very comprehensive and respected publication, both erudite and written with a wry sense of humour. For example, in a chapter on star identification he wrote of the constellation, Southern Cross, that,' … romantic young ladies love to gaze at it whilst the waters ripple by the side of the ship. The effect is enhanced if a good-looking officer should happen to be close by to explain matters celestial'. A sketch in the book illustrating the constellation shows the officer and a young lady, both in period dress, beside the ship's rail looking at the stars. The book was usually a treasured possession and highly valued by navigators during the years it was in print.

Reed's Nautical Almanac. A book, often found in the bookshelves of British merchant ships, which contained an enormous amount of useful data besides navigation ephemeris.

Brown's Nautical Year Book. Another annual publication full of useful nautical information, commonly found on the chart tables of many British ships.

Sight Book. This was a book provided by some companies, but personal to each navigating officer, in which, as the name implies, he recorded the results of his sight calculations including position, course and speed made good and the Estimated Time of Arrival (ETA) at the next port.

Fathom. For many years this was the nautical term for a measurement of six feet (1.83m) and was constantly used to express the length of ropes or depths of water, amongst other uses. An International agreement in the latter part of the 20th century did away with this unit on charts for depth of water and was replaced by metres which also became the unit for height. It became sensible to do away with the fathom for other purposes too but its departure left British seamen with a strong sense of losing an old friend. The loss of the fathom was mourned for many years.

Station keeping. Except in wartime convoys, and unlike warships which often operate as a squadron in company with one another, merchant ships very rarely had to keep station on another ship. Keeping station required a ship to maintain a set distance from the ship ahead, when in line ahead, and a set distance from the ship or ships abeam when in two or more columns. A simple hand-held instrument was available to assist in judging the correct distances. Many a shipmaster, particularly in the older, slower cargo ships, found it a very difficult requirement and was often the recipient of a convoy commodore's terse signal to 'keep station!'

Ahead (or Astern) of station. This term referred to a ship being either forward or behind her designated position in a convoy. It was also used figuratively when a person was early or late for an occasion, as in, 'I'm sorry I am late for our meeting but I found myself a little astern of station'.

Chart room. Until about 1960, in most of the steam ships built during between 1875 and 1975, the chartroom was entirely separate from the wheelhouse, usually behind and with a solid wooden bulkhead between them. In many cases the wheelhouse had an entirely separate entrance with access each side from the open bridge and none directly from the wheelhouse. (In modern ships the chart-table, chart stowage and navigation instruments are situated at the rear of the wheelhouse, abaft the helmsman, often with no more than a curtain separating them.

Consequently the term 'chart room' as such has largely disappeared.)

Bridge box. During the night watches tea/coffee/cocoa and sandwiches were usually available for the OOW who could not leave the bridge. In most cargo ships these items were provided in a wooden box sent up to the bridge before the cook went off duty after the evening meal. There was usually no need for a bridge box in passenger ships as a member of the catering staff was on duty throughout the night for passengers and would answer a call from the bridge for food and refreshments.

Colloquial terms referring to navigation:

Coming up with . . . . The expression was used when a faster ship was steadily overhauling a slower ship and was said to be coming up with her.

A rock hopper. A master with a reputation for passing close to land, often passing closer than more prudent masters were prepared to do. The term was sometimes also applied to coastal vessels.

Current Bun (Cockney). The overhead sun, an expression associated with a meridian altitude of the sun acquired by the sextant.

Sun gun. A sextant. Also **Ham bone** & **Jaw bone.**

Cast iron bollocks. A somewhat crude reference to Castor and Pollox, two prominent stars in the sky often used by navigators as suitable objects for star sight from which to obtain a position line.

Hurry-up tables. Speeding the calculation of sights, apart from any operational benefit this might provide, became a competitive exercise and a subject of pride for many navigators who, for this purpose, often pre-computed useful tables of their own, or collected miscellaneous ones in a notebook.

The Old Man's NOB. Before a master retired for the night when the ship was at sea he would usually leave his 'Standing Orders' and any special orders concerning navigation, for the

OOW's attention during the night watches. A special book, The **Captain's Night Order Book,** with his Standing Orders pasted in the front, and with nightly supplementary orders written on date-headed pages, was kept for this purpose and was often known by the book's initial letters as, **The Old Man's NOB.**

Flogging the Log. The *Deck Log, the record of the important events concerning the vessel's movements, including such details as, course steered, ship's position, weather etc., was kept by the OOW. (An appropriate log was similarly kept in the engine room.) All entries were expected to be made at the end of the watch after the OOW was relieved but sometimes this was overlooked and the necessary entries were made later, partly from memory. Any lapse of memory could sometimes lead to the entries being invented. Occasionally too, and often with the master's connivance, false entries regarding the weather experienced were made. These would exaggerate to force of the wind or height of the seas and were intended to strengthen the shipowner's case for refuting cargo damage claims on the basis of 'heavy weather'. This reprehensible practice of inventing or enhancing log entries was known as flogging the log.

Magnetic surfboard. A term introduced towards the end of the period for the deviascope, an instrument used during the Masters' Certificate of Competency examination to test a candidate's knowledge of ship's magnetism. Attached to a swivel pedestal it consisted principally of a magnetic compass mounted on flat, wooden, ship-shaped board vaguely like a surfboard.

Blind buoy. An unlit buoy.

MANOEUVRING AND SHIP HANDLING

Bridge/Engine room telegraph. Orders from the bridge to the engine room, and advice that the order had been received, were conveyed by means of a telegraph. The instrument fitted on the bridge comprised a handsome brass pedestal and dial standing about 4 feet (1.22 metres) high on the wheelhouse deck. Its dial, beneath a glass cover, was engraved with the manoeuvring responses required from the engine(s), and a pointer(s) attached to its operating handle outside the dial was moved to signify the response required. Another pointer(s) beneath the glass cover indicated the actual response from the engine room.

A similar instrument, but without the pedestal, was situated in the engine room adjacent to the manoeuvring platform where an engineer stood awaiting orders. Movement of the handle on the bridge moved the pointer under the glass of the instrument in the engine room and subsequent movement of the engine room handle indicated acknowledgement to the bridge. The sounding of a bell accompanied each handle movement and drew attention to the transmitting or acknowledgment of an order. By this method there should be no possibility of an order being incorrectly received. Typical orders conveyed to the engine room by this telegraph, and responses to the bridge were, 'Slow ahead', 'half astern' etc.

During the life of a ship, thousands of man hours accompanied the polishing of these brass telegraphs, most of which, in British built ships, were manufactured by Chadburn & Co Ltd of Liverpool. The earlier brass telegraphs were connected to one another by means of chain but later, painted telegraphs with semicircular dials and electrical connection, were introduced, some with devices for recording the time and detail of each order and response. Telegraphs have disappeared from many modern ships which commonly have direct operation of the engine(s) from a small instrument on the bridge consol.

Stand–by below. The master's order for 'stand-by' rung on the bridge telegraph shortly before requiring the engine for manoeuvring. This could occur either before arriving at or before leaving a port. When it occurred with the ship still at sea and about to arrive at a port, the time was recorded and taken as 'arrival' for statistical purposes. (When at sea it was usual to give the engine room telephone advice a short while, often half an hour, before ringing stand-by on the telegraph, to enable adjustments to be made for the change of revolutions. Ships had both a 'full speed' for ordinary steaming in open waters and a 'manoeuvring full speed', with restricted revolutions, when in close waters.)

Ring off the engine(s). The order given when the master has finished manoeuvring with the engine(s), usually following departure or after arrival at a port. At sea, prior to the order being given, the telegraph handle would usually be in the 'Full ahead' position but with the engines still restricted to their reduced manoeuvring revolutions. To ring off, the telegraph handle was quickly moved back to the 'Finished with engines' position and immediately returned to the 'Full ahead position', accompanied by a bell ring as always occurred when the handle was moved. This instructed the engine room to work up to revolutions for normal sea speed and its time was recorded as the time of 'departure' for statistical purposes. Also, **Ring full away.** The order to Ring off the engines was also used following arrival and securing at a shore berth and the telegraph was then left in the 'Finished with engines' position.

Double ring. Ringing the bridge/engine room telegraph twice from 'Full ahead' to 'Stand-by' and back to 'Full ahead' again (or from full astern to full astern again) – was used when in the reduced revolution manoeuvring mode if maximum revolutions were required urgently in an emergency during a manoeuvre. This might, for example, be used during berthing when, due to an error of judgment, striking a dock wall was becoming highly probable. A double ring, accompanied by the extra power that should follow, might prevent the impact. More often than not the double ring was likely to be for extra 'full astern' power.

Treble ring. When the last engine movement order has been given after arrival in port, with the vessel secured in her berth, the telegraph was rung to 'Finished with Engines'. When this took place on the completion of the whole voyage, not just of a passage, and usually with the vessel back in her home port, the telegraph was rung from 'Full ahead' to 'Finished with engines' and back again three times and left at the latter. This treble ring informed the engine room that, 'We are finally home!'

Passage. For statistical purposes this was the period between ringing off the engines at departure and ringing stand-by below for arrival.

Bridge Book. Prior to the mechanical or electronic recording of the times and orders rung on the bridge/engine room telegraph(s) a member of the bridge team, frequently a quartermaster, an apprentice or a junior officer, was required to note this information in a book kept for the purpose. Also **Movements Book** or **Bell Book.**

Docking telegraph. Similar to the bridge/engine room telegraph but fitted on the bridge and the poop, it was used, with different orders on its dial, to convey instructions from the bridge, and vice-versa, concerning the handling of mooring lines when berthing and un-berthing the ship.

Steering telegraph. Fitted on the bridge and poop, and similar to the other telegraphs but with steering orders on its dial. It was intended for use when steering by the bridge wheel failed and the emergency steering, operated by a wheel on the poop, was used.

CHAPTER SEVENTEEN

Communications

There have been many famous signals over the years, of which the two best known by British subjects were almost certainly Nelson's famous 'England Expects' signal before the Battle of Trafalgar, conveyed by flags using the code of the time, and the distress message transmitted by the radio officer of the White Star passenger liner *Titanic* when she tragically struck an iceberg in 1912.

At some time or another, messages of various kinds have been of the utmost importance to people all over the world, some urgent, some little more than routine and others causing amusement. Of the latter, many have originated at sea, particularly between the commanding officers (COs) of Her Majesty's ships. Two books recording a few were written after WW2 by a naval officer, Captain Jack Broome entitled, *Make a Signal* **and later,** *Make another Signal.* One CO, having just run his ship aground and being asked by signal what he proposed to do now, is said to have replied, 'Buy a farm!'

Messages were regularly passed between one ship and another or between ships and shore stations. The term **Signalling** was generally used for message exchanged by means other than radio although the term **Distress Signal** appears to belie the statement. It is however the exception, and of course distress signals were sent by many other means too. (**Distress message** is probably the more common term when radio is involved.)

Before radio became the convenient means of passing information, flags, and latterly more often the signal lamp, were commonly used. At one time, when passing a Lloyd's signal station, masters would often send a request to have their position and time of passing sent on to their owners. (Europa Point lighthouse off Gibraltar is a good example.) Also, during the square-rig sailing ship era, vessels were commonly required to report **for orders** when arriving off Falmouth, Lands End or Queenstown from distant places, and if a boat did not come off with instructions where they were to proceed to discharge their cargo, this information was communicated by flag or lamp signals.

In peacetime, most signals, whether visual or audible, between merchant ships or from them to the shore, were on a one-to-one basis, whereas naval communication was often to a number of vessels in a group, as with a squadron of warships operating together.

One notable exception arose with wartime convoys when merchant ships and their escorts assembled before sailing and the *Convoy Commodore called a meeting of all the masters, radio officers and the *Escort Commander. At this **Convoy Conference** anything concerning the conduct of the convoy was discussed and a most important part was that of flag signals and the use of the ship's whistle between the Commodore's ship and his charges.

At sea, radio messages from ashore could be received, but ships in convoy maintained radio silence to avoid giving away their presence to the enemy. At convoy assembly ports, flags and the signal lamp were extensively used, resulting in officers at sea during WW2 becoming very proficient at signalling.

TRANSMITTING INFORMATION AT SEA.

Three methods, flags, light and radio, have principally been used at sea to transmit information between ships, and between ships and the shore. The use of the first two has largely been superceded by the third as the technology has improved and, with one or two exceptions, they have become obsolescent or obsolete.

FLAGS

Ships flew many flags for different purposes. Some were **worn** as part of their *colours and others **flown** to convey information. For the latter purpose they were usually signal flags, the importance of which has steadily declined as the availability of the radiotelephone has increased. Since the end of about the third quarter of 20th century the use of flags at sea has diminished considerably in importance and flag etiquette has little meaning today except in some cruise liners. However there is still a legal requirement to show national colours on certain occasions.

Three factors which have largely done away with almost any flag etiquette:

(i) Many modern shipowners have little or no pride in their ships.

(ii) The proliferation of rod radio aerials and other electronic gadgets cluttering-up masts.

(iii) Frequently, the need to pay overtime to crew when involved 'after hours'. (Sunset, when colours are lowered usually falls well after normal working hours in port.)

Colours. The term has two related meanings:

(i) The flags normally 'worn' by a ship, mostly in port and sometimes at sea.

(ii) The name for the ceremony at which the colours are hoisted and lowered.

(The word 'ceremony' is used here with reservation because in many tramp ships there was certainly no ceremony and little attempt made to observe any semblance of flag etiquette at all.)

A British merchant ship's colours, (or 'suit of colours') consisted of:

(i) **Ensign.** Her national ensign, usually the **Red Ensign,** was worn aft on the ensign staff at the *taffrail when in port or at anchor, and at the mainmast gaff when under way. (**The gaff** is the relatively short staff angled at about 45° from the mast from which it lies in a fore and aft direction. In a sailing ship a sail, the spanker, is supported by it.)

(ii) **House flag.** Her company's house flag worn at the mainmast head (or at the one masthead in a ship with a single mast). If the masthead was cluttered with electronic instruments or short radio aerials – frequently the case in recent years – it was worn at the starboard yardarm unless it was already occupied by a 'superior' flag. A charterer's flag might be flown in addition to, or in lieu of, the owner's house flag.

(iii) **Stem Jack.** In port a stem jack was often also worn and this was usually either a small version of the company's house flag or a flag known as the *pilot jack.

The colours' ceremony. In liner companies it was usual in port to observe the customary times of hoisting the colours (0800) and lowering them (sunset) and to do so with all flags being hoisted or lowered at the same time if possible. This was achieved by stationing an apprentice (sometimes a deck rating) at each flag and for a junior officer on the bridge to blow a mouth whistle at the appropriate time. (In some passenger ships a bugle, or a recording of one, was played instead.) If it was not practical to hoist and lower flags together then it was acceptable to lower them one at a time, but the ensign was always first up and last down.

Commodore's burgee. The senior master in the larger British shipping companies was generally given the courtesy title, 'Commodore' and accorded the privilege of flying a special Commodore's burgee. It was usually the company's house flag with a swallowtail. As there are so few British ships and shipping companies of any note today the title of Commodore, and the burgee, are now rarely to be seen. (In the last quarter of the 20th century a P & O **Chairman's burgee** was introduced, to be flown when the Chairman went aboard one of the Company's ships – sadly this was one of P & O's final expressions of pride and ceremonial before its disappearance as one of the last great British shipping companies.)

Pilot Jack. A flag comprising a *Union flag with a white border. Little used latterly as a stem jack, and Orient Line was one of the last companies to use it consistently. (It had an entirely different significance if flown from the mast or above the bridge when it indicated that the ship required a pilot.)

Union flag. The national flag of Great Britain, commonly known as the **Union Jack.** However, in a maritime sense the term Union Jack is used only when it is worn as a stem jack, as on warships of the Royal Navy.

Blue ensign. Although the Red Ensign was the usual ensign for a British merchant ship, a Blue Ensign was worn by some ships instead. This could arise when a special warrant had been issued by the Admiralty after certain special conditions had been met. At one time, and the regulations did vary from time to time, the requirement was that the vessel had to be commanded by an officer of Her Majesty's Royal Naval Reserve with a specified number of the ship's officers similarly commissioned. The requirement was later altered to require only the former provision.

Defaced ensigns. Vessels owned by Port Authorities and other official bodies often wore a red or a blue ensign 'defaced' (the correct term) with its coat of arms or other badge in the fly. Also, Government owned ships flew the appropriately defaced Blue Ensign of the Department for which they operated, e.g. for Ministry of Transport owned troopships the ensign depicted a wheel in the fly. Several yacht clubs had defaced ensigns too.

Courtesy ensign. Another important flag commonly flown while in a foreign port was a courtesy ensign but it did not form a part of a ship's 'suit of colours'. This was normally flown at the starboard yardarm as a mark of respect for the country in which the vessel was lying. Although originally an act of courtesy it became a necessity in some countries where the lack of it was regarded as sufficiently offensive to warrant sanctions against the ship. The courtesy ensign was normally the country's merchant ensign if it had a separate one, otherwise its national flag. (Countries within the so-called, post WW2, Soviet block wrongly flew the national flag as a courtesy ensign even when a country had a merchant ensign. In the UK this meant that they wrongly flew the Union flag instead of the Red Ensign for this purpose.)

Destination flag. It was once common practice on the North Atlantic during the heyday of the Trans-Atlantic passenger liner, but only to a lesser extent elsewhere, to fly the national flag of the foreign country next to be visited. It was flown from the foremast before sailing.

The International Code of Signals. Early in the 19th century Sir Popham Home devised a system of flag signals for merchant ships. Captain Marryat improved upon it and introduced his *Code of Signals for the Merchant Service*, first published in 1817. The International Code of Signals was developed following a Board of Trade initiative published in 1857, and included 70,000 signals based on 18 flags. It received several revisions, principally in 1932 and 1965 (the latter after responsibility for it was taken over by the International Maritime Organisation (IMO). It provided many combinations of flags that could be hoisted together or separately to convey a message provided in the code book. Simple messages using a single flag, or two in combination taken from this code, were in general use in merchant ships but more complex flag signalling was largely restricted to use between warships, rarely being seen in the Merchant Service.

This method of signalling was naturally restricted to the range of visibility but it is still common to see a ship displaying one of a few but important single letter flag signals remaining in use to convey a simple message, such as 'G' flag meaning, 'I require a pilot', or 'H' flag, 'I have a pilot on board'. A small number of two flag signals remain in reasonably common use but for most purposed all other flag signalling to or from merchant ships has almost completely disappeared. (There was also a naval code incorporating some different flags, in use by the Royal Navy.)

Blue Peter. 'P' flag from the International Code of Signals signifying, 'I am about to sail, within 24 hours'.

The Yellow Peril. The International Code flag 'Q' but this name was a complete misnomer as it meant, 'my ship is healthy and I request a free pratique' (medical clearance).

'M' flag. The flag in the International Code of Signals for a ship having a doctor on board. (Ships of the P & O flew this flag in Tilbury Docks to indicate to other ships in the port the availability of a doctor in an emergency.)

'TE'. The two flag group in the 1931 International Code of Signals meant, 'you should proceed at slow speed while passing the vessel or station making the signal.' It was often flown by a ship in port lying at a busy river berth if concerned that ships might pass at a speed that could impose a dangerous strain on the mooring ropes. (Replaced in the 1969 code book by 'RY').

'WAY'. The three flag group from the 1934 addition to the 1931 Code Book meaning, 'I wish you a pleasant voyage or passage'. It was often flown by one ship wishing another 'Bon Voyage'. (Replaced in the 1969 Code Book by 'UW').

Making her number. This expression meant that a four-flag signal from the International Code of Signals, allocated to a ship when registered to indicate her name and nationality, was being flown to identify her. These four flags were usually kept permanently joined together, bent on ready for hoisting. They were often used on entering port, on meeting another ship at sea or being challenged by a warship. British ships' numbers began with the letter 'G' or 'M'. It is one of the few exceptions to the earlier statement regarding the obsolescent multi-flag signals.

Other flags flown from time to time:

A Royal Mail pennant. A white triangular flag with a red crown and the words 'Royal Mail'. It was flown by ships carrying mails under contract to the UK Government. When other mail was carried, the flag 'Y' in the International Code of Signals was sometimes flown.

A Regimental flag. When carrying a battalion of a regiment in peacetime, a troopship flew the appropriate regimental flag at the yardarm.

Special flags. There were occasions when a ship might fly an unfamiliar flag, or fly a familiar flag for an unusual reason, e.g. a ship bearing the name of a place sometimes flew the flag of that place. The *Columbus Queensland* flew the flag of that Australian State and there were other examples. In Singapore the troopship *Empire Fowey* flew the flag of the Royal Engineers which has adopted her.

There were also some interesting variations on the customary usage of stem jacks and house flags:

Brocklebank ships wore their house flag on the foremast instead of the mainmast.

Lamport and Holt ships wore a stem jack bearing the City of Liverpool Coat of Arms in recognition of the Company's contribution to the city's economic prosperity from 1845 onwards.

Clan Line ships wore a stem jack consisting of the tartan of the Scottish clan after which they were named. This was later discontinued, it being understood that Lord Lyon, the Scottish King of Arms, prohibited it for heraldic reasons.

H.Hogarth & Sons ships wore the Scottish white St Andrew's cross on a blue ground either as a stem jack or from the yardarm.

New Zealand Shipping Company ships wore a red, white and blue pennant above their house flag, and continued to do so right up to the time the company was absorbed into P & O. This was a hangover from the days when it was difficult to distinguish an early steamship with sails from a sailing ship – the former wore the pennant.

Cunard White Star ships. Following the amalgamation of the Cunard and White Star Lines in the 1930s their ships wore the house flags of the original companies, one above the other. White Star ships flew their original flag superior to that of Cunard and vice versa.

Ellerman Lines comprised a number of separate companies whose ships wore a dual house flag. It consisted of a pennant (with the letters J.R.E.) superior to an individual house flag for each member of the Group.

Miscellaneous terms:

Semaphore. The method of sending a message using the semaphore code by means of a signalman using two flags, each diagonally halved in red and yellow, attached to wooden handles and displayed in association with arm movements. It was never popular in the Merchant Service, unlike the Royal Navy where its use continued until the latter part of the 20th century.

Spoke. This term originated in the days of sail and flag signalling, when a message was passed between two ships, or between a ship and a shore station, consisting of the ship's name and where bound, often with little or nothing more. It was also used later when signalling was by lamp and after a similar signal exchange. In each case it was usual to make a log entry such as, 1745. Spoke *Queen Mary*, bound New York. The last known position of many a missing ship was often recorded only because she had spoken with another on the high seas.

Rags. Flags were sometimes referred to by this unworthy name.

By light

Signal lamps. Two types were common on merchant ships and certificated deck officers were required to understand and use the Morse Code for signalling by light at a speed of six words per minute. Messages were rarely exchanged at more than eight. This was slow compared with the requirement in the Royal Navy for specialist signalmen but was generally adequate for merchant ships limited use.

The Aldis lamp. Large naval type searchlights with shutters for use with the Morse Code were very rarely seen in merchant ships. For many years the hand-held Aldis lamp was largely used. Externally it consisted of a hand-held lamp housing with a pistol-type handle containing an on-off switch and a trigger, a low-powered telescope and a length of insulated electric cable.

Internally it comprised a high-powered bulb in front of a reflector that could be moved by the operation of the trigger. By this means a powerful beam of light could be momentarily directed by one operator to another in the distance. This highly directional light momentarily gave the distant operator a brief flash of light when the trigger was pulled and by means of which a Morse Code signal could be sent. It was bright enough for both day and night use and the lamp could be powered either directly from ship's supply or by its own portable battery. (It was not unknown for a meanly inclined OOW on the bridge of a passenger ship to shine this bright light directly at amorous couples 'hiding' under lifeboats. They rarely, if ever, thought to look above the level of the deck on which they were performing!).

The 'all-round' signal light. Ships were also fitted with a non-directional all-round white light on a short staff above the bridge, operated by a Morse key in the wheelhouse. It could be used when the intention was to signal all ships or shore stations in sight or to signal to one only when there were no others in visible range. (It was often also triggered by the operation of the sound signal apparatus (whistle or siren) so as to provide a visual, as well as a sound, signal for 'alter course' and fog signals.)

What ship? Where bound? It was common for the OOW of a ship meeting another at sea, to call up and make this enquiry. Sometimes the two-way exchange would extend to a wider enquiry as to cargo being carried and other points of general interest. It also provided an opportunity for signalling practice.

Naval/Merchant ship signal exchanges. Upon meeting a British warship at sea it was to be expected that a British merchant ship would be **called up** by lamp and, circumstances permitting, be drawn into a signalling exercise, the results of which were often passed by the Admiralty to the vessel's owners.

Heliograph. A simple mirror and sighting device carried in lifeboats during WW 2 to attract the attention of a potential rescue ship or aircraft by reflecting the sun's rays. In common with many of the wartime rescue and survival provisions heliographs remained in lifeboats for some time after the war ended.

BY RADIO

Note that the word **wireless** was used for many years but was later superseded by 'radio'.

Wireless Telegraphy (W/T). Flags or light transmission were the usual and only methods for communications at sea until about the end of the 19th century. Marconi was largely responsible for developing wireless as a practical means of communication in 1895 and it was first used for distress at sea in 1889 following the collision between a cargo ship and the East Goodwin Light Vessel. It then steadily improved in quality and range to become the long-range communications method of summoning assistance at sea in an emergency – the *Titanic*'s distress message being perhaps the most publicised case.

Following Marconi's further successful experiments early in the 20th century transmitters and receivers became more frequently fitted in ships. They were originally huge items of equipment and required a large compartment of their own. Wireless signals were transmitted in **Morse Code** using a Morse key, the device used by the operator to originate the pulse converted into radio frequencies by the transmitter. They were then converted by a radio receiver into an audible series of dots and dashes. This transmission system became known as wireless telegraphy.

Specially trained operators were essential for its effective use and they usually transmitted and received these Morse signals at a rate of about 16 to 20 words per minute.

Regular schedules were kept with specified shore radio stations which were used to pass messages to other ships out of range of the transmittingship, and to the ships' owners, agents and others ashore concerned with the ship's operation.

Under the **Area Scheme** the world was divided into areas controlled by radio stations at Portishead, Halifax, Cape Town,

Vancouver, Singapore, Wellington, Colombo and Sydney. A Radio Officer (R/O) would notify each area station when his ship moved from one to another so that traffic, (i.e. messages from owners and personal telegrams) could be forwarded to the appropriate area station. An R/O would listen to a roll call of ships' call signs every 4 hours. After the roll call, the coast station would await a call from any ship picking up its own call sign and would then transmit any messages to hand. Upon acknowledgment of receipt that ship's call sign would not appear on the next roll call 4 hours later.

The great advantage of the Area Scheme for British ships was that they could contact their local area station at any time, day or night, with a comparatively low power transmitter, unlike some others – Norwegian ships, for example – which needed much more powerful transmitters to enable them to make contact from anywhere in the world. The principal Area Stations in the United Kingdom with whom R/Os were most frequently working were Portishead Radio in Somerset, Niton Radio in the Isle of Wight and Rugby Radio in the Midlands. They were operated by the Post Office. Portishead Radio was the only H/F (high frequency) U.K. radio station for long distance communication but for local communication on M/F (medium frequency) on 500 kc/s there was a network of coastal radio stations, the busiest being North Foreland Radio, Niton Radio and Lands End Radio but also Wick Radio, Humber Radio, and Liverpool Radio amongst others. They could be used up to a distance of about 500 miles of the U.K. coast – further at night – for ship-to-shore traffic of all kinds. They also transmitted regular weather and navigation reports. Rugby transmitted a time signal (necessary for rating the ship's chronometer) at very low frequency, 15 kc/s, but was not able to receive messages

From about the middle of the 20th century the term 'Wireless' began to be replaced in almost every situation by 'Radio', although the W/T system of transmission retained its original name. Slight confusion ensued at first because voice transmission became known as *Radio Telephony (R/T). Today, all radio communication is by R/T; *Morse code and *W/T have now been superseded for radio communication.

Radio watches. These were kept at specified times (GMT) in different areas of the world and to facilitate this Radio Room clocks kept GMT. They had four three-minute sectors marked on them to indicate silence periods when they were required not to transmit but to listen for any distress messages. Two sectors (15-18 & 45-48 minutes past the hour) were marked in red and designated W/T silence periods and another two, in green (00-03 & 30-33 minutes past the hour) were for Radiotelephone (R/T) silence periods. For listening on 500 kilocycles (the international distress frequency) the hours of duty for a single operator ship were two on, two off, starting at 0800 and finishing at 2200. If there was a distress situation an R/O would remain on watch until it ended.

For much of the time at sea in wartime radio silence was observed, but a continuous listening watch had to be maintained and most foreign-going ships then carried three R/Os for this purpose. However, if a ship sailed short-handed with only two R/Os, each would be expected to do a 12-hour watch every day.

Auto-alarm. As a single R/O could not maintain a continuous radio watch the auto-alarm was invented some time after the *Titanic* disaster. Designed to activate when it received a special signal sent by a coast station, or by a ship in distress, it alerted the R/O to switch on and man his equipment. Having been alerted to a distress situation, the R/O would listen on 500 kc/s for the message and would then decide whether to report it to the bridge or, if clearly inappropriate, to disregard it and reset the auto-alarm. Automatic keying device (AKD). This was a sending device for use as a last resort when a ship was sinking and the master ordered the R/O to abandon ship. It was battery powered and keyed the emergency (battery powered) transmitter sending SOS 3 times, followed by the ship's call sign, followed by a number of 4-second dashes to set off any Auto Alarm receivers on nearby ships. It kept repeating this signal until either the batteries were exhausted or the ship sank.

Radio Telephony (R/T). It was not until about the 1960s that the radiotelephone, as a means of general communication between merchant ships and between them and shore stations, came into general use, but in succeeding years it steadily superseded all the earlier methods. Although its use was slowly being introduced into merchant ships shortly after the mid-20th century it was not until after about the 1980s, with the development of satellites, that its range and value increased dramatically. It is used extensively today, to pass messages between ships and between ships and the shore.

General Maritime Distress & Safety System (GMDSS). All the Post Office radio stations have now closed down and modern communication systems providing worldwide coverage using R/T have done away with the need for them. Long-range radio communication now involves satellites, tele-printers, faxes and the Internet, together with the General Maritime Distress & Safety System that requires a much lower level of training to operate satisfactorily.

Radio operators (See also Radio Officers in Chapter 2). Until comparatively recently marine radio equipment required a good deal of intensive training for its operation, and the training of specialist operators, was carried out by a number of colleges which grew up for this purpose. However, there were only a few radio companies that specialised in providing equipment and the operators for British ships, of which Marconi Marine was the largest. The employment of these radio operators remained largely in the hands of the specialist radio companies who then hired them out, with their equipment, to most of the shipping companies. Only a small number of shipping companies chose to employ their own radio operators. (Some small ships did not carry specially trained radio operators where their masters and mates were licensed to operate the equipment, some not even being fitted with W/T).

Ordinary Seaman and Wireless Watcher. Before auto alarms became available one way of getting over the problem of keeping a continuous watch on the Distress frequency in ships carrying only one Radio Officer, was to train an ordinary seaman to listen for urgent signals. He was then signed on in this dual capacity and spent part of his time in the Radio Room.

Wireless aerials. During most of the review period after the introduction of wireless at sea, the main aerial, comprising copper wires fitted with large porcelain insulators at each end, was spread suspended between the masts, with a down lead to the Radio Room.

Safety link. During times of hostilities the aerial for the main transmitter was fitted with a weak link so that if a ship was mined or torpedoed, and the explosion caused the masts to whip, it was less likely that the aerial itself would be parted. Doxford diesel engines in particular, fitted in a large number of cargo ships, could set up very significant vibration, especially when 'light ship' so these safety links remained in use long after hostilities ended.

Radio aerials – private. The crew frequently had their own broadcast radio receivers, often with short wave reception. To obtain worthwhile reception in a steel vessel an outside aerial was almost essential. Often the only means of achieving this was to hang a piece of wire from the end of a length of wood stuck out through a scuttle (porthole). The untidy appearance brought about by many such aerials often prohibited their use in port in passenger ships. (Woe betides the cabin occupant discovered by the chief officer to have failed to dismantle his aerial before arrival). The introduction of air conditioning in crew accommodation with its need for permanently closed scuttles, brought this practice to an end. However, personal aerials were replaced by a ship-fitted communal aerial amplifier system with outlet sockets in every cabin; and in some cases 'piped' radio also overcame the problem.

Spark transmitter. Before the introduction of more powerful valve operated radio transmitters ships were fitted with spark transmitters.

On watch on 'five ton'. Listening in on 500 kilocycles, the international distress, calling and answering frequency. (This was more a term used by amateur radio buffs than professional R/Os.)

SOS. Contrary to popular belief, the International W/T distress signal owes nothing to the letters being the initial of 'Save Our Souls'. (In other languages the initial letters of different words does not make up SOS.) In the Morse Code the letter 'S' was transmitted as a series of three dots and 'O' as three dashes, making the signal ... − − − ... (This is an easily transmitted group of letters, distinctive and simply remembered by those unfamiliar with the code). SOS was adopted following the Second International Wireless Conference in Berlin in 1906. When the Titanic sank it was used together with the previous British distress signal CQD. (Using R/T today the International R/T distress signal is **MAYDAY**, spoken three times. It comes from 'M'aidez' the French for 'Help me'.)

The radio shack. This name shack dates from the very early days of radio at sea, when ship owners did not know what to make of the new-fangled equipment and where to place the wireless operator in the ship's hierarchy. Was he simply a member of the crew, or was he a junior officer?

As there was rarely a spare cabin available for the R/O, a rough wooden lean-to was frequently hastily added at the after end of the boat deck. Often this was a combined radio room and sleeping cabin which, because of its match-boarding construction, was christened 'The shack' and the name stuck for many years. Later, the Radio Room was situated in the amidships accommodation, usually close to the bridge, and the R/O's cabin was placed adjacent to it, but the name tended to live on.

Radar hut. After radar was invented many of the ships to which it was fitted during and after WW2 had a special radar 'hut' built to accommodate it. This was another example of a late addition and in most cases it was fitted above the bridge and abaft the *monkey island.

In time, radar equipment became much more compact and small desk-mounted sets were easily accommodated in the wheelhouse or chartroom. As a result separate radar huts were no longer required.

Bentley's Code. A commercial code transmitted by W/T, which significantly abbreviated commercial messages between owners and their ships. Its object was to reduce the costs of messages sent through coastal Post Office radio stations which made a charge, except for safety messages, usually based upon the number of words in a message.

Company Codes. Some companies had their own confidential supplement to Bentley's Code. The object was to enable them to convey commercially sensitive information to their ships and vice-versa without it being understood by others.

Q Codes. This was a group of alphabets designed to save time and effort when using Morse code. Q Codes were used throughout the Services, but broadly speaking the Merchant Navy was allocated the alphabets QRA to QRZ, QSA to QSZ, QTA to QTZ and QUA to QUZ. It was an international language and the meaning of every single one had to be learnt by heart by Radio Officers, although many of them were never used in practice. For example, QRA stood for, 'What is the name of your station (ship)?' What no R/O ever wanted to hear was 'QSD' which meant, 'Your keying is defective'.

CHAPTER EIGHTEEN

Shipping Companies and their Ships

Today, many shipowners have companies owning single ships as a legal convenience, and are interested in them solely as investments, taking little or no part in their operation. The company management, the manning of the ships and the fixing of their cargoes is entrusted to others, many with a reputation varying from indifferent to disgraceful. In most cases the ships are registered under flags of convenience to minimise cost and responsibilities.

During the review period ship owning was a source of enormous pride to many highly respected shipowners. Often the shareholders in these companies valued their association, not simply as investments, but with a sense of great satisfaction in contributing to Britain's prowess in world trade.

There were hundreds of British shipping companies over those very successful years of British shipping. Many of these companies ranged from quite small firms, sometimes with little more than an owner/master of a small coaster, to huge conglomerates with some of the world's finest ships. More than one British shipping company, with its associated subsidiaries, owned over a hundred ocean-going ships and in a very large number of those companies the directors and management took an active part in their day-to-day operation. This was the era of the shipowner in every sense of the word, with a huge proportion of the world's tonnage under the Red Ensign. Cunard, P & O, Orient Line, Ellermans, Clan Line, Union Castle, amongst others, were household names in Britain and many of these companies were served by sea and shore staff who expressed great loyalty to their employers who took good care of them in return. Their masters, officers and seamen frequently also expressed pride in their companies and many served for their entire careers with one company. But there were others companies that operated sound ships with good crew but were less concerned with their employees' welfare and were hard taskmasters.

When a shipping company is mentioned in this book it is generally by its common or abbreviated name, it being felt unnecessary to give them their full title. Their full names usually included a reference to their maritime activities such as 'xyz Steamship Co. Ltd.,' 'xyz Shipping Ltd.', 'xyz Tanker Co. Ltd.', 'xyz Steam Navigation Co. Ltd.' But some used a trading name such as 'Shaw Savill Line' for 'Shaw Savill & Albion Co. Ltd'.

The companies almost always enjoyed limited liability, their names ending with Ltd. but a rare exception to this suffix was P & O Steam Navigation Company, a company incorporated under Royal Charter in 1840.

It is perhaps not surprising that many shipping companies acquired nicknames and some had a less-than-complimentary one. The prefix 'Hungry' was applied to several companies, principally tramp ship owners, sometimes with justification; but not all nicknames related to food, particularly where the liner companies were concerned. In some cases the nickname was not actually of the company itself but was related to some aspect of it.

Some of the most familiar nicknames:
Two of fat and one of lean. T & J Harrison, due to the funnel marking consisting of three coloured bands, the top and bottom of which were white and the middle one red. Their ships were known as **Apple Daddy boats** – this was a reference to a frequent dessert upon the menu. Also **Tom and Jerry's** (from its initial letters), **The Jam Butty Line** and **Hungry Harrisons.**
Hungry Harrisons. J & C Harrison, London. Another Hungry Harrison. A major tramp company.

Hungry Goose Line. Trinder Anderson. Although feeding may have had some bearing on this nickname, the funnel marking of a black swan perhaps invited it.

Are you (U) Sorry Now? (AUSN) Australian United Steam Navigation Co. The nickname suggests regret on joining the company.

Blue Flue. Alfred Holt ships usually had very large and prominent funnels painted pale blue, with a black top. In Liverpool, their home port, the company was known as The **China Line** for a time and **The Birkenhead Navy**, with its ships often being referred to as **Blueys.** Also, **Welsh Navy** on account of the number of Welsh officers in the company and a little unfairly, **Adolf Hitler Line** from the initial letters of the company's name.

Maggie Booths. Booth Line, a Liverpool based company running to South America which frequently loaded and discharged at ports a long way up the Amazon.

Hungry Hogarths. The house flag of H. Hogarth & Sons, Glasgow (also known as the Baron Line because of the names of its ships) displayed the two letters 'H' 'H'. Its ships were considered by some to be hard-working vessels and poor feeders.

Muck & Misery. MacLay & MacIntyre. Its nickname, also from its initial letters. A Glasgow tramp ship company.

The Three Rs. Ropners, Runcimans & Reardon Smiths were three of the best known of the well-established tramp companies, but reference to The Three Rs was not always complementary.

Ropner's Navy. Ropner Shipping Company of Darlington. One of the three companies comprising *The Three R's. It was a major British tramp company.

Cardiff Cunard. Reardon Smith Line. Another of *The Three R's and a major Cardiff company owning tramp ships whose funnels bore some likeness to the Cunard funnel with its red with a black top, although lacking the two or three black bands. Also simply **Smiths of Cardiff** and **Starvation Smiths.**

Slow Starvation & Agony. Shaw Savill & Albion. Most who sailed in their ships would not see this as a justified epithet but the nickname is another derived from the initial letters. Also **Shaw Swivel.**

Better Times are Coming. The **B**ritish **T**anker **C**ompany.

Peculiar & Ornamental. P & O Steam Navigation Company. Yet another name derived from the initial letters in a company's name and, in this case, also sounding similar. The term was used in a somewhat derisory manner particularly when referring to its officers whose rank braid on their uniforms, and their cap badge, was unusual. The derision also arose because they tended to consider themselves as serving in Britain's premier shipping company, the 'kid-glove line', and thus a cut above others at sea except those in the Royal Navy. Also **Poverty & Ostentation.**

Grey Funnel Line. A name often used to describe the Royal Navy whose warships, including their funnels, were painted grey.

Paddy Hendersons. P.Henderson & Co. a respected Glasgow company running passenger ships to Rangoon

Lousy and Hungry. Lamport and Holt, a respected Liverpool company.

Chatty Chapmans. Chapman & Willan, a Newcastle tramp company.

The Lavender Hull Mob. Union Castle Line. The colour of the hulls of their ships prompted the play upon the name of a 1951 film comedy, *The Lavender Hill Mob*. Also **Union Screw, Union Arse'ole** and **Union Cattle** (in South Africa), the latter two because of the somewhat similar pronunciation of the second word; and occasionally, **Blackwall Navy.**

The Shipping Company. The New Zealand Shipping Co. was frequently referred to simply by the abbreviated name preceded by the definite article.

The Union Company. The Union Steam Ship Company of New Zealand. Also, **Usually Sail Saturday** – shipowners liked to see their ships sail on a Saturday to avoid an idle weekend in port. This desire was completely reversed by the crew of their ships with their often muttered, 'Six days shalt thou labour and on the seventh proceed to sea' when they missed out on their Saturday night party ashore.

Joe Shell. Shell Tankers. Earlier the company was called Anglo Saxon Petroleum and then abbreviated to **Anglo-Sax.**

Every Sucker Signs Once. (ESSO) Esso Petroleum. Also, **Even Skippers Skin Out.** and vulgarly as **Eat, Sleep, Shit & Overtime.**

Please Send New Crew (PSNC). Pacific Steam Navigation Company. Also **Please Send No Cowboys.**

Hungry Hain. The Hain Steamship Company, a part of the P & O Group, ran a fleet of tramp ships, each with a large, white 'H' on a black funnel. Also **Hain of St Ives** (The company was formed in this small Cornish port).

Refuge For Alcoholics (RFA). Royal Fleet Auxiliary. Also **Roughest Fleet Afloat.**

Scottish Navy. The Clan Line. Its officers' ranks were denoted by cuff braid having a curl on the top stripe, similar to that of Royal Navy officers, although it was not the only company to have this braid distinction. Its ships were all named after Scottish clans but it was only one of several companies that could lay claim to the being Scottish. Ben Line with its ships registered in Leith was also sometimes known by the name.

Branch Line. The abbreviated form of 'The P & O Branch Line' and its name was used to distinguish its services from those of the parent company. P & O bought Lund's Blue Anchor Line not long after the disappearance of the latter's ill-fated passenger ship *Warratah* off South Africa in 1909, lost with all her passengers and crew on her maiden voyage. The newly acquired ships were then manned by P & O officers and ran to Australia, principally via the Cape, but were operated separately from the rest of the fleet for many years.

P-Nought B-One. P & O and BI Joint Service to India. The nickname may not be immediately obvious but is a play upon the similarity between nought (the numeral zero) & the letter 'O' and also between the letter 'I' & the numeral '1' (one).

MANZ Line. Montreal, Australia and New Zealand Line. This was more a service than a separate shipping company (but it had its own house flag) and resulted from three shipping companies, Port Line, Ellerman Lines and The New Zealand Shipping Company each contributing ships for a service from the East Coast of North America to Australia and New Zealand. For a time the Canadian manned *Ottawa Valley* was also on the run.

Hedlams Bedlam. Headlam & Son. Whitby. Tramp ship owners. Also **Hoodlum & Boodlum.**

Japanese Harrisons. Mitsui OSK, Japan. No connection with the British company but its ships had similar funnel markings to T & J Harrison.

London Greeks. The London shipping community had a number of Greek shipowners with offices in the City and ships on the British Registry. Some were single ship owners but others, including Counties Ship Management and London & Overseas Freighters owned or operated substantial fleets.

Medway Turks. Crescent Shipping Ltd.

The Liners. Manchester Liners Ltd, Manchester. Their home port necessitated their vessels constantly transiting the Manchester Ship Canal.

Wilson's parrots. Ships of Ellerman's Wilson Line of Hull carried some of the multi-colours of the bird after which they were named. Their hulls were green and their funnel red with a black top.

Stevie Clarkes. Stephenson Clarke Ltd. London, coaster operators.

Spanish Navy. McAndrew & Co whose small, white ships ran regularly to Spain.

Cauliflower on the funnel, nothing on the table. Prince Line. A reference to the Prince of Wales' feathers on the funnel.

Early Death Lines. Elder Dempster Lines. Their run was to

West Africa, notorious for being fever ridden. Their ships were also known as **monkey boats** in Liverpool. Also **Every Day Labour** and **Elder Gangster.**

The Lavatory Brush Line. Palm Line. This was a reference to the palm-tree logo on the funnel.

Glasgow Greeks. J&J Denholms, Glasgow. Another major tramp company, albeit with no particular association with Greek shipowners.

Happy Pappy's. Ellerman & Papayanni. Their small ships running to Portugal were known as the 'market boats' because they were back in Liverpool every fortnight with produce.

Crook Line. Indian crew name for Brocklebank Line.

John Robs Everybody. Ellerman Lines. The company's house flag, a pennant, bore the founder's initials, JRE. Also Jews Rule England.

Green & Slimey Weir. R.H. Green and Siley Weir, a London ship repair company, rather than a shipping company.

Also associated with shipping companies were:

The monkey and the nut. The Cunard Line officers' cap badge was sometimes referred to in this way because it depicted a lion with its forepaw on a globe of the world.

The little red monkey. The slightly disrespectful name for the red lion rampant on the Clan Line house flag. (The officers' cap badge had a similar silver lion rampant).

The ships of some companies also gained nicknames. Some were:

Slow greens. Union Steamship Company's cargo ships. Many were relatively slow and had dark green hulls latterly.

The Yellow Perils. The name by which the ships of F.T Everard & Sons were known, on account of their yellow hulls. Also **The 'ITY'** line on account of its ship names almost all ending in those letters, e.g. *Serenity.*

The Navvies. The ships of General Steam Navigation Company were often collectively referred to by this name.

The Treacle tankers. Ships of the United Molasses fleet involved in the molasses trade.

The sugar boats. Ships of Tate & Lyle.

The paper boats. The ships of Bowater & Co.

The Guinness boats. The small, specialised coastal tankers operated by the Dublin brewer from Ireland to Liverpool.

Butter Boats. The small reefer ships of Associated Humber Lines that plied between the ports of Hull/Goole and Copenhagen were known locally by this name because their return cargoes were mainly Danish butter and other dairy produce.

Banana Boats. Reefer ships that carried banana, particularly those of Elders & Fyffe. Also known, as **skin boats**, with the term being used more by dockers than seamen.

Bel Boats. C. Smith & Co., a Norwegian company with British connections, specialised in the carriage of heavy lifts with ships built for this trade. Their names all began with Bel, e.g. *Belpareil*.

Beaver Boats. The Canadian Pacific cargo ships whose names at one time were all prefixed by the word 'Beaver'.

Grocer boats. The small, white-hulled ships of McAndrew & Co. which were largely employed in the Mediterranean and generally carried a variety of cargoes which might be seen stocking a grocer's shelves.

The BA flyers. The four, fast refrigerated cargo-passenger ships of the Blue Star Line *Brazil Star, Argentine Star, Paraguay Star* & *Uruguay Star* which ran regularly to South American ports including Buenos Aires.

The love boats. The TV programme *The Love Boat* made it almost inevitable that some of the smaller ships of P & O Princess Cruises that figured in the programme would become known by this name.

Bass boats. The ships of Lambert Brothers which had a red triangle, point up, on the funnel. This was also the logo of Bass beer.

The double Bass boats. The ships of James Nourse & Co.

were distinguished by a circlet of red triangles, point-up, around the funnel. (See previous entry.)

Cork boats. Ships of the British and Continental S.S. Co,

Mosquito boats. The small tankers running between Lake Maracaibo in Venezuela and Aruba/Curacao in the Netherland Antilles.

The Bovril boats. The sludge vessels that dumped much of the sewage from seaport cities at sea. In some places they were known as **Cocoa Boats.**

Blackbirders. The name by which ships in the UK–West Africa trade were sometimes known. In particular, the occasional name of the Nigerian Black Star Line's vessels calling at Bristol, a port which thrived on the slave trade where the term originated a century or two earlier.

Some well-known ships with abbreviated names or nicknames:

The JVO. *Johan Van Oldenbarnevelt.* When the customary exchange took place between ships meeting at sea, What ship? Where bound?, the reply to the first question by this well-known ship on the run from Holland to the Dutch East Indies was JVO and most experienced officers readily understood it. But if it was suspected that the questioner was inexperienced the reply would be, a little unkindly, to spell out the full name of this Dutch passenger ship. The likely outcome was confusion for an inexperienced young officer who would struggle to read each letter and then have to remember them in sequence to sort out the vessel's name. (Her sister ship, sunk during the Second World War, would have been almost as difficult to comprehend. She was the *Marnix Van Sint Aldegonde*.)

Dominion Maniac. The *Dominion Monarch*, Shaw Savill's prewar and early post-WW2 flagship.

The Rotten Banana. The Union S.S. Co.'s ship *Rotomahana*.

Bargain Area. Cunard liner *Barengaria* (ex *Imperator*,) taken over from Germany as WW1 reparations.

The Maurie. Originally the four-funnelled and much loved Cunard liner *Mauretania* but the name was later applied to her successor.

Old Soup Tureen. Cunard liner *Tyrrhenia* later renamed *Lancastria*.

The Green Goddess. Cunard's post-Second World War *Caronia,* built largely for cruising from the USA, whose hull was painted a pleasing shade of green.

The Grey Ghost. The *Queen Mary*'s nickname during WW2. She was also referred to as The Peoples Ship by the Times newspaper when she was still on the stocks at John Brown's yard as Ship No. 534.

The Old Reliable. White Star liner *Olympic,* sister ship of the *Titanic.*

The Magic Stick. White Star liner *Majestic.*

The Great White Whale. During the Falkland Island's War in the 1980s P & O's *Canberra* acquired this name.

Oh Lord Never Again (OLNA). Said to be the despondent utterance of Royal Fleet Auxiliary crews on leaving the tanker *Olna* at the end of their time on board.

The Chocolate Box. Blue Star pre-war cruise ship *Arandora Star.* She had impressive and very appealing lines, painted all white but with her two prominent funnels in the colourful Blue Star Line colours – an ideal picture for a chocolate box.

CHAPTER NINETEEN

Nautical Institutions

There are and were a number of institutions of considerable importance to British merchant seamen, both officers and ratings. Concerned with aspects of their life at sea, particularly training, recreation, employment, and professional standards, many have disappeared with the decline in the number of British seafarers but some remain, albeit with reduced membership. In many cases there has been only a change of name and, where included below, the earlier names have been used. Others have seen little more than a small change in function but are included because of their importance to earlier generations of seafarers. (Training establishments do not appear below as they are to be found in chapter 3).

Two very special organisations providing education for merchant seamen:

Seafarers Education Service. Founded in 1919 the service's principal role was the supplying of books and libraries to ships for the benefit of British merchant seamen. At its height the service provided well over three million books.

The College of the Sea. Run jointly with the Seafarers Education Service, under the auspices of the Marine Society, the College assisted many seafarers to undertake university degrees and certificates of competency through correspondence courses. The name of Dr Ronald Hope will long be remembered in connection with both organisations.

Three miscellaneous organizations, each in a category of its own:

The Merchant Navy Comforts Service. Getting under way in February 1940 as a wartime measure this organization did splendid work during WW2 in providing, principally, warm clothing to merchant seamen who had been torpedoed or were sailing in unhospitable climates, especially those of the Russian convoys. All over the UK, ladies were provided with wool to knit into hats, gloves, socks and sweaters which were then distributed to merchant ships.

The British Ship Adoption Society (BSAS). Founded in 1936, the Society encouraged the association of schools with ships and those that manned them. Pupils visited their adopted ships, and ship's personnel visited the schools during their leave. The decline of the Merchant Service and lack of funds saw the Societies activities decline and it was amalgamated into the Seafarers Education Service in 1976.

Royal Merchant Navy School. The Merchant Seamen's Orphan Asylum was founded in the East End of London in 1827, to provide a home for the destitute children of merchant seamen. It moved later and became the Royal Merchant Seamen's Orphanage, moving again in 1921 to Bearwood near Wokingham in Berkshire where, in 1935, it was renamed Royal Merchant Navy School. Since 1970 it has been an independent school known as Bearwood College, but still provides some places for orphans of merchant seamen.

Some professional associations:

The Honourable Company of Master Mariners. Its stated objects are to promote and further the efficiency of the Sea Service generally and uphold the Status, Dignity and Prestige of Master Mariners in particular. Privileged as the only Livery Company in the City of London not referred to as 'The Worshipful Company of ...', The Honourable Company, founded in 1926, was the first new livery company to be admitted for over 200 years. Membership was restricted to those who had held a *Foreign-Going Masters' Certificate for at least five years but recently provision was made for senior naval officers, corporate and associate membership. Its floating livery hall on the River Thames at Temple Stairs, HQS *Wellington*, was originally a Royal Navy sloop of the same name, built in 1934.

Companies/Societies of Master Mariners. In the Commonwealth, particularly Canada, Australia, New Zealand and South Africa, there are organisations with much the same professional objectives as the *Honourable Company but they differ in not being livery companies. Their membership over the years has largely comprised British officers who have either joined local shipping companies or have *'gone ashore' and settled in these Commonwealth countries.

International Federation of Shipmasters (IFSMA). This organisation, with headquarters in London aboard HQS *Wellington*, represents the professional interests of shipmasters internationally. It is particularly concerned with legislation in the members' countries and its effect upon their roles and responsibilities.

The Nautical Institute. Founded as late as 1972, almost the end of the review period, the work of this organisation warrants inclusion on account of its sterling work for the profession and the high regard in which it is held. It finds a worthy place here as a very active name in the language of the British merchant seaman, with a membership comprising both qualified merchant and naval officers, together with other individuals with a serious interest in the profession. During its short life, now only a little over 35 years, it has endeavoured to maintain, even raise for some, professional standards at sea during an age when for many they are declining abysmally. Its role is not restricted to British interests and is truly international in its work.

Trinity House. The full title of this important organisation is 'The Corporation of Trinity House of Deptford-Strond'. Founded in 1514 by Henry VIII, **TH**, as it is often known to mariners, is both a charitable and a professional body. In its latter role The Trinity House Lighthouse Service is the General Lighthouse Authority for England, Wales, Channel Islands & Gibraltar, responsible for the lighthouses, buoys and other seamarks in those areas. Until comparatively recently it was also the principal pilotage authority for the United Kingdom.

Northern Lighthouse Board. Founded in 1786. In a similar manner to Trinity House, it was the General Lighthouse Authority for Scotland.

Commissioners of Irish Lights. The General Lighthouse Authority for Ireland.

Industry related organisations included:

The Chamber of Shipping. The British shipowners' representative body, concerned with almost all aspects of the industry, nationally and internationally, including legislation. It consults with government departments, seafarers' unions and others on matters affecting the British shipping industry. In 1975 it was amalgamated with the **British Shipping Federation** to become the **General Council of British Shipping**.

British Shipping Federation. Formed during WW2 to make the employment of seamen a less casual affair, it is usually known simply as the **Shipping Federation**, responsible for the recruitment, selection and shore training of most of the ratings employed in the Merchant Service.

The Pool. The common name for the pool of seamen available for employment. It was set up by the *Shipping Federation and operated through the *Shipping Offices around the country.

National Maritime Board. The joint negotiating forum in which pay and conditions of service were discussed by shipowners' and seafarers' representatives, temporarily created in 1917 and set up on a permanent basis in 1919.

The Merchant Navy Training Board. This organisation, consisting of company and union members, was concerned with training and education in the Merchant Service. It formulated policy and liaised with statutory authorities, preparing publications and running courses.

The Merchant Navy Association. Although not belonging to the period with which this book is concerned, it deserves a mention because of the valuable work it has done since being formed in 1989 to seek more recognition and respect for seafaring veterans, life at sea and Britain's maritime history. It was felt that nearly fifty years after the end of WW2 little was understood of the Merchant Navy and the suffering and sacrifice of thousands of wartime merchant seafarers. The Association's aims are the recognition of the Merchant Navy Veteran and the critical and strategic role of the Merchant Navy in times of war and conflict, while acknowledging those seafarers who died in the service of their country. It has developed a strong voice at a national level representing member's views to government and other key organizations, being accepted as part of the community of organisations that care for the interests of ex-service people.

An important United Nations (UN) Agency:
The International Maritime Organisation (IMO). With its headquarters in London the International Maritime Consultative Organisation (IMCO) was born when Britain still had a significant influence on world shipping. A UN conference in 1948 adopted a convention which establishing IMCO in 1958 but 'Consultative' was dropped from its name in 1982 to become IMO. With over 150 Member States, its work involves promoting conventions, most of which are later ratified by the world's maritime nations. Among these conventions some of the most important have been SOLAS (Safety at Sea), the Prevention of Pollution from Ships (MARPOL), the International Regulations for Preventing Collisions at Sea (COLREGS), Standards of Training, Certification and Watch-keeping for Seafarers (STCW) and others concerning load lines and tonnage measurement of ships. IMO also prepares codes and recommendations on a wide range of related subjects, almost all of which are intended to improve safety at sea and the environment in one way and another.

Two markets concerned with shipping:

Although the following two organisations are also still hale and hearty they are included as they played such a vital part with the support, albeit by no means exclusively, of British shipping during the review period.

Lloyd's. The usual name for Corporation of Lloyd,s, the world-renowned insurance market in Leadenhall Street, London, where a substantial part of the British merchant fleet and its cargoes have been insured by marine underwriters. The underwriters operated from their **boxes**, their very small offices where they transacted their business with insurance brokers on the **floor.** With origins in a mediaeval coffee house, it is marketed today as Lloyd's of London.

The Baltic. The abbreviated name by which the Baltic and Mercantile Exchange in St Mary Axe, London, is known throughout shipping circles. In the same way that *Lloyd's provides a market place for insurance business, The Baltic is the market place where shipbrokers, merchants, charterers and those concerned principally with fixing cargoes, freight rates, charters and ship sales, carry out their business on the floor. It has been of considerable importance to British merchant seaman because the business transacted 'on the Baltic' provided the basis of their livelihood.

The British Classification Society:

Lloyd's Register of Shipping. This Classification Society was founded in 1760 and, like Lloyd's, in a coffee house. A member of the **International Association of Classification Societies** (IACS) formed towards the end of the 20th century, it is commonly known simply as LR or as Lloyd's Register, and undertakes the classification of the majority of the British merchant fleet although also classing shipping worldwide. Until recently the world's largest classification society it is probably best known for it's publication of *Lloyd's Register of Shipping* listing details of the world's merchant fleet for which it uses the well-known designation, 100 A 1, for vessels and their machinery which are of its highest order. (Lloyd's Register took-over the British Corporation, a much smaller society, shortly after WW2.)

Maritime museums:

There are two principal maritime museums in the United Kingdom.

The National Maritime Museum. Founded between the two World Wars this museum at Greenwich, London, preserves a huge amount of British maritime history of both the nation's fighting and merchant navies. It is one of the world's leading maritime museums.

Merseyside Maritime Museum. Founded after WW2, this museum at the Albert Dock, Liverpool, has gone from strength to strength in recent years. It is concerned only with merchant shipping in its various forms.

Shipping newspapers:

Between 1875 and 1975 there were two renowned shipping newspapers in the United Kingdom but sadly only one has survived.

Lloyd's List & Shipping Gazette. Published daily except Sundays since 1837 this famous shipping newspaper is believed to be the world's oldest continuously published newspaper. With news, articles and information on shipping movements and casualties, it is usually known simply as *Lloyd's List*.

The Journal of Commerce and Shipping Telegraph. Generally referred to by its first name alone this respected shipping newspaper with offices in Water Street was published in Liverpool from 1861 until 1974 when it was obliged to close as the fortunes of that great port declined.

Shipping registers:

*Lloyd's Register of Shipping**, published by the classification society of the same name, is world renowned but two other less-known publications deserve mention as 'Institutions' because they contributed useful information in their day.

The Mercantile Navy List and Maritime Directory. This listed details of British merchant ships and included the Collectors of Customs & Excise, Superintendents of Mercantile Marine Offices and Registrars of Royal Naval Reserve, together with their office addresses. Examiners of Masters & Mates, and Engineers, Local Marine Boards, Officers approved to supervise the transfer of lascars in the UK, Persons lisenced to engage and supply seamen, and training ships for officers and ratings were also included. First published in 1849 it continued until 1976 (with supplements to the end of 1977) apart from the WW2 years. With the decline of the British merchant fleet it has now ceased publication.

Merchant Ships. The book of this name by E.C.Talbot-Booth first appeared as **British Merchant Ships** in 1934 with fleet lists of British shipping companies and details of their ships. Over 600 profile drawings at 150 feet (45.70m) to the inch (25.4mm) and funnel markings were included. This led in due course to a much larger tome, one and a half inches (40mm) thick, in landscape format, covering the world's merchant ships. With the number of drawings increased to 2200, it was a remarkable undertaking. It also included details of shipping companies and their fleets. There were numerous photographs of ships together with coloured drawings of house flags. So valuable was the book and author's work in helping others to learn ship identification, that during WW2 the subject was taught in the Royal Navy and the book carried in its warships. With the author's death and the high cost of production, the book has since appeared only spasmodically.

Welfare – Hotels, Hostels and Clubs:

The Merchant Navy Welfare Board. The history of coordinating the nautical charities caring for merchant seafarers goes back to 1927 when the **British Council for the Welfare of the Mercantile Marine** (BCWMM) was established. In

1940 the **Seamen's Welfare Board** (SWB) succeeded it and by 1948 had become The Merchant Navy Welfare Board (MNWB) comprising representatives from the shipping industry, the Government and many well-respected marine charities. Concerned with the welfare of British merchant seamen, it coordinated activities at home and overseas, providing many port hostels and later hotels.

Merchant Navy Hotels. A reduction in post-war demand saw many MNWB hostels close but in some of the major ports, including London, Liverpool, Glasgow, Middlesbrough, South Shields, Cardiff, Southampton and Swansea, Merchant Navy Hotels took their place with many seamen and their families taking full advantage of their good facilities. They prospered for a time, along with Clubs at Avonmouth, Milford Haven and the Isle of Grain, but the 1970s decline in Britain's Merchant Navy led to their being closed one by one. The last hotel to go was the very popular London hotel at Lancaster Gate, Bayswater, which closed its doors on 22 December 2002.

Merchant Navy Officers' Clubs. Although some clubs for officers serving in HM Forces have welcomed Merchant Service officers, and many ports had Merchant Navy Clubs during the wars, the club probably best remembered by those who visited it was the Merchant Navy Officers' Club in New York. Situated for a time at the Hotel Astor, it had other homes over the years, and gave comfort and support to the many officers who visited New York, particularly during and shortly after WW2. There was also a London club operating during a similar period, in Rupert Street, off Tottenham Court Rd.

The Cachalots. The name by which the Southampton Master Mariners Club, founded in 1928, is usually known and whose motto translates to 'In all respects ready and prepared'. Appropriately, its ordinary members are **Cachalots**, committee members are **Harpooner**s, the secretary is **The Boatsteerer,** the treasurer **The Storekeeper** and the Club's honorary members are **Stowaways**. The Club continues to provide a welcome to ship's officers although it lacks the glory of its halcyon years when Southampton was host to some of the world's largest liners commanded by many renowned and highly respected masters. It is also known in Southampton shipping circles for its annual **'Sea Pie Supper'.** (The name refers to a favourite dish in sailing ships days.)

British Apprentice Club. This remarkable club in New York, situated in the Hotel Chelsea at 222 West 23rd. Street, provided a home from home for British apprentices and cadets from shortly after WW1 until it closed in the 1970s. It was almost entirely run by volunteers and is remembered with great warmth by many who still vividly recall the outstanding hospitality they received there, particularly during WW2. The names of the Misses Mayo and Newell, the Club's founders, and **Mrs Spaulding**, its long-serving, resident secretary known affectionately to the apprentices as their American mother, will long be remembered.

The Mission to Seamen. Founded in 1855, and commonly known as **The Flying Angel Club,** the Mission to Seamen gave comfort and succour to millions of merchant seamen all over the world. Run under the auspices of the Church of England, its chaplains visited thousands of ships extending a warm welcome regardless of race, religion or creed. In the 1990s, reflecting the impact of equal opportunity of employment in many countries and the resultant changes at sea, it altered its name to **The Mission to Seafarers**. Sometimes referred to as **The flying tab-nab**. (This name reflected the Mission's warm hospitality, so often offered with, amongst other things, *tea and tab-nabs).

British Sailors' Society. Founded in 1825 with similar objectives to the Mission to Seamen but under the auspices of the 'Free churches', this organisation was also to be found in many ports around the world. Known in its early years as The British and Foreign Sailors' Society, later dropping the 'Foreign', it is currently **'The British & International Sailors' Society'.**

Stella Maris. In many ports of the world this renowned seafarers welfare organisation, known as **'The Apostleship of the Sea'**, is supported by the Roman Catholic Church.

Seafarers' Centres. In many ports, the three seamen's welfare organisations mentioned above have combined under one roof to provide Seafarers' Centres.

Seamen's Church Institute. This organisation, run on similar lines to those of the Mission to Seamen, provides support and a place of recreation and devotions for seafarers in the USA.

Seamen's Clubs. In ports where there were no clubs supported by the international welfare organizations there were sometimes other places which provided for seafarers' relaxation ashore. (The Seamen's Club in Shanghai, following the communist take over, was in the renowned Shanghai Club building on the Bund, once the bastion of British snobbery where one's position at the bar was determined by one's occupation or position. Its bar, over 100 feet (30.75 metres) long, was said to have been the longest in the world.)

The Mission. This term was not confined to the Mission to Seamen and was often used by seafarers to refer to all the seamen's welfare organizations, as in, 'I'm going ashore to the mission'. Often abbreviated to **The Mish.**

Chaplains. Ordained ministers in their respective churches, the chaplains in the above organisations were invariably worldly wise, understanding and especially helpful regardless of whether a seaman sought help or called simply to relax in pleasant surroundings ashore and to meet others. Known as Padres, particularly by those who had served in the armed forces, they were sometimes referred to as, **'The Man from the Mission'.**

Mission bum. The welfare organisation mentioned above made a point of welcoming all seamen regardless of their financial situation but a seaman who constantly visited the mission and appeared to take unreasonable advantage of its hospitality when he could reasonably afford other entertainment, was often known by his shipmates as a mission bum.

The Residential Hostel for Marine Officers. At 680 Commercial Road, London, this was opened in 1902 by **The British and Foreign Sailor's Society** (later BSS & BISS) and was sometimes referred to as the **Sailors' Palace.** Many ex-apprentices stayed here when 'up for their second mate's ticket' as the *King Edward VII Nautical School was in the same building.

The Empire Memorial Hostel. Known as **The Stack of Bricks,** this was also a *British Sailors' Society hostel for seamen in the Commercial Road, on the corner of Salmon Lane in the East End of London. It was an impressive building built after WW1 and is now a block of residential apartments.

The Sailors' Home & Red Ensign Club. This establishment in Dock & Ensign Streets, for boarding and lodging officers, seamen and apprentices was once very popular with seamen requiring accommodation not too far from the centre of London. Widely known as **Jack's Palace.**

Seamark Junior Officers (MN Club). Situated in the Minories near Tower Hill and started by the Rev. Tubby Clayton, the founder of Toc-H, this club was appreciated by the many apprentices who stayed there when studying for their mates' and masters' certificates nearby at "Cass's".

The Welsh Embassy. The Sailors' Home in Birkenhead where numerous Welshmen stayed before joining their ships, particularly those of the Blue Funnel Line.

Aulis. The name of the last of the hostels provided over the years by Alfred Holt's Blue Funnel Line in Liverpool for its apprentices, both deck and engine, who were in that city attending courses or standing by a ship in port on Merseyside.

A radio broadcast institution:

The Merchant Navy Programme. Intended as a welfare provision, the BBC broadcast a regular programme during and after WW2 on short-wave radio for those at sea in the Merchant Navy. It was a popular service with a mixture of programmes of interest to seamen, largely about events in Britain. The programme 'Shipmates Ashore', compèred for many years by **Miss Doris Hare** who was awarded an MBE for her services to the Merchant Navy, provided a regular opportunity for families and friends to remember their folk with music requests.

Trades Unions:

Officers' industrial organizations. There is now only one UK officers' union but at one time there were several organizations representing British officers throughout the Empire/Commonwealth, some of which later federated in **The Officers (Merchant Navy) Federation.** Some were:

The China Coast Officers' Guild

The Marine Engineers Guild of China

The Straits Merchant Service Guild

The Merchant Service Guild of Australasia (This later split into an Australian and a New Zealand Guild).

The Navigators and Engineer Officers' Union. (NEOU). This organization has seen a number of amalgamations and name changes. Its birth owes much to the Navigators' & General Insurance Co. whose tenacious and highly respected Captain W.H. Coombs worked so hard helping to establish an effective organization representing Merchant Service officers. In its own words,'… it has worked steadily for the attainment of unity in the Merchant Navy'. In 1956 the NEOU became the **Merchant Navy and Airline Officers Association** (MNAOA), then, the **National Union of Marine, Aviation & Shipping Transport Officers** (NUMAST) when it combined with the *Mercantile Marine Service Association and the **Radio & Electronic Officers Union** in 1985. (In 1990 the flight navigators and engineers transferred to the airline pilots union BALPA). In 2006 there was a further name change to *Nautilus (UK) when it amalgamated with a Dutch organization with similar interests.

Nautilus (UK) actively campaigns with shipowners for better conditions for its officers, and with politicians and the public for greater recognition of the vital role that shipping continues to play in the nations affairs. *The Telegraph,* its well-respected magazine, is widely circulated. (It is the only UK officers' union remaining and the major countries of the Commonwealth all now have their own guilds or unions).

Mercantile Marine Service Association (MMSA). Based in Liverpool and with roots dating back to 1857, this organization was concerned with the commercial interests of shipmasters and officers for many years until the officers became represented by their own union. It continued to represent shipmasters until amalgamating in the latter part of the 20th century with the officers union.

Radio Officers' Union. The Association of Wireless Telegraphists was established in 1912, and after amalgamating with the **Association of Cable Telegraphists** in 1921 it combined their names and was renamed the Radio Officers' Union in 1938. Its final name change in 1967 saw it become **The Radio and Electronics Officers' Union** and it amalgamated with *NUMAST in 1985. This was shortly before *GMDSS did away witha need for radio officers although the growth of shipboard electronics created a need for electronics officers and an opportunity for some ex-radio officers.

The National Union of Seamen (NUS). The ratings union. Originally the **National Amalgamated Sailors' & Firemen's' Union** (1887-1893). In 1926 it was reorganised and renamed The National Union of Seamen, under which name it continued to campaign on behalf of its ratings membership for improved industrial conditions. In 1961 it had almost 89,000 members but its strength substantially diminished with the decline of the Merchant Service and in 1990 it amalgamated with the National Union of Railwaymen to become **The National Union of Rail, Maritime and Transport** (RMT). (There was also a **National Union of Ships' Stewards, Cooks, Butchers & Bakers,** 1909–1921. It amalgamated with the **British Seafarers' Union** in 1921 to form the **Amalgamated Marine Workers' Union** that was later absorbed into the NUS).

CHAPTER TWENTY

People and Places Around the World

There were many place names, principally those of ports and well-known stretches of water, whose full name was often abbreviated by seamen. In some cases an abbreviated name such as The Gulf could mean more than one named gulf and an understanding of which one was being referred to would usually depended upon where the vessel was trading. Bound for The Gulf when crossing the Atlantic from the United Kingdom would usually mean the Gulf of Mexico, whereas in a tanker outward bound for the Middle East it would almost certainly refer to the Persian Gulf (now known as the Arabian Gulf).

Shipping's well-known streets:
Almost worthy of a place in the previous chapter on Institutions were some streets of shipping offices in seaport cities of the United Kingdom.

Leadenhall Street. London in the 1950s was the home of about a quarter of Britain's numerous shipping companies which, between them, operated well over half the British merchant fleet. Many of their offices were in Leadenhall Street where they owned some prominent buildings. For many years this street's name was almost synonymous with 'British Shipping', an honour it shared to a slightly lesser extent with **St Mary Axe, St Helen's Court, Fenchurch Street** and a few other streets in the 'Square Mile', as the City was known. Other ports had a their shipping streets too – Glasgow's **Bothwell Street**, Cardiff's **Bute Street** and Liverpool's **Water Street** were all once a part of shipping's language.

Seafarers' names for many countries, sea areas, gulfs, rivers & ports:

Alex. Alexandria, Egypt.

BA. Buenos Aires, Argentina.

The Bay. The Bay of Biscay.

The Bight. The Great Australian Bight.

The Cape. The Cape of Good Hope, known to the early mariners as, **The Cape of Storms.**
'The Cape' was sometimes also used simply as a name for the Cape Town area.

The Coast. Usually said of the ports of a country to which a ship was trading regularly and at which it usually spent much more than the odd day or two. There was a distinction between ports on the coast and ports on passage to and from a major country destination. Typically, to those serving in British India or Clan Line ships the coast was the Indian Coast whereas to those in Port Line or Shaw Savill ships it meant the coasts of Australia and New Zealand.

The Ditch. The Tasman Sea, between Australia and New Zealand.

The Downs. The area of the English Channel off the Southern part of the Kent Coast in the vicinity of Deal and inside the Goodwin Sands.

Gib. Gibraltar.

The George Cross Island. Malta. Also **The island of hells bells and smells.**

The Horn. Cape Horn. Also known as **Cape Stiff**, a hangover from the sailing ship era.

The Leeuwin. Cape Leeuwin, South West Australia.

The Line. The Equator.

The Loo. Woolloolmooloo, Sydney. Australia.

Rio. Rio de Janeiro, Brazil.

Tiger Bay. An area of Cardiff dockland. Also once an area of the East End of London around Cable Street.

The London River. The River Thames.

The Western approaches. The waters to the West of Ireland from which emerge the sea routes to the River Clyde, River Mersey and the English Channel.

The Chops of the Channel. The Western part of the English Channel.

The Western Ocean. The North Atlantic. Also known as **The Herring Pond.**

Paddy's milestone. Ailsa Craig, an island on the West coast of Scotland.

Hell's Gate. The channel to the east of Perim Island at the Southern end of the Red Sea, providing a very restricted alternative to the Strait of Babel-Mandeb.

Longitude 40° West. This meridian of Longitude, running through the middle of the North Atlantic, was of particular significance during WW2 when vessels outward bound for southern ports, or approaching the United Kingdom from the South, usually made for the approximate Longitude of 40° West, well off the French Atlantic Coast. This was to avoid being within range of German long-range reconnaissance aircraft which would otherwise shadow them and report their positions to U-boats.

E-boat alley. The narrow seas off the Suffolk and Essex Coast where the East Coast convoys were frequently attacked by German torpedo boats (E-Boats).

Convoy assembly points. During the two World Wars merchant ships were herded together and formed into convoys with naval escorts for transiting the areas most heavily frequented by lurking U-boats. Three of the principal assembly points in the North Atlantic U-boat war were Liverpool, Halifax and Freetown.

The Meddy. The Mediterranean Sea. This term was probably more often used in the Merchant Service; the Royal Navy favoured **The Med**, although it too was used by merchant seamen.

ABC Country. Tasmania. The part of Australia favoured for its Apples, Beer and Cider. (The word cider in this expression was usually replaced with 'cunt 'by licentious seaman, ever with an eye open to opportunity).

Trinco. Trincomalee. Ceylon (now Sri Lanka). For many years it was almost exclusively a naval base but later became a more significant commercial port.

Mena apple-daddy. Mena-al-Ahmadi, an oil port on the Persian Gulf.

Prick-town. Tanjong Priok, in the Malacca Straits, as it was known to tankermen who frequently called there.

The Bar. Usually referring to the sandbar at the entrance to the River Mersey unless otherwise specified, although the Hoogly Bar was also a particularly well-known one.

The Royal Docks. This enormous areas of impounded waterway in the Port of London, built during the early part of the 20th century, comprised three docks –the King George V Dock, the Albert Dock and the Victoria Dock. (No longer dockland, this area now includes the London City airport and recreational waterways.) These docks were at the height of their importance in the years immediately preceding and after WW2. The largest ship ever to enter the King George V lock was the new *Mauretania* in 1939.

KG Five. King George V Dock. Usually referring to one of London's *Royal Docks, there were also docks of this name in other UK ports.

The London Docks. This was not simply a generic term for London's Dockland but referred to the specific dock area located just east of the Tower of London. With the exception of St Katherine's Dock, retained today largely for pleasure boats, the docks in this part of London have now all gone, filled in for housing estates and commercial enterprises.

The Upper and Lower Pool. The reaches of the London's river immediately upstream and downstream of the London Docks. The name remains but this once very busy part of the river, full of overseas and coastal shipping, retains little commercial shipping connection with the Port of London today.

The Firemens' Lighthouse. Beckton gasworks on the left bank of the River Thames just below Woolwich. The sight of this landmark encouraged the firemen in the old coal-burners, when homeward bound, to work hard to keep up the steam pressure in the boilers. This ensured maximum speed to help the ship catch the tide at the dock entrance and so berth at the first opportunity.

The Overhead. Liverpool Overhead Railway, 1893–1956. The famous light railway which ran along the River Mersey's north shore from Dingle to Seaforth Sands above street level. It ran past the head of many of Liverpool's docks during the city's heyday as a port. Sometimes referred to as **The Irishman's umbrella** or **The dockers' umbrella.**

Pier head. An important part of Liverpool's waterfront and the site of the Landing Stage where ships embarked and disembarked their passengers.

The Liverpool of the East. In the years before WW2 Shanghai was often referred to by this name.

Siberia. A large dock in Antwerp which seamen considered lived up to its namesake's reputation for bitter cold and misery in wintertime.

Pier 90. Of all the piers in the Hudson River on the West Side of Manhattan, New York, this would have been the best known to many British merchant seamen. It was the regular berth of the great Cunard liners, particularly the *Queen Mary* & *Queen Elizabeth.*

Ocean Terminal. The Southampton berth of the *Queen Mary* and *Queen Elizabeth* but of more recent origin than Pier 90 in New York, having been completed in the 1950s.

The coat-hanger. Sydney Harbour's impressive bridge. Known locally as 'The car strangled spanner'.

Ming Ming. Immingham, a UK North East Coast port.

The hole in the wall. Several confined areas between navigation hazards have been so named. Amongst them is

Seaham Harbour (A UK port familiar to coaster crews) and a stretch of sea on New Zealand's East Coast used by ships seeking to shorten the distance between Auckland and Wellington.

Sailortown. Not so much a geographical locality as a term for an area around certain ports. London and Liverpool had good examples of dock area frequented by seamen containing principally their doss houses, eating places, cheap clothing shops, pubs and other entertainment places catering especially for them. The replacement of many old dock areas by new container terminals, often in different areas, has almost entirely done away with the traditional sailortowns.

Portishead. The name and location of one of the best known Post Office operated radio stations, in Somerset, through which a substantial portion of wireless messages from/to ships at sea were passed. Modern methods of communication have done away with the need for these Post Office radio stations.

Some 'red light' districts well known to seamen:
The Reeperbahn and **Winkelstrasse.** Hamburg (San Pauli).
Schipperstraat and **Schippers kwartier.** Antwerp.
Katendrecht. Rotterdam.
Amsterdamse walletjes. Amsterdam.
Lockhart Rd & **Hennessy Rd.** Hong Kong.
Kings Cross. Or simply, **The Cross.** Sydney.
General Camara Street. Santos.
Vinte cinco de Mayo. Buenos Aires.
The Gut. Valetta. Malta.
Grant Road and **Torres Road. Bombay**
Bugis Road. Singapore
Kilindini Road &**The Shacks**. Mombassa.
Napier Street. Karachi.
Watgun Street. Calcutta.
Campo Legro ('Happy Valley'). A particularly large brothel in Curacao, a major oil port in the Dutch West Indies, catering for the many visiting tankermen who had often been at sea for long periods without female company.

Some well-known seamen's pubs:

Charlie Brown's & **The Brown Bear** in London's dockland.
The Round House in Woolwich, just around the corner from London's King George V Dock. (No longer a pub, it has been converted into apartments.)
Joe Beefs in Montreal.
The Bunch of Grapes, The Big House and the **Union** in Sydney.
Aggie Grey's in Apia, Samoa.
Tombo Mary's on the west coast of Africa.
The Mad House in Curacao.
Ma Gleesons. In Auckland, on the corner of Fanshaw & Hobson Streets, was a well known sly grogging shop in the days of New Zealand's infamous 'six o'clock swill'. Also **Ann Powell's** (The Criterion), **The Blood House** (The Ambassador).

Some Liverpool bars and the companies' whose crews were said to regularly frequent them:

Elm House (North End).	Furness Withy
Langdon Castle (North End).	Mud pilot's shore gang
Seven Steps (South End)	Harrison & Elder Dempster
The Devil	Booth & Mersey Docks &HB.

Other places and expressions:

The Long Room. Designated ports of entry into the UK had a Custom House, and it was in the Long Room that a shipmaster officially reported a vessel's arrival and paid her dues. Import merchants also paid their duty here.
Shuttle run. The name by which the short sea route between Venezuela and Curacao or Aruba in the Netherlands Antilles was known by Esso and Shell tankermen who constantly made the crossing.
Shore-side. A general term for the shore, as in, 'I'm going shore-side'.
Rubbity Dub. A Pub. (Cockney.)

The arse hole of the East. Port Said, situated at the end of a canal leading to the East.

Narriman's Cut. A name used to describe the Eastern Branch of the Suez Canal when it was first opened. Narriman was a wife of King Farouk at the time.

Simon Artz. The famous department store adjacent to the Western bank of the Suez Canal at Port Said. A huge 'Johnny Walker' whisky advertisement stood over its large building. Both the store and the advert became familiar landmarks to seamen over the years.

LEFO. Land's End For Orders. Before the days of radio communication ships would leave their loading ports in Australia or the Far East bound for Land's End; there they would expect to receive orders regarding their discharge port or ports in Europe. Lands End was almost never a destination after radio communication became commonplace as further destination orders would be received well before arriving there. Queenstown and Falmouth also became familiar destinations 'for orders'.

USNH. The US coast north of Cape Hatteras, an area on the northern part of the coast of the USA on which are situated most of the major East Coast ports outside the Gulf of Texas.

WCSA. West Coast South America.

Some names for people, regional and national:

Limey or Limejuicer. A British seaman. It was generally intended as a derogatory term, used principally by American seamen, on account of the Board of Trade's requirement from 1844 for lime juice to be made available as an anti-scorbutic in British ships. It remained a requirement until some years after WW2 although lime juice was rarely issued in the later years since refrigeration ensured that fresh vegetable were then readily available at sea. The term was sometimes used by Americans for all British people.

Stornawegian. A seaman from Stornaway in the Outer Isles of Scotland's West Coast.

Chucthas. (Spelling varied: Chukta, Cheuchters or Teuchters). The name also used for seafarers from the Hebrides and Western Isles. The men from these islands, usually excellent seamen, often signed on in Glasgow.

Shelties. Also fine Scottish seamen, from the Shetland Islands.

Geordie. A native of Tyneside from the Newcastle area, but not including Wearside. Any misnaming would cause offence to both parties.

Westos/Cornese. Plymothians and Cornishmen.

Bluenose. A seaman from Nova Scotia, Canada.

Liverpool Irish. Many living in the poorer parts of Liverpool were of Irish decent and some found their way to sea, particularly as firemen and trimmers in the coal-burners.

Cardiff Arabs. Firemen of Arab descent who lived permanently in the Tiger Bay area of Cardiff and generally gave good service in the *black gang.

Glasgow redskins. Deck hands and firemen hailing from Glasgow. Although drunkenness was a frequent problem regardless of origin in the UK, those recruited in Glasgow were particularly noted for their violent behaviour.

North Sea Chinamen. Derogatory name for seafarers from Tyneside and Wearside, especially those in the collier trade.

Scouse. One who hails from Liverpool – a Liverpuddlian. It also refers to the Liverpool dialect and a type of stew. Also **Scouser** when referring to the person.

Whack. Liverpuddlian for friend, pal, mate.

Judies. A Liverpuddlian term for women generally, particularly those of Liverpool Irish origin. The word appears in sea shanties.

Our Judy. My girl (Liverpuddlian.)

A moosh. A member of the crew from the Southampton area.

Kroo boys. Natives hired to help work ships in the West African ports and anchorages. They supplemented the work of the deck crew for whom the high temperatures and humidity were particular exhausting.

Dutchmen. An occasional slang name for all northern Europeans. (During the review period most in the British Isles did not regard their country as being part of Europe.)

Square heads. Northern Europeans, particularly Germans and Dutch. Also **Box heads,** especially Latvians and Estonians.

Ruskies. Russians.

Scowegian. A seaman from Scandanavia. Also **Scandawegians.**

Scrobs. Derogatory name for all Scandanavians. Also **Scandahooligans.**

Smoked Scotsmen. Coolies or Indian seamen on Clan Line ships and those of some other companies.

Ham shanks. Yanks.

Dago. Usually used in reference to a person of Latin extract, particularly from South America.

Frog or Froggie. Frenchman.

Gippo. An Egyptian.

Itie. Italian. Also **Wop.**

Brazzies. Brazilians. (Some Booth Line ships carried Brazilian ratings.)

Chinks. Chinese.

Wogs. A derogatory term used for Egyptians and often also for others of Middle Eastern origin:. 'wily oriental gentlemen'.

Niggers. This term is now considered particularly offensive and only the foolish and insensitive would use it today for Africans and Afro-Americans.

Norsky. A Norwegian.

CHAPTER TWENTY ONE

Miscellaneous Terms and Expressions

Most of the terms and expressions appearing so far have readily lent themselves to being placed in categories according to their usage, or location in a ship. Those that follow do not have the same convenient categories and are more inclined to relate to traditions and to various other aspects of life at sea.

More days : more dollars. The longer a voyage lasted the more wages would be earned by the crew. This expression was often used when a voyage became unexpectedly extended and the crew would make this comment, often with some pleasure, or at least appearing philosophical about any inconvenience, seeing the financial benefit as a consolation.

Different ships : different long splices. Used in reference to anything on board where there was more than one version or method of doing almost anything. Its origin lay in there being more than one form of long-splice for joining two wire ropes together. One ship might use one method and another ship a different one. The method adopted was usually determined by the mate or the bosun. (The corresponding term in the Royal Navy is, 'Different ships : Different cap tallies' and refers to a cap ribbon having the name of the ship in which the rating was serving).

Every turn of the screw is a turn nearer home. The 'screw' being the propeller, these were words of consolation to a homesick seaman. A variation on this, used in letters and phone calls to sweethearts, was; **Every turn of the screw brings me closer to you.**

Oil and water don't mix. A saying which, in some ships

expressed the unfortunate fact that the deck officers and the engineers did not mix more than was absolutely necessary to run the ship. Fortunately, there were some happy ships where this was certainly not the case.

To swing the cabin lamp. Used when a group of seamen, in a social environment and often after a few drinks, yarned about their past ships, shipmates and seafaring life. Some tall stories usually emerged and it was said that they were swinging the cabin lamp. More often than not the theme would be 'the good old days at sea'.

Every finger a marlinspike : every hair a rope yarn. This expression, intended to convey that a particular seafarer possessed exceptional seamanship skills, was used much more by landsmen speaking of seafarers than by seafarers speaking about other seafarers.

Wiping the slate clean. Originating in the days when the OOW kept his record of courses steered with chalk on a *slate board this expression has since come into everyday use in the English language.

Gold Bricking. Spin doctoring or telling small or large fibs.

Before the mast. Originally a term of the sailing ship era when only seamen were berthed in the fo'c's'le, ahead of the masts. Although later firemen were berthed there too it was still used later, to a lesser extent, to refer to seamen who shipped out before the mast and distinguished them from officers or others who were berthed further aft.

Up through the hawsepipe. An officer who began his seagoing life as a seaman in the fo'c's'le, rather than learning his profession as an apprentice or cadet, is said to have come up through the hawsepipe or to be out of the fo'c's'le. (The hawsepipe is the pipe running almost vertically through the fo'c's'le as a containment through which the cable attached to the anchor is led upwards to the windlass above. The expression is a reference to this suggesting a 'pipeline' through which a seaman could rise to become an officer.)

Moved amidships. The same meaning as 'Up through the hawsepipe' because a seaman who gets his *'ticket' and become an officer will no longer be berthed in the fo'c'sle but will have a room (cabin) in the midships accommodation.

Slipped his cable. Reference to a seafarer having died. (The cable is the anchor cable and if slipped (uncoupled) from the ship while she was anchored, would cast her adrift). There are several other terms with a similar meaning including, **Crossed the bar, Gone aloft, His sailing has ended, Paid-off for the last time** and – a sailing ship term – **Gone to Fiddlers Green.** (Whether Alfred, Lord Tennyson's famous poem 'Crossing the Bar' took its theme from this seafaring term or vice versa, is uncertain. The bar referred to is the sandbar at the mouth of a river which an outward-bound ship would cross en route to the open ocean.)

Flying fish weather. A frequently used expression for fine, warm weather at sea, the typical conditions in tropical areas where flying fish are commonly seen skimming the waves. Seamen who remained in ships plying mostly in fine weather areas become known as **Flying fish sailors** or **Blue-water men.**

All hands and the cook. Commonly used in general conversation to refer to everyone on board. It is derived from sailing ship days where the maximum number of people were required to take in sail when bad weather endangered the ship.

The Liverpool fireman. A fictitious thief who was given the blame when something went missing on board. Also **The man from Liverpool** who was responsible when things went wrong. (Doubtless not a term used in ships whose home port was Liverpool.)

Tealeaf. A thief; a particularly obnoxious creature in the confines of a ship.

Down by the head with .... An expression referring to a ship, but not necessarily used to relate to a situation on board, when there is a surfeit of something; e.g. The office was down by the head with all the extra staff. (Too much weight of cargo in a forward hatch or too much water in a fore peak tank would cause a ship to trim 'by the head'.)

A one-bell yarn. A tall story purported to be told by seamen sitting in the mess room waiting to go on watch after being called at *one bell.

Stand-by. Apart from 'stand-by' being an order to the engine room to be prepared for engine movements for manoeuvring the ship, it was also a term used when the deck or engine room crew were required to be at their *stations during the transit of a restricted waterway. The term would, for example, be used as in, 'that was a long stand-by', meaning that the crew had been at their stations for a long time as might occur when a ship was transiting a long river leading to or from a port, or was in either the Suez or Panama Canal.

Black Friday. Needless to say shipping did not grind to a halt on Fridays but when things went wrong traditionally superstitious seamen were likely to attribute this to having signed-on, joined or sailed on a Friday, the worst of them being Friday 13th of the month – Black Friday.

She's up for ...(a specified time). When a time was set for sailing, especially after agreement had been reached with the port authority for the time the pilot would board and the tugs take up station, it was usually expressed in this manner, e.g. the ship would be said to be up for 1800 and this time was posted at the gangway. (The 24-hour clock was invariably used.)

Only fools, firemen and first trippers sit on rails. Cautionary remarks given to inexperienced crew who might unwisely sit on shipside rails, risking a watery grave.

Officers of the Royal Navy (RN) were 'gentlemen trying to be seamen; officers of the Royal Naval Reserve (RNR) were seamen trying to be gentlemen; and officers of the Royal Naval Volunteer Reserve (RNVR) were neither, trying to be both.' Merchant Service officers were occasionally to be heard making these broad, harsh and often unwarranted generalisations.

The three Sea Services. It was sometimes said, usually

sarcastically, that there were actually three sea services – The Royal Navy, the P & O and the Merchant Navy. This was a 'dig' at the P & O, many of whose officers were in the RNR and were thought by some to consider themselves superior to officers in the Merchant Navy.

Gentlemen of the P&O, Officers of the BI and men of the other companies. This was also said sarcastically of the officers of the P & O which was sometimes referred to as 'the kid glove line'.

The Fourth Service. This term was coined when referring to the Merchant Navy, in recognition of its major contribution with that of the three Armed Services during WW2, to the preservation of the country.

Built for comfort and not for speed. Occasionally said of a ship which was relatively slow for her trade but was sea-kindly and had good accommodation. It was also often said of a woman of ample proportions.

A Forced draft job. A large woman with more than adequate bosom and bum who was also often referred to as **a blast job** or **a double-ended job.**

Arse like a BA fender. As above but refers only to her backsides. (The reference is to large fenders used at Buenos Aires (BA) for berthing ships.)

Cake & arse party. Said of a smart party on board, as that thrown by the master or a shipping company for guests from the shore. Such a party might be intended to thank shippers as an inducement to ship cargo in the company's vessels.

Put it in the big locker. This expression, with the four others below, all mean the same – to throw something over the side into the sea. It was usually galley waste that was thrown over the side at sea but all kinds of both floatable and sinking rubbish went over with little regard for the environment. Although the dumping of biodegradable waste is still acceptable when well out to sea, international law now prohibits the disposal of almost all other in this manner. Also **Throw it over the wall, Give it**

a float test, Give it a passage, and **Give it the Deep Six.** ('By the deep six' was the call from a seaman taking soundings with a hand lead-line and reporting to the bridge on finding six fathoms (approximately 11 metres) once considered reasonably deep water for a ship.)

The drink. The sea generally. Sometimes **Og-wash, Oggin** or **Briney.**

A greybeard. A very large wave encountered in high latitudes.

Chatty but happy. Sometimes said of a rather rust-stained old tramp ship that was nevertheless a happy ship.

New chum. In the training ship HMS *Conway* new cadets were referred to by this name. (John Masefield, a 20th century Poet Laureate, was a cadet in her before going to sea briefly and wrote his autobiography with this title. Also **Quarter boy.**

Tankeritis. After being cooped up in a ship for long periods, particularly in hot weather without air-conditioning, and with little or no opportunity of shore leave to relieve the boredom, a seaman was said to be suffering from this so-called mental condition. Ranging from mild eccentricity to full blown psychosis, it particularly applied to those serving in tankers, often for weeks on end with little time ashore in a 'civilised' port. This was the case in many tankers trading to the Persian (now Arabian) Gulf. It was also known as **Abadan fever** or **Abadan blues**, since Abadan was one of its principal oil ports. **Abadaner.** One who was suffering from Tankeritis/Abadan fever.

The Channels or **Channel Fever.** This has nothing to do with illness but to the contrary. It was the excitement felt when a voyage was nearly over and a ship was nearing a home port, or any port where the crew would be paid off and free to go home.

Channel Night. The final night before arrival back in the UK at the end of a voyage. Sometimes *channel fever would get the better of some of the crew who might have a final 'piss-up' together.

Kiss-my-arse latitudes. The name by which a discontented crew, probably having complained about almost everything to do with the ship, including the food and accommodation, and usually accompanied by a high incidence of *loggings, might refer to the approaches to port where they were about to pay-off and leave the ship. In high spirits with *channel fever they would adopt a could-not-care-less attitude at this final stage of the voyage and suggest that the master can 'Kiss my arse and say goodbye'.

Feeding the fishes. Being seasick and depositing the results over the ship's side.

A seven-bell dinner. An early lunch at 11.20 for the 12-4 watch that was on duty at Noon. (See Chapter 5 – Meal times)

Bombay canary. A very large cockroach. Also **Bombay Eight Wheeler.**

Gone ashore. Although, of course, this can refer to a seaman simply leaving his ship temporarily for a few hours ashore, it was also applied more definitively to explain that he has ceased to follow a career at sea in favour of permanent employment ashore.

On the beach. Usually said of a seaman when temporarily unemployed and awaiting another job at sea, but was sometimes said of one who had left the sea permanently.

Swallowed the Anchor. Somewhat similar to the above but only used where the seaman has permanently left the sea to settle ashore.

Finished with Engines. This ship-handling term was sometimes used when a senior officer retired, as in, 'He's finished with engines'.

Coffee pot sailors. A derogatory term used by sailing ship crews when referring to those in steam ships. (A 20th century variation on the use of this term was applicable around the end of the review period where, on at least one occasion, the then very powerful New Zealand Seamen's Union prevented a ship from sailing when her crew refused to take her to sea until their coffee pot had been repaired.)

Left the sea and gone into steam. A sarcastic remark often made by sailing ship men of those who had shown a preference for joining slightly more comfortable steam ships.

Iron ships and wooden men. A derisive comment for seamen in early steam ships by sailing ship men who considered themselves to be iron men in wooden ships.

Chundering along at eight knots and an onion. The onion was a fraction of a knot. The expression conveys a vision of an old tramp ship squeezing every last ounce of steam out of her boilers to make the best speed possible which, in this case, only just exceeded eight knots.

Banjiboo. A party or 'knees up'.

Phoo Phoo band. Comb and paper band formed by the crew of some North Atlantic liners before WW2. They are said to have paraded ahore in New York and other ports on the North American seaboard and Eastern Canada.

The sun's over the foreyard. Originally the expression is believed to have referred to the sun being high in the sky and the heat being so oppressive that those working on deck were allowed a rest period. However, latterly it has come to mean that it's a respectable time for the first drink of the day.

Down the hatch. A goodwill toast immediately prior to taking a drink; now commonly used ashore as much as at sea.

Galley wireless. The mythical source of all rumours and gossip. They often related to the expected loading ports or routeing of the vessel later in the voyage after discharge of the outward cargo, or to personnel joining or leaving – particularly the next master or mate.

Scuttlebut. Gossip – anything originating from the *Galley wireless. A scuttlebut was a cask of fresh water once provided for the crew, and consequently a popular gathering place. (Probably of naval origin).

To get alongside a person. To get to know somebody with a view to establishing a rapport with them.

One hand for the ship (or company) and one for yourself.

It was important for a seaman to pay close attention to personal safety when working in dangerous places. This frequently meant allowing one hand to be kept free for his safety alone while working for the ship with the other. Failure to observe the maxim has seen more than one careless seaman fall to his death.

To knock eight bells out of someone. A beat-up of one person by another.

Stow it! A forceful appeal to a shipmate to 'Shut up!'

Whistling up the wind. Whistling at sea was frowned upon and if caught whistling a seaman would often be severely rebuked by an officer. There was a superstition that whistling brought about freshening winds which, except occasionally in extreme heat, was usually unpopular in steam ships.

Albatross, seagull or shitehawk. Seamen spoke of almost all sea birds as falling within these three categories. If a bird was not a seagull or an albatross, both readily identifiable birds, they were lumped together as 'shite hawks' for lack of basic ornithological knowledge. (The latter term was sometimes applied especially to Frigate birds which are birds of prey found mostly in the Tropics.)

Albert Ross. Albatross.

Bo'sun bird. The Tropic bird with tail looking a little a marline spike.

Mother Carey's chicken. The Storm Petrel.

Cape dove. The Brown petrel.

Cape Hen. White-chinned petrel.

Stinking Nellie. The Giant petrel.

Nobbies. Sharks.

Honeymoon revs. At certain engine speeds and in some conditions almost all ships vibrate. Particularly in motor ships when approaching critical engine revolutions, this vibration can be heavy and gives rise to the suggestive expression.

I haven't seen that face at the *shipping office before. Said of a crew member displaying a bare backside when bending over.

Going like a fiddler's elbow. A simile for any reciprocating motion, but usually used when referring to sexual intercourse.

Up and down like a whore's drawers. Used to refer to anything being frequently hoisted and lowered.

Dobi and dobying. Hindustani term for personal laundry and the act of washing. Before washing machines became common equipment in ships, dobying was often done in a bucket by boiling the water with a portable immersion heater. Dungarees were then sometimes rinsed by towing them astern on a rope in the propeller wash for a few moments, although this was hard on them. (The author learnt a salutary lesson on his first voyage when he boiled his woolen socks!)

Dobi dust. Washing powder.

Western Ocean roll. The almost constant movement of a ship at sea requires an innate sense of balance to counteract it and can lead to a seaman having a slightly rolling gait when walking ashore. It was particularly associated with the heavy weather of the North Atlantic, hence 'Western Ocean Roll', but it was sometimes a deliberately exaggerated swagger in order to impress those ashore.

Ten to the Rock, Four to the Dock. An old saying, almost a lament, which applied to slow ships homeward bound after clearing the Suez Canal. It referred to the passage time in days from Port Said to Gibraltar and then on to the UK port where the voyage would finally end.

Gig boats. Moorting boats used by mud pilots. (Liverpool).

A North Cape Telegram. The mate's note to a seaman who was not welcome back next trip (NZ).

Bombay biddy. A prostitute; hence the often heard comment by some seaman, 'Bombay biddy, bot acha' – the Hindustani phrase for 'Bombay prostitute, very alright'.

The Cages. The abode of prostitutes who were displayed in cages at Bombay. In some ports, Hamburg in particular, they were often displayed in glass-fronted buildings in the Winkelstrasse.

POSH. A term suggesting a high degree of smartness, even superiority. It is said to be formed of the initial letters of Port Out Starboard Home and to have originated in P & O in the nineteenth century with the tickets of travellers to India being stamped POSH. This was said to convey that they had been allocated a cabin on the port side outward bound and on the starboard side homeward bound, meaning that for the hottest part of the voyage, in the Red Sea, they had the cooler side of the ship. Here the ship's course was roughly north and south and the morning sun is less aggressive than the afternoon sun. (P & O does not have any record of this practice.)

Chimney in the middle. A term used to differentiate traditional steam and motor ships from tankers and some coasters. Until Shaw Savill had the *Southern Cross* and *Northern Star* built in the latter part of the period, most passenger and cargo ships had their engines and funnels amidships while almost all tankers, and many coasters, had their's aft.

Every finger a marlinspike and every hair a rope yarn. Said of a particularly good seaman who was well versed in the art and science of sailorising.

Short hand money. When a ship was short-handed, necessitating extra work on a regular basic by other members of the crew, it sometimes (but not very often) occurred that the wages of the missing crew member were shared among those doing the extra work.

He's only been at sea for a dog watch. A derogatory expression said of an officer or rating who has been at sea for a very short time only and was ignorant on many important seafaring matters.

She would roll on wet grass. Said of a ship with a propensity for heavy rolling.

A fair weather friend. Said of a person who is a friend when the going is smooth but fails to give the support of a true friend when the going gets rough.

Hollywood sailors. Flashy, overly dressed 'precious' sailors.

In the Deep Tank. This oblique reference to the special, deep cargo-oil tanks in some cargo ships was used to refer to a seaman's savings of money for a rainy day.

The night of the long knives. The name by which the dramatic changes in the structure of the P & O Group in the early 1970s became known. Some of Britain's most respected liner and tramp ship companies saw many of their ships sold or renamed. Most that remained were reorganised into either a Passenger, General Cargo or Bulk Shipping Division of P & O. So sweeping were these changes that individual companies within the Group almost completely lost their identity and more than a hundred years of British shipping was consigned to the history books.

As tight as a duck's arse. An expression intended to convey that something is totally watertight. It was also used for a mean a person reluctant to part with his money to treat a shipmate.

Passenger ship material. In a company having both cargo and passenger ships, an officer possessing the necessary social graces and other qualities for service in passenger ships was often reported upon as being potential, passenger ship material.

The Blue Riband (Ribbon) of the Atlantic. Although not a seafarer's term, the coveted Blue Riband figured strongly in the lives of many who sailed in the great North Atlantic liners. It was won by the vessel making the fastest Westbound and Eastbound crossing between Bishop's Rock Lightship (Scilly Isles) and the Ambrose Light (New York). Originally a mythical award, the Hales Trophy was later instituted and the winner received a blue pennant to be flown by her.

Armstrong's patent. Human muscle power as distinct from power derived by the use of machinery. Sometimes referred to as **Norwegian steam.**

Outward Bound. A ship is said to be outward bound when she leaves her home port, or one in a country where she is based, for a voyage and continues it in a general direction which takes her further away from it. Alternatively, if not used geographically, the term might be applied until she has completed discharging her outward cargo and before loading for a home port. It was often difficult to pin-point where tramp ships ceased to be outward bound as they might be away from home for a year or two making many passages between ports, loading and discharging several times. The opposite of outward bound was **Homeward Bound** and it would not be until she loaded for a home port discharge that a tramp would at last be said to be Homeward Bound.

Worse things happen at sea. Not a particularly meaningful expression, it is often used by seamen when something unsatisfactory occurs ashore and they seek to make light of it with this remark. It is said that it originated in Deal, on the Kent Coast, following the Great Storm of November 1703 that devastated the area, drowning 2,000 people but the survivors still suggested that worse things happen at sea.

Changey-changey. A name for the bartering that took place between bum boatmen or itinerant quayside vendors, and passengers or crew in Egyptian ports.

Wakey, wakey, rise and shine, hands off cocks and pull on socks. A wake-up call only used when calling another of the same or junior rank.

Rise and shine. 'It's gone Seven o'clock; not a whore in the house washed, and a street full of sailors.' Another, tongue-in-cheek, wake-up call for the crew. (This may have been the wake-up-call attributed to only one particular tramp ship bosun.)

Wakey, wakey, rise and shine, for the P & O Line. A 'Wake-up' call often used when one officer awakened another for duty. (Any other shipping company name could be substituted for P & O. as appropriate)

When in danger and in doubt, call the old man out. Good advice to the OOW when confronted with a worrying situation during his bridge watch at sea. Also, and very much less constructive, **When in danger or in doubt, run in circles, scream and shout.**

I'm in the Lifeboat. Simply, this meant to hell with anyone else, I'm OK. Also, **'Pull up the ladder Jack, I'm inboard'.**

She (referring to a ship). For centuries ships have been referred to in the English language by the pronoun 'she'. In the latter part of the twentieth century political correctness has moved to suggest that this practice is no longer acceptable. Almost universally seafarers abhor this attitude which appears as yet another effort to remove any colour from everyday life and to stereotype it. Although there have been several jocular explanations for the use of 'she', rarely have they been intended to denigrate women. Although not every ship was regarded with affection at the time by those serving in them, nor is there a universal liking for the appearance of many modern ships, there generally remains a similar feeling of warmth and affection for ships as befits a man's regard for the opposite sex.

What is the speed of a convoy? Not so much an expression as a question, this was often asked of a young seaman. The answer was simply, 'The speed of the slowest ship'. Wartime convoys were either fast or slow convoys, every effort being made to group together suitable ships so as not to hamper and unduly risk the faster merchant ships. The fastest ocean liners, usually used as troopships, were sometimes routed independently and relied upon their speed to avoid attack by enemy forces.

Golden rivet. There was a wholly fictitious story that the very last rivet put into a vessel's hull during the era of riveted ships, was made of gold. A First tripper was often teased by his shipmates by sending him off to find the golden rivet which, it was suggested, might be found in particularly places difficult to access, such as the engine room bilges. There was also a rather vulgar interpretation placed upon the instruction to 'go and see so-and-so and ask to see the golden rivet,' as the penis is of somewhat similar shape to a rivet.

Where does the last rivet go in a ship? A question asked of a first tripper. The answer is simple, and obvious – in the last rivet-hole!

Fog locker. This is another of those mystical, fictitious items used in the process of teasing embryo seafarers who might be sent to collect something from the fog locker. It was also the place where items of gear long since missing, or never even supplied to the ship, were said to be stowed. There was literally no such thing as a fog locker although the locker in which the *fog buoy was stowed for wartime convoys came as close as anything to it.

A long stand or a long weight. Another teaser for the greenhorn who would often be sent down to the engine room for one of these mythical objects. (The long stand, like the long weight, actually involved a long wait). The chief or other engineer to whom the request was made would play him along for as long as he felt inclined.

Fetch the key of the keelson. Another instruction to a hapless greenhorn to fulfil an impossible task.

Red oil. Still another fruitless mission for a lad sent to ask the lamp trimmer for some red oil for the port sidelight. (Even after the introduction of electricity, oil lamps continued to be required for many years as emergency lights, red, green and white, in case of a power failure. The oil burned white and only the glass shade around them affected the colour of the light.)

The Spurlash. The similar sounding 'Spurling' pipe is a professional term for the pipe guiding the anchor chain from the windlass down to the chain locker. Being familiar with it many an unfortunate cadet has been sent forward to report on the spurlash when anchoring, only to learn that anchors do indeed make a splash when dropped into the water.

Food for the Panama Canal mules. The seamen's' *peggy (messman) was frequently a first tripper and when a ship's voyage was to take her through the Panama Canal the hapless peggy might be instructed to save any stale bread scraps to feed the mules when they later towed the ship through the canal locks. His embarrassment can be imagined when the 'mules' (they were correctly known by this name) turned out to be huge diesel powered locomotives on the side of the lock running on a toothed track, used for towing into each lock.

As cold as the fluff on a polar bear's chuff. An expression of concern when referring to very cold weather. It is a vulgar equivalent of, **Cold enough to freeze the balls of a brass monkey,** an expression of naval origin which has passed into common English usage and does not relate to a monkey's testicles. Also, **As cold as a nun's cunt, As cold as a whore's heart** and **More running noses than standing cocks.**

Put some hair around it! A vulgar expression addressed to a seaman who, for example, might be experiencing difficulty in finding the place to insert a bolt, or other object, into a hole. The implication is that he would have no difficulty in finding his way into a female's genital organ.

Boat train. Not strictly a seafaring term but relevant to ships, it refers to a special train operated specially to carry passengers to the embarkation port for a voyage.

Donkey's breakfast. A seaman's straw mattress that had to be brought with him when joining a ship. By about the end of the WW2 this item of a seaman's kit had just about disappeared as almost all shipowners were providing mattresses by then.

Xmas tree on the foremast. Traditionally, seafarers have celebrated Christmas by securing a Christmas tree at the foremast head.

A Lump of coal for the engineers. In some ships a lump of coal was delivered to the Engine Room at New Year, 'With complements of the Deck Department'. Presumably this tradition arose because so many engineers came from Scotland where the celebration of New Year is so important. There would have been few ships where one would have found a lump of coal after the mid-1950s unless it was part of her cargo.

The 'farewell' whistle signal. Three long blasts on the whistle were often given as a friendly farewell gesture when leaving a port. The three long blasts were also used as a greeting when two ships of the same company passed close at sea on opposite courses. (This is not to be confused with the manoeuvring signal under the Collision Regulations of three short blasts heard when a ship is about to go astern when manoeuvring to leave a port and indicates, My engines are going astern.)

Making one's number. The term sometimes used of an officer joining a new ship and introducing himself by reporting to his captain or senior officer for the first time. The term is probably more used in the Royal Navy than in the Merchant Service.

Speed money. It is said that a bonus was once paid in General Steam Navigation Company to deck officers who sailed in their fleet's faster ships, such as Golden Eagle and Royal Daffodil whose speed exceeded 16 knots.

Paddy's lantern. The moon.

Paddy's hurricane. A flat calm or a condition on board of no wind due to a following wind and the ship' speed being identical. Gentle Breezes from Gentle Jesus. A reference to the weather reports from Cabo Torinana (Spain) rumoured to be broadcast from a monastery. The term owes its origin to its weather forecast on one particular day for, zephyrs and light breezes, which turned out to be a howling gale.

Ringbolt. To ringbolt meant to travel illegally in New Zealand coastal ships between ports as a non-fare paying passenger. Usually concealed by the crew on their own initiative, or sometimes as part of a well-organised illegal operation with their acquiescence, the term was also used as a noun. (NZ)

Shore-side. This term was sometimes used simply to refer to 'on the land' e.g. 'I left it shore-side' but often as an adjective referring to something not aboard a ship as in 'a shore-side crane' or a 'shore-side person'.

Three sheets in the wind. Drunk. Also **Half seas over**.

Mash up. Said of a seaman badly injured after being caught on deck by a big sea coming aboard. This not infrequently occurred in the square-riggers.

Shipping them green. Said of a ship in heavy weather when large seas, rather than light spray, are breaking aboard and dumping quantities of water on deck.

Signing his name in the water. Said of a helmsman steering a bad course. The ship might wander all over the place and leave a very complex wake astern.

Who's on the fucking wheel? Often said in anger to blame the possibly innocent helmsman when, in bad weather, a vessel lurches violently or ships a large sea thoroughly wetting the speaker. The implication is that the helmsman was off course, thereby altering the ship's profile to the prevailing wind and sea.

Pissing into the wind. When throwing away anything light over the ship's side at sea, a seaman was usually careful not to do so on the weather side as it might blow back on board. The same obviously applied to urinating over the side but it was said that one could do so with impunity if one had been around Cape Horn.

The four Esses. Shit, Shave, Shower & Shampoo. Before going ashore for an evening's entertainment seamen would often crudely state that they would go and have the four Esses first.

Broaching the cargo. Sometimes said of a seaman's dalliance with a female passenger. It has, of course, a literal meaning dating to the period when seamen would often get amongst the cargo in the hold and steal attractive items. This was not an infrequent problem before sealed freight containers became common.

An umbrella, a wheelbarrow and a naval officer. These three items are said by merchant seamen to be the three most useless objects on a ship. The latter was intended to be deliberately derogatory and the second was certainly not true of the old coal-burning steamers where wheelbarrows were used to convey coal from the bunkers to the stokehold, and in the New Zealand coastal scows where their crew frequently wheeled sand and gravel aboard from the beaches, across a gangplank. (Concerning the umbrella, the author joined a Russian four-masted barque in recent years and was fascinated to see the sail-maker working on a sail on deck in the rain under an umbrella held by a seaman.)

Steam murgi. An aircraft. Although not a nautical term it was used by Indian crew when flying to join or leave a ship. It literally meant 'a steam-powered chicken'.

Bumped. During WW2 a seaman who had been sunk under him due to torpedoes, bombs or mines would say that he had been bumped.

Skyhook. A mythical item of ship's equipment often called for when the only apparent way to get to a high part of the ship for maintenance or painting appeared to call for a bosun's chair with a hook that could be hooked into the sky above to support it.

Ship's women. As sometimes used this might not refer to 'loose' women but to refer collectively to woman assistant pursers, stewardesses, telephonists and other female staff. It was said in a slightly derogatory sense by those who were les than favourable disposed towards having women in the crew of ships.

The Fishing Fleet. The many unmarried young ladies, principally from Britain but also from Australia, who travelled before WW2 to Ceylon and India in search of a husband, often a tea planter or army officer. They usually travelled during the cooler North East Monsoon season, mostly in P & O and Orient Line ships, and stayed with friends or relatives. (Neither this nor the next entry were strictly nautical expressions but would have been in common use on board the ships in which the ladies travelled.)

Returned Empties. Those young ladies who comprised the *Fishing Fleet but failed to find a husband and went home unmarried were said, in brewery terms, to be Returned Empties.

One night of love. Said of the overnight passenger ferry services, Wellington – Lyttelton (New Zealand) and Melbourne to Devonport (Tasmania).

It's not my first trip, you know. Often said when someone on board was spinning an unlikely yarn or giving some improbable explanation for something, possibly absence from duty, and the receiver wished to point out that he was sufficiently experienced to be wise to such unlikely stories.

May I come back next trip, Sir, if I work my watch below. A person seen to be currying favour with the master or mate might have these words chanted to him very pointedly by his shipmates indicating they were well aware of his sneaky behaviour in sucking up to his superior.

Clearing one's yardarm. Taking care to ensure one is not held responsible for an incident.. (A sailing ship going alongside a wharf or another ship often had to brace her yards inboard to make sure their outer ends (yardarms) did not foul an obstruction.)

Loblolly for the captain. Rowing the master ashore or to other ships. (Sailing ship term).

The Great Bitter Lakes Association. On 5 June 1967 a convoy of 25 ships was northbound in the Suez Canal when the Six-day War broke out between Egypt and Israel. As was customary, the northbound convoy anchored in the Great Bitter Lakes to allow the southbound convoy to pass. The tankers leading the northbound convoy then proceeded but before the cargo ships could do so the Egyptians blocked the Canal. Fourteen ships, representing eight nationalities, of which four were British, were trapped for many months. After a while a huge camaraderie sprung up among the crews who, needing to overcome boredom, organised a number of makeshift entertainments and competitions, pooling their resources of food and equipment. They then formed a unique 'Association' and the master's wife on one of the Swedish ships, the only woman involved, became known as, **The Lady of the Great Bitter Lakes.**

The Lady in White. Thousands of service personnel passed through Durban in troopships, hospital ships and naval vessels on their way to and from the Middle and Far East during WW2. From April 1940 until VJ-Day in August 1945, the remarkable Perla Siedel Gibson welcomed and farewelled them, and the crews of the ships, as they arrived in port in every kind of weather, day or night. An opera singer, she was a familiar sight on the dockside in her white dress and large red hat. Carrying her megaphone, she sang the patriotic songs the servicemen and women longed to hear. She even returned years later when the Suez Canal was closed in the mid-1950s, to greet the peacetime troopers as they passed through South Africa again. After her death in 1971, a monument to her memory was erected in Durban Harbour.

A typical British coaster of the mid-20th century.

Indices

INDICES

Guide to using the index

This book was originally intended as a simple dictionary of colloquial terms and expressions but it developed into a more comprehensive discourse on seafaring customs as well. However, the index fulfils the original intention in providing **a comprehensive reference to terms and expressions** rather than as a general index. Consequently, with few exceptions, the index contains the terms and expressions shown in bold print throughout the book.

There is a basic index showing each chapter's content with the page range. This is intended to assist research into any general subjects covered in the text, and there is also a full alphabetical index following it. There is a separate index for ship names.

Generally in the index, the key word is alphabetically indexed except in chapter 21 where some expressions are indexed from their first word. Although not without limitations this is likely to be more helpful than by breaking some of them down to a key word.

Bold page numbers indicate illustrations. Where a page number appears twice against an entry it indicates that there is more than one similar entry on the same page.

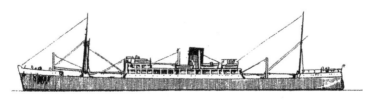

A refrigerated cargo ship on the
Australia-New Zealand run after WW2.

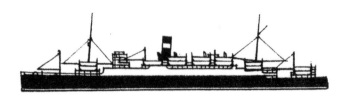

A post-WW2 emigrant ship running to New Zealand.

SUBJECT INDEX BY CHAPTERS

ALPHABETICAL INDEX

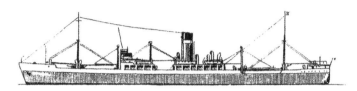

*A cargo ship on the Indian run during
the middle of the 20th century.*

ALPHABETICAL INDEX
Ship names are at the end of this index

INDEX TO SHIP NAMES

Notes

Notes